PRAISE FOR

ARE YOU READY FOR LASTING LOVE?

"An important and beautiful book. Important because heeding
the advice and practicing the exercises can transform your
relationships and bring great joy into your life. Beautiful because
your heart will open as you give and receive love more directly
and more honestly. I highly recommend this book."

—BRIAN WEISS,
author of *Many Lives, Many Masters* and *Only Love Is Real*

"A complete course on life, love, and everyday spirituality.
By sharing her intimate experiences and most vulnerable moments,
Dr. Welles has created a masterpiece and personal guide.
This is a book you can read over and over."

—PAT LOVE, Ed.D., coauthor of *Hot Monogamy*

"Love is a gift and a responsibility. Paddy shows us all how to enjoy
the gift more deeply and stand up to the responsibility. Her book
holds many of the answers to the challenges we face as individuals
and as families and communities. I highly recommend it."

—NANCY ROSANOFF,
author of *Intuition at Work* and *Intuition Workout*

"If you are weary of looking for it, running after it, struggling for it,
grasping for it, Paddy Welles will show you how to stay put, to
cultivate home grand, to sink roots, to dwell together, in lasting love."

—SAM KEEN,
best-selling author of *Fire in the Belly, To Love and Be Loved,*
and *Passionate Stages of Life*

PADDY S. WELLES, PH.D., received her doctorate at Syracuse University. She has been granted numerous professional awards, and is a member of many honorary and professional organizations. She has served as a child psychologist for the Prenatal/Early Infancy Project sponsored by the National Institute of Mental Health and the Robert Wood Johnson Foundation, as the supervising teacher and therapist at the prestigious Hoffman International Institute, and as an educator and lecturer on numerous campuses here and abroad. A devoted wife, mother to four children and two stepchildren, and a grandmother of six, she practices marriage and family therapy near Elmira, New York, where she lives with her husband, Tim.

Are You Ready *for* Lasting Love?

A revised and expanded edition of
To Stand in Love: Untangling the Webs We Weave

Are You Ready *for* Lasting Love?

A PERSONAL GUIDE TO CREATING FULFILLING RELATIONSHIPS

PADDY S. WELLES, PH.D.

MARLOWE & COMPANY
NEW YORK

ARE YOU READY FOR LASTING LOVE?:
A Personal Guide to Creating Fulfilling Relationships

Published by
Marlowe & Company
An Imprint of Avalon Publishing Group Incorporated
161 William Street, 16th Floor
New York, NY 10038

An earlier edition of this book was originally published in hardcover in 2001
by Giest & Russell Companies, Inc., under the title *To Stand in Love.*

Library of Congress Cataloging-in-Publication Data
Welles, Paddy S.
Are you ready for lasting love? : a personal guide to creating
fulfilling relationships / by Paddy S. Welles
p. cm.
Includes bibliographical references.
ISBN 1-56924-519-3 (trade paper)
1. Interpersonal relations. 2. Love. 3. Marriage. 4. Family. I. Title.
HM1106 .W45 2002
158.2—dc21   2002141446

9 8 7 6 5 4 3 2 1

DESIGNED BY PAULINE NEUWIRTH, NEUWIRTH & ASSOCIATES, INC

Printed in the United States of America

Are You Ready for Lasting Love? is dedicated to my love

teachers: my father, Ronald, who lived love to the fullest and

to my mother, Esther, who expanded and gave depth to my

definition of love; my children: David, Stephen, Karen, and

Karla, who have increased my capacity to love and taught me

more than I ever could have imagined needed to be learned;

my stepchildren, Henry and Eric, who gave me a new

perspective on love; my grandchildren: Nina, Matthew,

Michael, Andrew, Carder, and Madison, who allow me to love

in its purest and most joyful form; and my husband, Tim, who

chose to stand in love with me "after we fell." We have not

had an infallible relationship, but have grown and matured in

love together throughout the past twenty-eight years.

Contents

Preface

BEFORE YOU BEGIN this book, it is important to me that you understand there is no concrete concept that defines or encompasses real love. Just as a rainbow cannot be confined in a bottle for analysis, real love is beyond the reach of language; it is understood through experience. Real love happens "after the fall," or when illusions have faded and we begin to stand together to cocreate a loving reality that "grows us" through the frustrations, irritations, and trials of day-to-day living. Real love is not limited to romantic relationships. It is the essence of quality living from the cradle to the grave—and perhaps beyond.

It is easy to be energized by falling in love, but remaining energized through "standing in love" requires that we learn more about both ourselves and the people we love—our parents, siblings, partners, children, and friends. We are a culture that loves to fall in love, yet the staggering divorce statistics and the large numbers of couples that choose not to marry at all suggest that we are also a culture that tends to jump ship when the inevitable storms of love and life shatter our illusions about our love relationships. We'd rather *idealize* than *realize* most of our relationships. Idealization and the fantasy that "another will make me happy" are necessary for falling in love, but realization and the acceptance that happiness can be found only within ourselves are necessary for growing into committed lasting love.

Because timing is important, and we are living in a time when one disturbed individual without love in his life could push one button that could annihilate life in a large sector of the world, it is imperative that every effort be made to understand and cultivate the only power that will prevent this kind of destruction. The power base of love lies within each individual's mind and heart. We must develop a deeper understanding and acceptance of ourselves to be able to love. We are able to love others only to the extent we love ourselves. It is impossible to give away what we do not have. When we have unresolved anger, fear, and despair, these are what we pass on to others; this is what underlies terrorism, including the tragic events of September 11, 2001 and school shootings such as Columbine. It is the reason children slay their parents and anyone else who gets in the path of their rage. It is the reason that an average of eighteen teenagers per day commit suicide in the United States.[1] It is the reason for the cruel murders of homosexual Matthew Shepherd, African-American James Byrd, Jr., and of six-year-old Kayla Rolland by desperate people filled with fears and empty of love.[2] This is not a comfortable concept for our culture to absorb. However, until we commit to making the priority changes necessary for children to value themselves, there is no way they can value others.

The purpose of this book is to guide you through your memories and personal experiences so that you will both appreciate your own unique love story and be able to complete it knowing the "wonderfull" experience of real love. As Anthony de Mello has written, "Concepts are always frozen. Reality flows."[3] Each of us participates in creating the reality in which we live. It is easier to blame others for the lack of love within our reality than to assume personal responsibility for the ebb and flow of love in our lives.

There are Reflection Exercises throughout each chapter to encourage you to focus on your personal love story and the reality you are creating through your thoughts and actions. I hope you will write out your answers in response to these exercises, and thereby become more conscious of your own thoughts about love, as well as how and why you make the choices you make each day. *When our hearts speak, we need to listen and take good notes, for with every choice we make we will add to, or subtract from, positive energy and love in our lives, and therefore, in our world.*

A friend sent me a card last year entitled "In God's Kitchen," which portrays God taking a globe cake out of the oven, and muttering, "Something tells me this thing is only half-baked." Reading this book without doing the reflection exercises would have the same half-baked result, just as studying a map without taking the journey. I urge you to take this journey and discover your personal power to love and be loved.

Within each of our minds and hearts the mystery of our world's condition is held. We must be willing to honestly investigate the workings of our individual lives if we desire peace in our world. Permanent peace will never come from violence, wars, public demonstrations, or even the most well-intended laws and rules. Peace will only come when we each make our daily decisions from a place of love, for all life is interconnected.

The Introduction deals with seeing endings as new beginnings and with wake up calls. Endings and wake-up calls are usually not welcomed in our lives, but are necessary to increase our awareness of what love demands of us. Chapter One explores the differences between love and sex and the requirements for building lasting love. Chapter Two explains how life's webs become tangled through our early definitions of love and why we tend to cling to those definitions throughout the remainder of our lives. The first level of all love is attachment, which must happen for us to survive; however, as we mature, we must develop empathy and compassion to become a loving person. The necessary steps to becoming a mature loving person, who can make wise decisions about choosing partners and about whether a relationship should last, are presented in Chapter Three. We must become aware of our conditioning and our potential to grow beyond it if we want to untangle the webs that often reduce our ability to form lasting and fulfilling relationships.

The ways we are attached—connected—to all that exists are examined in Chapter Four. We are one united web and the consequences of any single thought or act affects more of the web than we could ever imagine. Chapter Five helps us assess our relationships and analyze our development as passionate persons. Chapter Six offers insights into how to improve our relationships, as well as how to end unhealthy involvements. It also sheds light on the crucial differences between male and female and explains how to build bridges of understanding and appreciation among genders, cultures, and races.

Chapter Seven explains why we must first love ourselves, and how we can improve our relationships when we treat ourselves lovingly. Love heals, and its healing aspects are delineated in this chapter. The emphasis of Chapter Eight is that love involves making choices and taking risks. Many of the choices are difficult, such as choosing between love and money or between time at home and time at work. Love involves balancing rather than juggling our priorities.

The ways therapy can enhance our awareness and help us become lovers in the finest sense of the word are probed in Chapter Nine. Chapter Ten redefines love and presents the guidelines for achieving lasting love—our only chance for terminal dignity.

My deepest sense of knowing at this stage in my life continues to remind me that in our drive to compete for financial, military, political, and technical power in the world today, we have forgotten the power of cooperative nurturing of ourselves, others, and the universe. In experiencing cooperative nurturing, the power of real love happens. Women seem to have a natural edge on this power, but I fear we have traded it in for what we *perceive* to be more valuable power. The results have been devastating.

These results are visible in our relationships, in our lack of intimate commitment, in our homes, or empty houses, in our longings for something to fill the aching void in our lives. We try to fill it with food, with television, with sex, with violence, with commodities, with work, with novelty, with money, and with addictions. We seek more and more, hoping to find a place where the aching stops. Instead we become addicted to the processes of accumulating and hoarding. We become victims of "affluenza," a rampant, cultural disease no annual shot can cure. Only cocreating love can stop the aching.

I have changed the names of most clients throughout the text. A few have requested that I use their real names and are excited that their stories are being shared. The names of family members and a few others in my personal life are used with permission.

Are You Ready *for* Lasting Love?

Are You Ready *for* Endings *and* Beginnings?

*WHEN OUR WORLD LEARNS THE LANGUAGE OF LOVE, WARS WILL
CEASE AND RIOTS WILL STOP. THERE WILL BE PEACE ON EARTH.*
—RONALD E. WALL

SITTING ON MY parents' back porch, watching the old man rock tediously back and forth in his wicker chair, I tried to imagine where my *real* father had gone. My *real* father was a distinguished minister, whose sermons I'd heard since conception. He had defined my life and written books that inspired thousands. He had taught me about God and love. He had told me that God is love. As I searched the vacant face of the man in the rocker, I wanted to scream at him to help me understand this supposedly loving God who allowed Alzheimer's disease to steal away the magnificent man I adored and leave what appeared to be this empty shell of a human being.

A wrenching pain tore through my being as I felt the powerful influence of this man on my life. I couldn't bear to think that his physical life was reaching its end when there were still so many things I needed to learn from him. I'd always turned to him for answers, for comfort, for an example of the loving life. But his brilliant mind had shut down, his wit and good humor had dried up, his wonderful laughter had ceased. He had been a deeply emotional person, who often tried to conceal the depth of his emotions, lest he not be able to control them if they leaked through his armor. Like most men of his generation, he was carefully and subtly taught that expression of emotion was a fatal weakness in a male—and often in a female as well. At that moment, I was feeling such despair that I feared he somehow might pick up telepathically on my intense frustration and unanswered questions.

Then, before I could censor my thoughts, the questions simply spilled from my mouth: "Daddy, what th' hell is life all about? What makes all this pain worth bearing? Do you still believe there is a loving God, or is there some maniac running the show who makes a mockery of everything you've professed to believe? If we were created in God's image, then what drives us to be so inhumane, greedy, selfish, jealous, fearful, and biased against anyone we see as different from ourselves? What is important in all this insanity?"

I knew he wasn't even aware that I had spoken. I felt as though my soul were screaming at him to give some meaning to the pain and confusion of these last few years of his life. Looking after him twenty-four hours a day had exhausted my mother and created havoc for my brother, sister, and me, as we argued endlessly over what should be done to help our parents. I also wanted his advice about my almost twenty-year marriage, which seemed to be unraveling, regardless of my efforts to make it better. I did not feel valued by my husband and he did not feel accepted by me, although we claimed to love each other.

Suddenly my father's deep blue eyes shifted into focus and looking directly at me in his most gentle pastoral voice, he said, "Nothing but love really matters, honey. Nothing else. Only love."

That was it: the last question I asked him, the last question he answered. He had no further need to participate in earthly conversation, and died shortly thereafter. I am continuing the conversation with you, the reader.

That was ten years ago. Not a day has passed since that I have not remembered his last words and seriously pondered where we have gone so wrong with love that children are murdering other children, our elementary schools have to search students for weapons and illegal drugs (A high and rapidly rising number of kids are on prescribed drugs, which is equally tragic), and many homeless people would rather live on the streets than be subject to the injustices of our welfare system. Most present-day children don't even think in terms of a "happy home life," for home has become a place to drop by and pick up some food or to sleep. Far too often there is no parent there to prepare or share the food or to tuck the kids into bed at night. As for telling bedtime stories or saying prayers, too many children are now going to sleep with their TVs or computer games as their sole companion. The only prayers many know are "Please don't let Mommy and Daddy get a divorce," (and we know that over half of the mommies and daddies do) or "Don't let Daddy come home drunk and hit Mommy," or "Please let someone come home before morning. I'm scared. God . . . God . . . God, are you there? Is anyone there?"

The greatest gift we can give our children is the gift of our presence. This is becoming increasingly difficult as more children are raised in single-parent homes, yet children need to have someone present to love them, or they cannot know love. The fastest-growing statistic in our culture over the past thirty years is that of childhood crime. We can blame the NRA, the schools, television, and other media; however, we have always had guns, schools, and some form of media communication. Over one million elementary school children go home after school where there is a gun and no adult supervision. The dominant difference between the past and the present circumstances of young children's lives is that more children are raised today without consistent parenting. Children, and adults, give up on love when it is not consistently available. Without consistency, there is no trust. Without trust, there is no internal truth. Without internal truth, there is no real love. It is often easier and less painful to deny our need for love than to feel the pain of living without enough of it.

Reflection Exercise

▶ Do you have the love you want in your life at the present time?

▶ Have you ever given up on love? When? Whom do you blame?

▶ Take a few minutes to think seriously about your present and past love relationships. Do not limit yourself to "romantic" relationships. Often these have more to do with fantasy than love. Focus on people to whom you've been significantly attached.

▶ Who has been present for you? For whom are you present?

▶ What is the first emotion you feel when you think of "love"?

▶ What are your childhood memories of love?

EARLY CONFUSION ABOUT LOVE

AS A YOUNG child lying in my bed at night, during the early 1940s, I also lay terrified and praying—praying that the Germans or the Japanese wouldn't drop bombs on us. In the east coast town of San- ford, North Carolina, where I lived, we had air raids and "black-outs" during which we were not allowed to have any lights on. Entire cities would literally be "blacked out" so that enemy planes could not find us. Horrible sirens pierced the air to teach us what "it"—an attack— would sound like. I would bargain with this God of my parents that if He—it was inconceivable in my four-year-old brain that God would be other than a Caucasian male—would keep the planes away I would be *so* good that I'd never tell another lie, and I'd be super nice to my little brother.

My parents would remind me that God was taking care of us and that I need not be afraid, but it was clear to me that He wasn't taking care of the children in Germany and Japan. Often, rather than pray to a God I couldn't understand, I'd suck my thumb for comfort and make up stories about how the world might have begun and about who could be "running the show." Who would allow war and killing and make little children have to stay in the dark, afraid of bombs falling on their heads? To help me make sense of this confusion, I made up a fantasy, which, in my grown-up life, often feels as if it could be closer to the truth than some of the things I was told as a child in Sunday school. The fantasy was:

Once upon a longer-than-I-could-imagine time ago, before there was a world at all, there was only a big yellow spider, with eight black dots on her back to match her eight black legs. This giant spider crawled around in the huge black sky and wove her web. The web was yellow, like her body. That was nice because then she could always see her web, and she could find herself against all the black. But after days and days of making a web, the spider got tired of weaving and wanted someone to play with her, someone who would tell her that the yellow web was beautiful. One day she got so lonely that she started crying. She was watching her tears fall when a teardrop stuck onto a strand of her web and turned into a little person. The spider was thrilled and crawled over to the little person.

Each thought the other looked funny, for they were very different in design, although they magically knew they shared the same need to be loved. They smiled and laughed together.

The spider and the little person were happy playing in the web until the little person became bored and wanted more webs to explore. She demanded that the spider make more yellow webs. The poor spider wanted to please her little friend, so she made webs until she was exhausted, but her friend still wanted more. She cried in frustration, for she could sense that her friend was never going to be satisfied and would always want more and more. As the spider's tears splattered throughout the webs, little people began to appear everywhere. Her first friend was delighted to have so many new playmates; however, she became so busy playing with them she soon forgot all about the yellow spider.

The spider crawled off to rest and contemplate. While she was asleep, the little people tangled up her web. When she awoke, she was very sad again, but decided not to cry this time. Instead she became angry and started weaving a tight web around the little people to trap them all in one place. She then crawled to another part of her beautiful web and cried to see if she could create one more little person whom she could have all to herself. This person would be her only best friend. She made this new friend a beautiful red color so she could tell her friend from the first group of yellow people.

Although a far-fetched fantasy in the mind of a frightened child, this story comforted me. It led me back to the possibility that perhaps we were created to keep an entity from being lonely. My fantasy diminished my fears and loneliness and gave me some primordial ideas of love. Of greater value, it challenged me into a more careful observation of human behavior. It offered some light when my world was dark. I've often looked for "light," or knowledge, knowledge in unique places, especially when I felt confused and afraid.

LATER CONFUSION ABOUT LOVE

THE EARLY CONFUSION over love and war gave way to massive confusion over love and sexual attraction when I was struggling with my first romantic love relationship in high school. I was constantly concerned that my boyfriend was going to dump me for someone cuter, or with a more sparkling personality, or that he would just stop liking me. This kind of anxiety over abandonment runs rampant throughout our lives, but is painfully strong during our first romantic involvement. It was only bearable at the time because my closest friends were suffering the same malaise. We wanted the assurance that we were loved by the persons we chose to love. Four of us pooled our money and sought that assurance from an elderly blind psychic, who called himself a "personal advisor." He charged twenty-five dollars an hour, which seemed outrageous to us at the time, but by saving up six dollars and a quarter apiece, we could swing it. Other friends had conferred with this man, and their reports had been fascinating and intellectually seductive in that we would obtain verboten knowledge, like Adam and Eve by tasting the forbidden fruit that would make them as wise as God.

It has taken many years for me to grasp how gifted this psychic sage really was. He did accurately describe quite a bit about my life at that time. Then he began to foretell the future and asked me to take notes, to which I make reference as I write. There were many predictions, which life has proved accurate, such as the initials of my first and second husbands, neither of whom I knew at the time. His last prediction was that I would write three books after I had lived through many hardships that would ultimately enable me to understand what was really important. I quipped something to the effect that nothing could be more important than whether or not my current boyfriend loved me. Smiling, he responded, "You're already in the ball park, but you know nothing about the game you've come to play."

I'm glad he did not tell me more. That was almost a half-century ago, and it has required every minute of my life since for me to begin to understand the game we've all come to play. The name of the game is Love. It is not always fun. The rules sound simple: love thy neighbor as thyself, be ye kind one to the other, do unto others as ye would have them do unto you—but these often prove difficult to follow in our daily lives. Yet, it is impossible to live a fulfilling life without love. We desperately need it. We sometimes shun it when it is offered due to our fear that it cannot last. We're often afraid to trust it as a result of unhealed wounds. Do we really understand what it is? Do we know the source of its power over us?

WAKE-UP CALLS

I AM CONVINCED that unless we are ready to seriously consider what we mean by love, unless we are willing to love responsibly—ourselves, our parents, our children, our lovers, our neighbors, our earth, our universe—we will soon destroy the ball park and all the players. The only game worth playing will be over.

I'm increasingly concerned that we are facing the final innings when I hear the morning news. The unthinkable, unimaginable events of September 11, 2001, brought each of us Americans to our knees, humbling us and reminding us that we are not immune to the atrocities caused by hate and fear. We became aware of our vulnerability and of our ability to support each other through tragedy.

Authentic horror stories have become a sad part of our daily expectations. In recent years we've all read or heard about parents brutally abusing and murdering their children, children murdering their parents, mass murders by children and adults. The ones that verify a lack of understanding love and continue to send shock waves throughout my mind and soul are: Susan Smith, who allowed her car to roll into a lake with her two young sons strapped into their car seats, sacrificing their lives so she could be free to have a romantic relationship with the man of her choice; the equally hideous case of another mother whose young sons literally roasted to death strapped in their car seats for over ten hours with 120 degrees of heat in the car while she "partied" in a nearby motel with four men; and the most brutal and inhumane of all—the father who beheaded his thirteen-year-old son while the nine-year-old brother watched. The father claims the son was possessed by the devil. The brutal beating of Matthew Shepherd by two young men who were deeply threatened by Matthew's courage to lead an honest gay life and the dragging murder of James Byrd, Jr. by three men filled with fear of their own weakness attest to how pathetically intolerant of differences many remain. Intolerance of differences always stems from ignorance, personal fears, and insecurities.

Sexual molestation and murder have become common, everyday occurrences, and often the people committing these crimes go unpunished due to our faulty judicial system. During the mid-nineties, the cases of O.J. Simpson, who allegedly murdered his wife, and Rodney King, who was beaten nearly to death by a group of white Los Angeles policemen, have made a continuing mockery of our criminal trial courts. Polls taken during the past year in elementary schools indicate that the majority of children now believe a perpetrator can commit a major crime and go unpunished if he has fame, fortune, or power. The bombing of the Federal Building in Oklahoma City by people who justified their actions by claiming to be saving us from a bigger monster—our federal government—defines our society as one in which chaos, confusion, and fear are prevalent.

Many of us feel sickened when we are made aware of these events. We rail at the terrorists, the courts, the NRA, the government, criminals, God, and society. *We forget that we are society.* We do not like to be reminded of this. Some have become so hardened that they feel absolutely nothing when made aware of these barbaric events. This is terrifying, for blocking our feelings allows us to ignore our responsibility to care for one another, and reduces empathy in the world. This was driven home powerfully last year through reports of the horrific torture and murder of beautiful six-year-old Elisa Izquierdo at the hands of her crack-addicted, deranged mother. Neighbors and social workers in New York City were found to have known of the abuse, but out of fear, apathy, or being too busy, no action was taken to save the child's life.

When I first read Eliza's story, I felt physically ill with anger, disgust, and grief. I admit that I felt I could murder the mother, or even the social workers, and even more frightening, I believed for a moment that I could justify such a murder. I put the paper down and had to pray for the moral courage to continue reading. My soul knew that I had to read it, to feel it, to get in touch with the pain, the anger, the confusion, and then get in touch with my own potential to abuse. Until we are aware that under certain circumstances we are each capable of anything, we set ourselves up to use our innate potential to abuse or to turn away in the face of abuse. When Mother Theresa was asked why she began her work with the diseased and dying indigents of Calcutta, she replied that she knew what she must do the day she discovered there was a "little Hitler" inside her.

We each have a "little Hitler," a few saints, a few devils, and a few angels inside us. On a plane last year, I picked up a copy of *USA Today*. The front-page story carried photographs and stories of several women who claim to have had sexual involvement with the president, positioned next to a photo of President Clinton claiming that he had not had sexual relations with these women. With disgust I turned the page and saw another photograph with a story of a Texas prison inmate who wanted to give his second kidney to his teenage daughter, to whom he had given the first, three years ago, when he knew she had diseased kidneys. I cried. We each make choices moment by moment that activate our saints, angels, or devils. If we deny that we have negative thoughts and feelings, those negative thoughts and feelings will grow inside of us like monsters. The monsters surface as lies, crimes, cancer, high blood pressure, strokes, heart disease, and thousands of other physical and psychological illnesses. There is a popular expression in the therapeutic community that the body expresses what the mind represses. Until we can be honest enough with ourselves about ourselves, we will blame much of the negativity, which we help create, on others.

Reflection Exercise

▶ What are you doing that causes pain and negativity in your life? In the lives of others?

▶ What have you done recently to intentionally cause pain?

▶ How many lies have you told this week? Who suffered as a result?

▶ Are you basically honest? (Or do you just want everyone else to be?)

▶ Are you willing to take an honest inventory of your own behaviors? (Or do you tend to focus on what's wrong with others?)

▶ Do you take your responsibility as a woman to be an effective change agent? Or do you fall into blaming men for all the ills of the times? (Reverse the genders, if you are a male.)

▶ Do you focus more on how you think others should change than on how you could change? How do you try to change others?

The most familiar question initially asked in a marriage and family therapist's office is how can I make my spouse, my child, or whomever else is causing me pain, change.

Once a precocious ten-year-old boy asked, "If my parents really love and accept me because I'm me, like they tell me, then why are they always trying to change me? I always feel like they want to make me into someone else. I don't feel like they really love me."

The only person any of us can ever change is our individual self! We must change the aspects of ourselves that block love if we want love in our lives. Hoping and sometimes demanding that others change will never create love. These behaviors create an illusion of control and always separate rather than connect us to another. Injustices of every kind, abuse in all of its sordid forms, criticism that cripples the spirit, and lies that break our hearts often happen "in the name of love." We frequently behave in unloving ways while expecting that what we call "love" will happen for us. We, like Blanche Dubois, want it to be magic.

AFTER THE FALL

IF YOU WERE to discover that real love is not magic, not something you fall into, could you still get high on it? All the clients who come into therapy saying, "I love my spouse, but I'm no longer in love with him," might have a chance for a lasting loving relationship if they were to redefine what love really is. When they come in thinking they are passionately connected to a new person, often they are on a collision course that will drive them into states of depression, heartache, financial disaster, and worse. The passionate connections are usually below the belt and are short lived once the reality-based problems of divorce demand attention. *Real love is not perpetual lust, but is developed through our implementation of caring decisions that lead us from dependence and obsession into interdependence and truth.* It involves sharing the good and passionate times, but more importantly, it demands standing together through frustrations, irritations, selfishness, stubbornness, grief, and tears, having the pain kissed away by love that forgives and whispers, "I do love you."

RECENT CONFUSION AND PAIN

ONLY A FEW years ago I believed that my life was in fine shape. For the first time in my adult life, I felt reasonably content. I was professionally more successful than I'd ever dreamed possible. I had a large private therapy practice in a beautiful office that encompassed a waiting room, conference room, playroom, and a perfect therapy room filled with thriving plants that contributed to an ambiance of growth and love. I loved it. In fact, I loved it to the extent that I often spent twelve to fourteen hours a day there, including Saturdays. Sundays were reserved for billing and insurance forms. Any time I dared be away from my clients, I was teaching workshops or courses on therapy. I had the sense that I was truly helping people, that I was reducing pain in their lives by caring for them and listening to them. And perhaps that was true.

The people I no longer had time to care for or listen to were the ones I loved the most: my husband, our grown children, our grandchildren, and my friends. To show their respect for my time, friends stopped calling me. My children would begin their conversations with, "Mom, I know you are busy, but could I have a few moments of your precious time?" I simply didn't get it, although there were many warnings. I rationalized that I still did the "big, important things," like going to help when grandbabies were born or when there was an honest to God crisis in our family. I was overlooking an ongoing crisis. I hadn't figured out that the things I told my clients, such as, "It's the little day-by-day things that truly show others your love for them," also applied to me. I denied that the most important people in my life did not feel loved by me.

Reflection Exercise

▶ Take time to list the top five things (include relationships to specific people) in your life to which you give the most time and energy.

▶ Now list the five most important things in your life.

▶ How well do your lists match up?

▶ Do the people you claim to love feel loved by you? Ask them.

The things to which we give time and energy usually work for us. The things we neglect, or take for granted, die or leave our lives.

MY HUSBAND, TIM, and I did a weekend couples workshop to help us rekindle our love. It was a wonderful, quality-time weekend. We returned home feeling that we were in love again. We did not allow ourselves to realize that we felt this way because we'd shared forty-eight hours together. We quickly resumed our normal routine of a quick breakfast together, and then rushing our separate ways to do our demanding, important jobs. If our schedules permitted, we'd have dinner together on the nights we were both free of other "priorities." His weekends were spent flying planes and gliders, while mine were spent "working," or helping others—and myself—feel worthwhile.

We were on a fast track to marital disaster, all the while promising each other that "it"—an affair—could never happen again because neither of us had time. But then "it" did happen. It happened because someone else showered the kind of attention on my husband that I had not taken time to do in any consistent way for years. He had denied his need for loving attention because he stayed busy enough to keep his deeper needs repressed. Both he and I were living in denial of what love requires to be kept alive. This affair was the "last call" for our marriage. The pain was big enough and constant enough that I could no longer work it away. Meanwhile, my husband was losing his self-respect, feeling confused and afraid, and developing high blood pressure.

On the day I was to sign a legal separation document, he called to say he really loved me. I hung up. He called again. He got my attention by leaving a loving message on the answering machine. I cried. I arrived at the attorney's office in tears and couldn't sign the separation papers. Afterward, I called Tim to apologize for hanging up on him and asked him to join me for lunch. He canceled an important meeting to meet me. Each of the above acts was a behavioral change—I'm not big on apologizing to someone who has hurt me, and he'd never canceled a business meeting to meet with me. We began an honest dialogue, putting aside our defenses and blaming to really hear the other's story. After weeks of continuous honest communication, we slowly came to our senses. We woke up before the last bell tolled. We each made a choice to love the other from a place of commitment and respect. Love always involves a choice. We realized that we would have to rearrange our priorities and our lives, which is never easy. We learned that precious gifts can come in painful wrapping paper.

I walked away from my lovely therapy office, gave up my practice, and began to redefine love from a deeper perspective, one that involves increased attention, time, and energy. He slowed up a bit and made a commitment to expressing honest feelings rather than repressing them. It has paid off. This does not mean that every day is easy, but it does mean that everything is dealt with in a more committed and caring way. It means we have discovered something more valuable than making money or being popular with clients. We have discovered that creating and keeping a loving relationship requires that the relationship receive priority energy and time. It requires opening up and sharing honestly everything that is important. It means that we must no longer take each other for granted.

I am not claiming that we have discovered all the answers, but I am admitting that I have had most of the problems and have learned to ask myself many of the right questions, which I share with you throughout this book. I've learned that answers don't come when my heart and mind are closed, or when I'm stuck in unconscious patterns of behavior. Life has a way of not allowing us to stay stuck for long without whamming us with an "experience club" that delivers a powerful enough blow to get our attention. Then we have to make some significant choices and take some risks.

This book explores the questions and concepts with which I have struggled. It cannot give you truth or love. It can only help you open your mind and heart to discover your own truth and how you can make more responsible loving choices. If the majority of us do not commit to implementing loving choices, I fear our time of choice will soon end. Look around you. Of greater value, look within yourself. Deep within you is your truth—your love story.

We have to open our minds and hearts to our memories, which program us, and to the truth about ourselves to know love. As the fox says to the little prince in the beautiful love story *The Little Prince* by Antoine de Saint-Exupéry:

> "It is only with the heart that one can see rightly; what is essential
> is invisible to the eye."

"What is essential is invisible to the eye," the little prince repeated, so that he would be sure to remember.

"It is the time you have devoted to your rose that makes your rose so important."

"It is the time I have devoted to my rose—" said the little prince, so that he would be sure to remember.

"Men have forgotten this truth," said the fox. "But you must not forget it. You become responsible, forever, for what you have tamed. You are responsible for your rose."

"I am responsible for my rose," the little prince repeated, so that he would be sure to remember. [1]

Each day of your life offers you an opportunity to learn more than you knew the day before and each moment offers you a choice. Are you ready to remember your love lessons?

Are You Ready *to* Understand What Love Really Is?

LOVE IS THE UNIVERSAL THIRST FOR A COMMUNION,
NOT MERELY OF THE SENSES, BUT OF OUR WHOLE NATURE.
—P. B. SHELLEY

Birds do it. Bees do it. Even monkeys in the trees do it. So let's do it . . . let's fall in love." This popular tune makes "it" sound easy, as if falling in love were a natural stage in the life processes of all living organisms. If that were the case, isn't it strange that after four million years of "it," we are unable to produce enough love on this planet to raise the majority of our children in loving homes or to cure loneliness? Is it possible that the popular "it" actually has little to do with love, and much more to do with lust? Lust leads to sex, which is so plentiful that the planet is dangerously overpopulated, sexually transmitted diseases are rampant, and adultery ostensibly remains the leading cause of divorce. Is it possible that having sex is the easy and natural thing to do, but that creating love demands far more of us than we've wanted to realize? Author John Gray asserts that women need love to open up to sex, while a man needs sex to open up to love. While there may be some cultural truth to his assertion, I am convinced that we each need passionate love, but are giving love short shrift by limiting our definition of love to sex.

Love and sex are not even distant cousins. They both involve attachment, but attaching his to hers does not attach all of him to all of her. Could we be confusing our hearts with other parts of our anatomy? Most of the world's dominant cultures use sexual overtones to advertise everything from foods to laundry detergents. Movies and television are filled with demonstrations of "it." We are always seeking new ways to do "it." Sex sells! Can we say the same about love? Without sex, there would be no continuation of life, but without love, what kind of life would there be? Sex may make the world go around, but love makes the ride worthwhile.

Reflection Exercise

▶ Divide a piece of paper into two columns. Write, "Love is............" at the top of one column and write, "Sex is............" at the top of the other. Fill in as many words as come to your mind under each heading. You might note for starters that sex is a noun, while love is a noun and a verb.

▶ How are your lists similar? And how do they differ?

▶ Have you been harmed in the name of love? By whom? How? (Include physical and emotional harm and note whether you are harmed in the same ways by more than one person.)

Your parents had sex. Did they have love? Your grandparents, their parents, and their parents all had sex. Did they have love? Each of us began as a continuation of "sometwo's" sex life. Do you feel you are a continuation of anyone's love life? Consider what criteria you used to determine your answer.

When I think of "lovers" in my family history, the first image is always of my maternal grandparents. My grandmother was a Dickens, of the Charles Dickens clan, and her family was considered important in the community. Her mother died when she was ten years old, and her father remarried quickly to have help with his five children. The "wicked stepmother" tales became a reality for these children, especially for my grandmother, who became "Cinderella," as she was expected to do the housework and look after her siblings while her stepmother attended the social events. The handsome prince showed up when she was fifteen years old, but he did not invite her family to a masked ball. He was an eighteen-year-old nomad who had wandered into town from across the hills looking for work. He found a job—and my grandmother. They fell in love. Knowing their marriage would not be acceptable to her family, she tied the proverbial bed sheets together, climbed from a second-story window, and eloped with him. They raised five children and were together for fifty years. Shortly after their golden anniversary, as she was walking through a park close to their home, she was attacked by a large stray dog. Her heart stopped.

I will never forget seeing my grandfather after the accident. His light had gone out. His body seemed withered. His familiar chuckle seemed to be stuck in an irretrievable place beyond our reach, and he told us plainly that he could not endure being alive without her. It was true. His pain was visible in every aspect of his being. Even his hands, which had always been busy, were listless. He died a few years later—of grief. At the time of his death, I felt a profound sadness that he'd never rallied from losing her. As I've matured, I've realized that they created and shared something most of us would die for—that rare and beautiful love that happens only when two people have totally entrusted their hearts into the other's keeping.

Taking a walk with him several months after her funeral, I asked him what their secret had been. Looking up into the heavens, he replied, "She loved me *just as I am*. That's the most wonderful thing that can happen to anyone. Most people don't have any idea what love really is."

"What is it?" I persisted. At age twenty, I was beginning to understand that I probably didn't know.

It took him a while to reply. "Well, you have to discover it with someone else helping you," he began. "It's like discovering that you are a king and live with a queen in a beautiful castle. We never had very much in the way our world puts values on things, but we really had everything—because we shared all we had."

That was over forty years ago. I doubt that I've ever heard a more precious definition of love—love does not involve what we own, but what we share. It allows us to experience ourselves as grand because the person we love treasures us. When we are seen through the eyes of love, we are able to love ourselves. I'm deeply grateful for their love story and equally grateful that my mother was a product of their sexual union, which was a union of love.

THE UNION OF LOVE AND SEX

EACH OF US became a reality in a small web created by two people who had sex in the context of larger webs, woven by our families, communities, religions, and other broader cultural influences. The act of sex was, and is, the easy part. The context in which the sex happens becomes more complicated. After puberty our hormones are raging, driving our bodies to "do it," long before we can handle the consequences of "it." Our peers want to know if we've "gone all the way." Males are under pressure to use their "little heads" rather than their larger heads. An attractive female client came into the office for her first therapy appointment with me, and without waiting for me to say a word, she blurted out, "Penises, penises . . . I'm so sick of penises. I can't even remember who they belong to. Guess you could say that my problem is I'm fucked out."

I laughingly replied that she was terribly young—early thirties—to be "fucked out." I hurt for her because I knew what she was really saying was that she had never felt loved by a significant other. She was looking for lasting love and fulfillment. She'd settled for "quick fixes" to make the pain of needing love go away. It works—temporarily, which is why many get "fucked-out" without knowing love.

Reflection Exercise

▶ How do love and sex interface in your life?

▶ How are they compatible or incompatible?

▶ How important is sex in your life?

▶ Make a list of your sexual partners. Indicate with which ones you shared life beyond the sexual relationship.

▶ Have you been harmed through sexual experiences? By whom? How?

THE CRITICAL ELEMENTS OF LOVE

WE USE THE word "love" to mean just about anything from enjoyment of a corned beef sandwich to a sincere desire to share our lives with another. We talk about loving our children, loving chocolate, loving a piece of jewelry, loving a sport, loving the way someone laughs, loving the snow, loving spring. Are there any common denominators underlying the meaning of this word?

Of course there are different kinds of love, various levels of love, multifaceted variations of love, special moments of love. Erich Fromm, in his classic book, *The Art of Loving,* delineates parental love, brotherly love, erotic love (defined as romantic, sexual love), self-love, and spiritual love; however, he states that *all meaningful love* must have the basic elements of *care, responsibility, respect, and knowledge.*[1]

CARE

CARE IS MOST evident in a devoted parent's care of a child. Roberto Benigni, who plays the father in *La Vita e Bella (Life is Beautiful),* exhibits this depth of love for his young son as he attempts to protect the child from the horrors of their concentration camp experience. Using his incredible imagination up to the final moment of his life, he designs a game that saves the life of his son.

Mothers give us our first definition of love, which begins in utero. Dr. Carla Shatz, a neurobiologist at the University of California, Berkeley, has found evidence to prove that there is meaningful neural activity in the brain of a fetus as early as ten weeks after conception that actually changes the shape of the brain as it carves circuits into patterns. These patterns will enable a newborn to recognize the feel and feelings of its mother and be able to distinguish her from others immediately after being born. There is considerable research to support that a calm, healthy pregnant woman who looks forward to raising her baby will produce a calmer, healthier, and even smarter baby. The reports from neurobiology laboratories all over the world are encouraging parents to slow down and take time to be at home with their baby. Babies (and fetuses) in love-deprived environments not only suffer emotionally, but their brain development suffers as well.[2]

There is a growing body of research that indicates that plants also thrive when they are tended by someone who loves them, talks to them, and protects them. All living things require care at some level to maintain existence on our planet. At the deepest level of quantum physics, we know that all things are living, and therefore have requirements to maintain life. Caring means responding and attending to the physical, mental, emotional, and psychological needs of living things we love. *Caring is nurturing something so that it is better able to realize its highest and fullest potential.*

In the mid 1950s, Dr. Harry F. Harlow, director of the University of Wisconsin's primate laboratory, carried out several experiments to determine if love between a mother and infant is based upon associations built between them while the baby is feeding. To analyze the situation, he constructed substitute mothers, one made of wire, and the other of wire covered with a soft cloth padding. Both could hold propped bottles. Eight infant monkeys were separated from their real mothers shortly after their births and placed in cages with the substitute mothers. Four baby monkeys were fed by the wire surrogates and four by the cloth surrogates. The four monkeys fed by the wire surrogate approached her only at feeding times, but all eight monkeys spent most of their time trying to cling to the softer cloth surrogate. They each demonstrated a need for the softer touch, and all were calmed while they were clinging to the soft mother substitute.[3]

Later, Dr. Harlow raised a few monkeys in total isolation. They had no surrogates and were fed by a bottle wired to the side of each cage.

He discovered that these isolated monkeys were more fearful and more aggressive than the monkeys raised by the surrogates. This research suggests that love may be more a result of comfort and touch than meeting the basic need for food. It also suggests that feeling warmth and comfort reduces anxiety and aggression.[4]

A lesser-known fact, but of immense importance to our love and sex topic, is *not one of these monkeys deprived of mothering ever became sexually active.* They did not lack the ability to present a sex drive, as males would approach females, and females would present themselves for sex, but neither gender could carry through with sexual intercourse. Psychologists who have studied this data conclude that it indicates there is a strong connection between deprivation of mothering and a fear of intimacy in adult life.[5]

When a group of these isolated females was impregnated artificially and reproduced, they showed no interest in caring for their offspring. The conclusion of this research is that not only is sexual behavior severely impaired by a lack of mothering and/or lack of love, but the ability to mother is also severely impaired. When we study the statistics of sexual abuse in humans, we learn that people who are sexually abusive tend to have had little or no parental love as young children. Most sexually abusive adults were sexually abused children and were raised without responsible, caring parenting. The bottom line is that children must have both their emotional *and* physical needs met in order to learn to care for themselves and others. When children are raised without security and love, they cease caring about themselves—and others. To actively care for something requires that we value the object of our caring. We only learn to value ourselves when we are valued by others.

Reflection Exercise

▶ Write your personal definition of caring.

▶ List the people you value enough that you are actively involved in meeting their needs—physical, emotional, mental, and psychological. I hope you put yourself on your list. How do you show each person, including yourself, that you care?

RESPONSIBILITY

RESPONSIBILITY, FROMM'S SECOND criterion for love, requires that we take competent action *as soon as possible* to respond to a need so that the pain caused by the need diminishes, and pleasure, or comfort, ensues. A common idea in the first half of this century was that it was healthy to allow babies to cry for fairly extended periods of time, but we've since learned that in reality the longer an infant remains in distress, the more anxious and fearful she becomes. Instead of continuing to cry in discomfort, the infant gives up—losing trust in the caregiver and in her ability to survive. Over time, she becomes withdrawn and passive, as if her "life force" were draining away—which is exactly what is happening. We each have needs, and unfulfilled needs cause pain. This can be as simple as hunger or as complex as needing to be in a relationship.[6]

We need to be in a relationship to know that we exist, and unless someone acknowledges our existence, our humanness begins to die. C. S. Lewis has written: *We love to know that we are not alone.* Infants cannot survive alone. To be in a relationship with someone who will share the responsibility of our existence allows us to honor and trust our humanness. It allows us to love. When a child feels loved, the child does not harbor violence. Violence stems from the fear of not getting love. A human child has the most extended period of dependency in the animal kingdom, which translates into the most allotted time to be taught love. I believe this is to ensure our humanity. We tend to treat others as humanely as we have been treated.

Rapists are usually men who have lost their humanity because no one loved them responsibly. Jim is an example. He was born to drug-addicted parents. As an infant, he was left alone in his crib for hours at a time without food. It was not unusual for him to be found by a neighbor, or social worker, eating his feces. He was finally taken away from his parents and put in foster care where he was fed, but was also physically and sexually abused by the partner of his foster mother, who claimed to love him. The sad truth was that she enjoyed having sex with her abusive partner more than she enjoyed being responsible to Jim. During his tragic childhood, he lived in three different foster homes. Today he is in prison for rape and murder. He is still a human, but one who never had a chance to value his humanity because no one shared responsibly in his existence. His basic need for love was reduced to a need for contact to prove his existence. Jim's story has been filled with sex, but without responsible love his life has been an unending tragedy, which has led to pain, grief, and tragedy in the lives of many others.

This story is extreme and not likely to happen in a middle-class society, but when I first met Jim in a group of prison inmates who were participating in a human relations class, I painfully remembered the afternoons I had been detained at the college and allowed my eight-year-old daughter to come home on the school bus to an empty house. It was easy for me to convince myself that she could manage, and that I would be home soon. I rationalized that I was teaching her independence and responsibility and that she would be proud of my professional success. What selfish bullshit! I was wrong. Being a more responsible parent would have helped my daughter far more than an extra hour at work ever helped anyone. To the extent I caused her to feel lonely and afraid, I taught her not to trust me, or my love. With my resources, compared to the resources of Jim's mother, I was as wrong as she had been.

> ### Reflection Exercise
>
> ▶ Write down what responsibility means to you.
>
> ▶ List the people for whom you feel responsible (yourself, children, other family members).
>
> ▶ With whom do you share a responsible existence? When does that responsibility become a burden for you?
>
> ▶ How could you change this? It is always possible to change your perception of a situation even if the dynamics of the situation cannot be changed.

This last question evokes the memory of a story told by my paternal uncles. My paternal grandfather shared the ownership of a large lumberyard and mill with two of his brothers, and the boys in all three families grew up working in various jobs around this occupation. The older, larger boys worked on the big saws. There was an accident in which one of my uncles sawed through his hand. Only one of the younger boys was near enough to help. He tore off his shirt to wrap his brother's wounds and ran several miles for help. (This was in pre-telephone days.) That evening, he was recognized as a hero, but his reply was simply: "He is my brother." Responsible love spurs us into action when there is a need.

Just this morning I visited an elderly client, Alice, who is terminally ill and knows that she will die within weeks—perhaps days. She has not been an easy woman to love. When she was an infant her mother had left a large cauldron of boiling water in the yard for the wash while she ran inside to attend Alice's wails. Her two-year-old brother fell into the scalding water and died before the mother returned. The grief-stricken mother became unable to give Alice the responsible loving attention she needed. When Alice became old enough to understand what had happened to her brother, she assumed her needs as an infant caused her brother's death. As a result, she's been terrified to express any needs for love for most of her life.

Her defenses became denial and criticism of anyone who did express love needs. She refused to show any vulnerability and sabotaged kindness when people tried to give her attention. Although she craved it deeply, she felt she did not deserve it. When she realized that she was very ill, she literally went to bed, refused to ask for help, and refused to tell anyone of her agony. Her husband of forty stormy years, who is a stroke victim, discovered that she was unable to get out of bed—even to go to the bathroom. He began cleaning her, bathing her, feeding her, and sought medical attention although his verbal skills are severely impaired. At long last, she was able to respond to love because she had been taught by someone who loved her responsibly that she was lovable—even covered in shit. Their adult children were awed by their father's ability to show this depth of devotion to their mother who had criticized him and nagged at him for as long as they could remember. One of the major reasons was that he had had a mother who adored him and loved him responsibly. He was able to share the gift of his mother with his wife when she was no longer able to reject it.

RESPECT

FROMM'S THIRD CRITERION, respect, requires that we honor our humanity, our individual ways of developing, our similarities, and our differences. We must be able to see the good in ourselves and in others to have respect in our lives. It happens in a context of appreciation, gratitude, and concern for our natural "unfolding," or developing as unique members of a group. It happens best when there has been, and is, responsible caring. Respect guarantees freedom from rigid control and exploitation.

One of my clients, a talented, beautiful girl with professional employment, recently committed suicide. People were shocked, as there had been no public exhibits of pathological behavior. Several of us knew she had been a childhood beauty queen. When the goal of parents becomes to form a child into an object to enhance their own self-esteem rather than respecting the normal limits of childhood, the child will suffer. Respect for the natural beauty of childhood and for nature's unfolding is forfeited.

Responsibility and respect are often intertwined. Many children of alcoholic parents assume the adult care-giving role, while the alcoholic parent behaves as an irresponsible child. With the addict's lack of self-respect, there is no respect for the needs of the child. I sadly remember Bonnie, who told me that during her childhood, her mother would get so drunk on weekends that all she ever had to eat from Friday night through Sunday night was canned soup because it was the only thing she could prepare. Bonnie would heat up the soup for herself and for her mother, who would be in bed with her gin. Bonnie remembers taking hot soup to her mother and trying to spoon-feed her. Her mother was so drunk that she hit her daughter, scalding her with hot soup, and then raged at her to mind her own business. Bonnie grew up trying to take care of everyone—except herself, and died an early unnecessary death because of it. Psychological wounds inflicted upon children by disrespectful parents are often never healed. These children grow up bleeding internally from repressed pain and anger, choking on the "family secrets." The price of parental disrespect is high.

Respect is transmitted in the ways we look at someone or listen to someone. I sadly remember many children in elementary school classrooms and in therapy sessions who would draw their parents with scowling faces and leave off the ears! Children who are not seen or heard by their parents are not able to internalize respect. They live in a fog of fear that they are somehow unworthy and unlovable. This fear is difficult to overcome in adulthood.

Penny had a father who put her down because she was a female, because she gained weight in puberty, and because he falsely believed that she would respect him if he made her feel inferior to him. She hated him. Today she hates her husband, who criticizes her for having no self-esteem and no respect for him. Without self-respect she will not consider leaving him, for she does not believe she deserves respect. Real love eludes her.

Then there is Bob, who seems to have the Midas touch. Everything works for him. He is an excellent student, star athlete, and leader in several organizations. When asked about his secret, he replied that when he was a four-year-old bed wetter his parents once praised him for continuing to sleep through the night in a wet bed (which no one realized was wet until the next morning) out of respect for their need to sleep. He claimed that he never wet his bed again. I can believe that. His parents gave him respect for something many children are shamed for—in return, he respects himself and others. He was well loved.

Reflection Exercise

▶ Write down what respect means to you.

▶ List the persons you truly respect. Beside each person's name, write what you respect about him/her. (I hope you are on your list. If not, get in touch with why not.)

▶ Do you respect the people you claim to love?

▶ Do they respect you? Without self-respect, we tend not to respect the people who claim to love us. (They would have to be stupid! Right?)

Reflection Exercise (continued)

▶ How do you treat people you do not respect?
  How do you treat those you love?

▶ Do you have sex with people you do not respect?
  (If so, what does this do to your self-respect?)

KNOWLEDGE

AT FIRST, KNOWLEDGE may not seem to fit into our ideas about love as easily as care, responsibility, and respect, but knowledge frees us from illusion. Acquiring knowledge requires committed time and effort. Fromm is referring to our willingness to know the depth of others and to make an effort to understand their needs and struggles. Real love cannot grow through illusions, although falling in love is initially based on our illusions of how we want a person to be—an illusion of hope. It is easy to have a sexual relationship based on illusion, as most of us can sustain an illusion for a few hours, especially between the sheets. As the popular song *Both Sides Now* says, "It's love's illusions I recall, I really don't know love at all." Getting to know someone intimately is a lifelong challenge, which most of us do not readily accept.

Frequently, during a therapy session a client will ask why "love" rarely seems to last beyond a few months. The process of falling in love (including the lusting for constant contact—that feeling of "I can't get enough of you") only lasts a few months, for that's about the length of illusion. When we come to the sometimes brutal realization that this new love object cannot make us happy all the time, that he has some faults and comes with a set of his own problems, reality takes a whack at our hearts—and minds. Twenty years ago I would listen empathically when someone would come into my office with that sad, guilty look, and admit, "I still love my partner, but you know, I'm just no longer in love with him." I would nod that I understood, and I knew we were headed for "the new lover who is everything I've ever wanted" saga. After years of listening to how the next stage of this saga almost always develops, I wised up, or grew up, and began to respond to the introductory statement with, "Fantastic, now you might be ready to learn what real love can be. It helps to have your first lesson in reality with a partner where there is no illusion left."

Reflection Exercise

▶ How well do you know the people you claim to love? Do you allow them to know you?

▶ List the people you believe you fully know and understand. Are you on your list?

▶ How much effort do you put into understanding another person's point of view?

▶ Are you often surprised by the behavior of people you think you know well? List a few of your latest surprises.

▶ Does it matter how well you know the people with whom you have sex?

▶ Test your knowledge factor: Sit down with a significant other for the purpose of sharing what you assume each knows about the other. Then share something you might not have shared before about yourselves. An exercise known as the Johari Window (Appendix A) can guide you through a test of your knowledge about your significant other, and add to your knowledge of yourself and the other. Be prepared for several surprises—and a few shocks!

TIME AND ENERGY

MY EXPERIENCE HAS taught me another critical element required for cocreating love in our culture suffering from "affluenza" (the accumulation of things) is that of priority time and energy. Fromm did not need to mention this specifically because during the first half of the last century it was taken for granted that love required time and energy. Wives and mothers were expected to put their major time and energy into "keeping the home fires burning." Husbands and fathers were expected to come home by five o'clock to be warmed by those fires. Keeping a family together was a top priority before World War II. However, during and following the war, women became used to having to do it all, discovered they could, and also discovered they could depend on each other for a kind of support that they did not get from their men. Some of these discoveries brought about positive changes for women, but our children, homes, and relationships are paying a high price for some of the changes we *assumed* would be positive.

My "fucked out by too many penises" client happened to be a highly skilled, successful, and well-paid businesswoman. At the conclusion of that first session, she burst into tears and sobbed, "I'd give up this damn job tonight if I could fall asleep in the arms of a man who really loved me and had time to share life with me, instead of just his prick and the good times!"

A case of the grass is always greener? I wondered then. I no longer do. Balancing our time between home and work is a partial answer to this problem, but this balance is difficult to achieve with the pressures of a professional job. This is especially true when our goal is to "get to the top" professionally. No one tells us that the top is a lonely place when we've forgotten that creating love in our personal lives also requires time and energy. This is a complex and very real problem. In his book, *Must Success Cost so Much?*, Paul Evans writes that the demands of work involvement often have a negative effect on private life and significant relationships; however, he suggests that the reason may be not only the work pressure, but that many people have never developed the attitudes and skills needed to make relationships work. It is easier to blame work than to take an honest inventory of other problems and develop skills that will enhance our relationships.[7]

I agree with him. I have been accused of implying that I thought all women should stay at home barefoot and pregnant, which is not what I believe, or mean to imply. What I know is that raising children is at least a ten-year career, and unless we are willing to work out ways to give that career a high priority and committed time and energy, we should forego parenthood.

During a recent play-therapy session with four-year-old Sarah, I watched her pretending that she was a mother putting her children (dolls) to bed. She let out an audible sigh, and said to the dolls, "Of course I love you, but Mommy's tired from work and I don't have time to read to you. I can't wait until you go to school and can read to yourself."

At this point, I asked her if she would like to be able to read to herself. She ignored my question, did not look up, but asked in a very soft voice, "Do you have time to read to me?"

I nodded. She'd cut through all the excuses—and cut out a piece of my heart. She knew what her mother did not yet know: that loving requires taking the time to put love into action. As she picked out a book and climbed into my lap, she grinned up at me and asked, "You do love me, don't you?"

I knew both of her parents were busy professional people. Sarah had gotten the message clearly that her parents' jobs were more important to them than she. Her parents did provide for her physical care, but they did not provide the responsible caring she needed in order to meet her emotional and psychological needs. She desperately needed to feel connected to them. They paid me to connect to her for an hour each week. Sarah's parents were the ones who should have been in the office, but they did not have time!

We each have the same twenty-four hours in a day. It is what we choose to do with it that determines what is really important to us. Children know this in a way that many modern parents do not. Limited time results in limited knowledge, which results in limited and conditional love. Limited time also allows us to *idealize* rather than *realize* the people we claim to love.

Can you imagine having a flourishing vegetable or flower garden that never required us to take time to expend the energy to weed, water, or cultivate? These aspects of care, responsibility, respect, knowledge, time, and energy aptly apply to gardening, hobbies, sports, and other things we claim to love. My husband and I love to fly gliders and airplanes. Studying the science and skills of flying and taking time to practice are requirements for staying current in the field, as well as for staying alive! Unfortunately, we did not work on our relationship with the same amount of effort we put into flying—until our marriage suffered "engine failure."

Reflection Exercise

▶ List the top ten roles (ways you identify yourself) in your life today. This would include your work, your extracurricular activities, hobbies (even watching movies, TV, the stock market, sports, etc.), and relationships (such as parent, child, spouse, lover, friend, sexual partner, etc.). Check with the last reflection exercise in the previous chapter to be sure the things you listed there are included.

▶ Beside each role, jot down an estimate of the average amount of time you give that role in a "normal" week's time.

▶ Next, write down how you feel while participating in that role.

▶ Then prioritize your roles, from most important in your life to least important. (Think in terms of those you would like to give away or could have a more fulfilling life without versus those you would not want to have taken away from you.)

▶ Are you spending the majority of your time and energy in roles that are truly the most important to you?

▶ How could you rearrange things so that you and your significant others feel more loved? How do you implement self-love? (Without care, responsibility, respect, and knowledge of ourselves, there will be none for others.)

FORGIVENESS

A CLOSE SECOND to committed and consistent priority time and energy on my list of criteria for real love is a willingness to forgive. Henry van Dyke defines love as the heart's immortal desire to be completely known and to have all forgiven. Forgiveness means accepting your power to pardon, to extend grace—meaning that you forfeit demanding reasons and suspend judgement. Forgiveness is viewed by some as a weakness. In truth, it is a strength. Oskar Schindler said it best in the movie *Schindler's List* when he tries to explain to the power-hungry Nazi, Amon, that the emperor who grants pardon to the thief has more real power than the emperor who has the thief executed. Forgiveness is not forgetting. It is a conscious decision not to fuel the fires of blame, self-righteousness, or victimization. Not forgiving always hurts us more than the person we refuse to forgive. Hate tends to destroy the hater in that it fills us with negative energy, which often converts into negative behaviors.

To err is human, to forgive divine. A quote first spoken by Alexander Pope, and often repeated by my mother, a wise woman.

Reflection Exercise

▶ Do you hold grudges? Against whom?

▶ Who has forgiven you recently?

▶ Are you able to forgive yourself?

▶ Make a list of people you have not forgiven. Concentrate on each one. Write down what you would like to say to that person. Visualize having the conversation. If you believe it would be of value to actually contact the person and initiate the conversation, do so. If not, then let it go. You could have a private ritual and burn what you have written. Just as the paper is transformed by the fire, your negative energy can be transformed into neutral, or even positive, energy.

HONESTY

NO LIST OF love's criteria can be complete without honesty, or truth, yet we each tend to lie most often to the people we claim to love the most. If I had to name the most corruptive force in relationships, it would be a lack of honesty. Truth is a complicated and multifaceted concept. Gandhi is attributed with saying that only God has access to absolute truth; that any human's understanding of truth can change from day to day with new information. Our commitment must be to the truth of the moment rather than to consistency. This will keep us as honest as possible.

A friend recently said to me, "I think I could really love if I could force myself to always tell the truth." His statement overwhelmed me as one of the wisest and most insightful I'd ever heard. Love has to be based on truth, or there is no trust, and without trust, there is no real love—only a painful need and longing. We've each felt this pain when we were lied to by someone we loved. A client expressed that when she discovered her husband had been lying to her about seeing another woman, she literally felt like she'd been shot through the heart with a poisoned arrow. The poison had saturated her being until she could no longer be in her husband's presence without feeling she might kill him.

A common defense of lying is to convince ourselves that we lie to protect someone's feelings, or not to hurt them with a truth we believe they cannot handle. The deepest truth is that the person we are trying to protect is usually ourselves, and the lying only works temporarily, for as Roger Gould writes in *Transformations:*

> The truth, as best as we know it, must be our goal, no matter where it leads us. Every self-deception causes erroneous judgments, and bad decisions follow, with unforeseen consequences to our lives. But more than that, every protective self-deception is a crevice in our psyche with a little demon lurking in it ready to become an episode of unexplained anxiety when life threatens. The self-deceptions that are designed to protect us from pain actually end up delivering more pain. We fortify our deceptions to protect them from the natural corrections of daily life. The larger the area of our mind we find it necessary to defend, the more our thinking processes will suffer. We will not allow our mind to roam freely because new information might contradict our self-deceptions. The larger the self-deceptions, the larger the section of the world we are excluded from.[8]

Life has taught me that he is right. The extent to which we lie, to ourselves as well as to others, correlates negatively with love. In other words, the more we lie, the less we love. It is not the quality of the lie, but the distance lies create in a relationship that will harm the relationship.

Reflection Exercise

▶ Keep track of how many lies you tell in the course of one day. (Lies of commission and omission) To whom did you lie? Why? What good can come of it?

▶ Do you want others to trust you?

▶ How could telling the truth change the situation in the long run?

▶ Visualize doing this, and then follow the same instructions as given in step four of the previous reflection exercise on forgiveness.

SPIRITUALITY

WHAT ABOUT SPIRITUALITY as a criterion for lasting love? Primary love is dependent upon attachment, connection, or union. Spirituality is experiencing the sacred in such a way that we connect to it, recognizing the sacred within ourselves. Spirituality involves our souls.

I once read that before we are sent to earth, God sings us a lullaby, hugs us lovingly, kisses us, and then sends us on to the struggle we know as life on Earth. Although this is not a conscious memory, there remains deep in our souls a hint of memory of the song, the hug, the kiss, and the love. If this is true, it would verify that our first feelings of love grow from our original spiritual connection to the Divine Creator of all life—in whatever form one may exist. I have to consider the validity of a Divine Creator's love each time a young child tells me that he doesn't feel loved *anymore*. That *anymore* haunts me.

There is a deep and abstract part of each of us, regardless of our age, that *knows* and yearns for more love, or more connection to something we seem unable to capture for long. We may grasp it for a moment while viewing a sunrise over the ocean, the reflection of a sunset in a mountain lake, a majestic mountain against a clear blue sky, or a beautiful butterfly. My soul feels loved when I listen to the opera singer Andrea Bocelli sing "Nessum dorma" or Maria Callas sing "Te Deum." The music fills me—I am passionately in love with life, with everything and everyone. I know that I became a better person in these spiritual moments, but the better person gets lost quickly. Or perhaps I simply forget her—forget that she is a part of divine creation and has a responsibility to be kind and loving.

My father wrote a sermon on divine love in which he stated that love in its ultimate form is always present and always available to us, but that we mortals do not take time to respond to it. Could it be that the lack of love we feel is instead our lack of response to the divine love within each of us and our unawareness of who we really are? We are the species in charge of the known universe. Perhaps it is divine love, spiritual love, from which all love extends. When I allow myself to feel the miraculous existence of each of us alive on our planet, I have to stop in my tracks. It makes me cry—tears of awe and wonder.

Reflection Exercise

▶ Is your soul love-starved?

▶ How often do you consider the question "Is this all there is?"

▶ When have you been poignantly aware that you needed more? Where did you turn—to whom or to what (the bar, the refrigerator, a book, television, a computer, music, art, etc.)? Did it work to fill your emptiness? For how long?

▶ Have you tried meditation, or prayer, or a spiritual practice?

> ### Reflection Exercise (continued)
>
> ▶ Does a sexual experience fulfill your need for connection?
>
> ▶ List some of the special times you felt connected to all of creation and were filled to your capacity for union.

THE UNION OF SPIRITUALITY AND SEXUALITY

SEX IS ALSO union and can be a deeply spiritual experience—*when it happens with love.* When sexuality and spirituality are in conflict within us, we are in trouble in both realms. The deepest need of the human soul is to overcome the anxiety of separateness, the feeling that we do not belong, or are not loved. Sexual needs compulsively drive us to form a union that can prevent our psyches from carrying us off into total emotional alienation. If we are able to feel that we belong, that we are desired, the experience will diminish our anxiety—*if only for a few moments.* If we are allowed the continuation of union through companionship with our lover, the security of knowing we are loved, are therefore lovable, and can love in return, we are able to endure almost any hardship. Consensual sexual passion consummated does make us feel alive and connected. Creating within us this desire for union could have been not only the Absolute's plan to populate the earth, but also the way to keep us connected passionately to each other. The knowledge of how to bond in sexual union is innate, a basic part of our DNA, but what about the knowledge of how to bond in love? *Is it possible that the Absolute's greatest gift, and greatest challenge, is to allow us to discover and work out the practice of love?*

At the age of ninety-two, Will Durant, author of the eleven-volume *The Story of Civilization,* was asked what the most valuable information was that he'd learned from his studies and his life. He replied, *"If only we could learn to love one another, there need be few other lessons."*[9]

Are You Ready *to* See How *the* Webs Are Tangled?

*THE NEXT TIME YOU SEE A FAMILY, ANY GROUP OF BEINGS
"DOING" LIFE TOGETHER, REMEMBER THAT SUCH A GROUP IS THE
BASIC BUILDING BLOCK OF OUR WORLD, THE PLACE
WHERE THE MIRACLE OF "US" TAKES PLACE.*
—PAUL PEARSALL, FROM *THE POWER OF THE FAMILY*

WATCHING MY ELDEST grandchild take her first breath remains the most spiritual moment of my life—instant love. I felt as if I could see her breathe in her spirit and become more than a physical body. To breathe is to inspire, to take in: breath, spirit, life, and love. As great a miracle as our conception is the breathing in of life on earth. It could be considered our first independent act—the physical acceptance of our soul, or spirit, from that unknown reservoir where souls must be stored and cared for by angels. When our birth parents shared the elemental genetic essence of themselves that created us, their genes formed the combination that distinguished us as unique, but at the same time guaranteed that we would be more like them than like others, to whom we are not directly related. They gave us form; however, with our first breath we became more than physical form. The birth of each of us alters the energy of the world.

FAMILIES

WITH THE BIRTH of a child, a new family is also born, a new web is woven within the larger webs that are anchored in place by our extended families, communities, and cultures. Every family is a whole, but also a part of something larger. This is true of everything— individuals, families, neighborhoods, cities, and so on. There is no perfect family, yet, at a deeper level, every family has its own perfect reason for "doing life" together. This holds true for biological families, stepfamilies, adopted families, foster-care families, homosexual families, and reconstituted families.

Several philosophical and religious theories postulate that we will "do life" with souls with whom we have accumulated unresolved issues, or karmic debts, during past lives. Whether this is true or not, I am certain that we do life with the people who will challenge us, irritate and frustrate us, and ultimately will "grow" us—help us refine our souls to know more about love. It seems simple for infants to respond to love. When an infant's needs are met, he settles into contentment. The adult caregiver feels rewarded and they become attached—the primary stage of love. However, as we grow up, we learn to block our natural responses to love because we've often been hurt *in the name of love*. We've been lied to, controlled, betrayed, and sometimes abused. It becomes more and more difficult to accept and trust what someone calls love. By adulthood, everyone has become one of the "walking wounded," and we tend to remain faithful to our wounds. Everyone has a few holes in their hearts, but some have gaping craters—those whose innocence was betrayed through sexual abuse or total abandonment. Our hearts and minds cry, "Why?"

Perhaps the only viable answer to "why" is well portrayed by Eleanor of Aquitaine in one of the most poignant scenes of the movie *The Lion in Winter*. The three sons of Eleanor and Henry II are arguing with their father over whom he should choose to be the next king of England. Richard, the eldest, who is a homosexual and his mother's choice for the throne, is holding a sword to his father's throat, while John, the youngest son and his father's choice, is having a temper tantrum. The middle son, who knows he is not the choice of either parent, is complaining to his mother about how her deviousness has divided their family. Henry decides to disown all three sons and have his marriage to Eleanor annulled on the grounds that she had probably slept with his father. She waltzes from the room with the comment: "Well, I guess every family has its ups and downs."

Touché, Eleanor. Families can be very different, but each will have its share of difficult times. Individual members of families are also different; however, the people who come together as a family are more alike than different. When each aspect of ourselves is considered, we are all more alike than different, for the entire family of mankind shares 99.9 percent of human DNA. You could line us up from imbecile to genius, from the most loving to the most hateful, every race, color, and creed; the similarities will outweigh the differences cell by cell. We all have the same basic needs and emotions and need to be loved before we in turn can love others. On the other hand, each one of us remains a unique miracle—when you consider that, of the millions of sperm struggling for connection at your conception, only one connected to the unique egg that became the unique you.

The differences begin to outweigh the similarities due to the circumstances (genetic interactions included) from which and into which we are born and raised. If our circumstances were identical, we would each be capable of any evil act or act of kindness that has been done, but the total circumstances are never identical. The most influential set of circumstances with which we must deal can be summed up in one word—*family.* When we are children, we cannot see the world as it really is, but as we are conditioned by our families to see it.

Being in a family guarantees the beginning of an endless waltz— the shadow waltz we each dance with the realities, memories, illusions, and fantasies of our parents and other childhood caregivers. Orphans and children raised in foster homes are destined to dance with many partners. The music, giving rhythm to each dance, plays on throughout the generations of every family. All life is based on the rhythm of sex and death, of connection and separation. As long as there is life, these rhythms blend into a cosmic symphony where each of us is a contributing composer.

Reflection Exercise

▶ List the people you consider members of your family. Write how you feel about each one.

▶ If you were to write a book about these people doing life together, what title would best capture the story?

▶ Jot down things that come to your mind as you reminisce about your family—values, traditions, special events, special moments, both positive and negative.

▶ What unresolved issues do you have with your family?

You are basically made from the genes of your birth parents. These genes unite to determine your color and colorings, your basic size and shape. They influence how you move, eat, think, and even how you feel. They influence many diseases and addictions with which you may struggle. They etch the blueprint of the way you were, are, and will be, and they greatly influence your children and your children's children. It is important however to understand that your genetic makeup does not remain stable. It is subject to changes throughout your lifetime due to varying environmental circumstances, including addictions, medications, drugs, and diseases.

Most of us know that we physically resemble our parents and relatives, but we have a more difficult time admitting that we often behave like them. However, our genetic relatedness does not mean we have to "become" our birth parents, or be locked into their patterns. *It means we are given all they can give, and then given an opportunity to develop beyond them.*[1]

FAMILY TANGLES

THE ABOVE TRUTHS were driven home to me during therapy sessions with the Albertsons. The six adult members of the Albertson family were seated at the round table in my office conference room. Their family symphony had deteriorated into cacophony bouncing from the walls that was painful for my heart to hear. I had been listening to sections of it for weeks, and it was time to combine the sections into a full score. I insisted that the four adult children (two males and two females) and their aging parents come to my office for a lengthy session if they had any desire to reunite as a family. Fred, the eldest brother, had been arrested for sexually molesting one of the teenage daughters of his oldest sister. The niece told her mother, who believed her, because Fred had also molested her when she was a young girl. She had not told her own mother for fear of not being believed, or of breaking her mother's heart if she were believed. She had not told her father for fear he would have beaten Fred to death.

In a prior session with her sister, she had learned that her sister had been molested by Fred as well. Neither told during their years in the original family out of fear that the family would fall apart. Rather than fall apart instantly, they drifted apart by distancing themselves each from the other. They created physical and emotional space without building bridges of communication—no one wanted to travel over a bridge that supported such secrets and pain. Never did they congregate at home for the holidays, as the mother had hoped they would. The mother's heart was breaking at every fault line, for she assumed that the distancing of the family must somehow have been her fault. Each family member knew his personal reason for staying away, but no one knew anyone else's reason. The recurring minor themes in their family symphony were suspicion, fear, denial, doubt, and pretense. Yet, the therapist in me trusted that a more dominant theme of caring and love had brought them together in this room. Without some desire to reunite, they would not be present. They were connected in their shared history and even through their unshared secrets, for each secret had been kept as a way of trying to protect another's feelings. This never works in the long term, as truth does seem to have a way of emerging, even though it often takes its own not so sweet time. They had thought their secrets were safe until the niece discovered she was not safe with her uncle—and saw no reason to protect him.

The offending brother had been mandated to six months of therapy prior to his trial, which was scheduled three days hence. He was a successful, charismatic businessman, and was exceptionally handsome. His early goal in therapy had been to convince me that his niece had mistaken abuse for a friendly gesture of an uncle's admiration. He claimed that he was willing to apologize, but not to be blamed and punished for something that he did not do. I had invited the niece and her mother, Fred's sister, to come in for an appointment with him, so he would have the opportunity to make his apology. They showed up, but he called to say he would not be able to make it. While I listened to him on the phone, my gut confirmed what I suspected—that he had consistently lied during his earlier appointments.

The appointment turned into an emotional "clearinghouse" for the mother and her daughter. The mother told of the abuse she had suffered and why she had been afraid to tell. She confessed that she had always believed that Fred was her mother's favorite son, since he was the child who looked the most like her, and this caused her to fear that her mother would not believe her even if she had told. She and her daughter shared their stories and their tears, promising to support each other in telling the truth to the whole family, beginning with the older parents.

This session turned into one of the most painfully intense hours of each of their lives. The mother of the entire tribe admitted for the first time, after repressing the information for over sixty years, that in the foster home where she had been raised she had been abused in every way by her foster father. He had threatened to give her back to the "welfare lady" if she ever told. She never did. She'd turned to the church and become a devout, but silent, Christian. The father had married her out of pity because he had gotten her drunk and pregnant. He had become an alcoholic over the years, as was his father, but had recently stopped drinking when a doctor told him he would never live to teach his grandsons to fish, unless he gave up the booze. When he was drunk he had been verbally and emotionally abusive to every member of his family, especially to Fred, whom, he confessed, he had never trusted. "Interesting," he mused, "I never knew what was really going on, but intuitively, I somehow knew he was doing something wrong. I have to admit that I suspected what might be happening, but I just could not accuse my own son without some

proof. I took the easy road. Oh God, can I ever forgive myself—
or him?"

In subsequent sessions, he accomplished both. Fred finally
stopped lying, lowered his defenses, admitted his abuse of his sister
and of her daughter, apologized to everyone, and asked for their forgiveness. He and his father ended their joint session sobbing in each
other's arms and left together planning a fishing trip.

Sessions continued over weeks with different dyads and triads
sharing their stories and their tears. In each session secrets were
revealed that broke down barriers, or washed them away by opening
the holding tanks of deceit, fear, guilt, and sadness buried deep in
their psyches. Most of us have such tanks, which have the power to
drown us in depression when kept sealed, or bathe us in fresh vital-
ity—when opened by choice.

As I looked over this group that had spent the last two months
untangling the webs that had been woven throughout their family, I
was struck by the ways they physically resembled one another. The
mother was small and appeared fragile, as did one of her daughters
and Fred; however, these two had the lips and nose of their father.
The father was larger and more robust, as were the other two siblings,
however, these two had their mother's nose and mouth. If anyone had
walked into the room, he would have recognized this group as a "family." Two kept their hands tightly folded in their laps, as their mother
did, and tended to look down rather than make direct eye contact.
The father and the other two folded their arms across their chests and
tended to look straight out, making direct eye contact. There was
something aggressive and almost bullying in their eyes. The three
with downcast eyes included the two who had been sexually
abused—and the abuser. It was impossible for me to know which
traits and behaviors were genetic and which had manifested from the
quality of nurturing provided by their environment.

The niece in the Albertson family had somehow developed beyond
the level of the prior two generations. Her genes were altered by the
contribution of those from her father, and equally important were the
alterations in her social culture. She viewed things from a perspective
ushered in by her peers, the early nineties adolescents, who studied
psychology in high school and participated in support groups where

they shared what was upsetting them. Their generation became the base for a society in which most girls do not tolerate abuse. They had stopped giving awards for being quiet, or for being victims. They are young and powerful lionesses who support each other in taking risks, expressing emotion, and telling the truth. This niece began the process that freed the entire family from their tangled webs of lies and secrets. Her courage energized them, and gave them a new spirit.

During this extended family session the tears of three generations mingled in the joyous freedom of truth, a freedom not known previously in this family. Protecting their secrets had drained the energy from individual members. Honesty frees your energy to deal with problems and also energizes your relationships, keeping them vital and alive. As Starhawk writes in *Walking to Mercury:* "What we don't say divides us. Secrets carve Grand Canyons of separation through our relationships."

The family proclaimed concern, love, and forgiveness for Fred, but they were united in wanting him to be punished. The mother, smiling through her tears, could say lovingly to her son, "We, and that means our family, have made our first group decision. We want you to straighten up, son. We want you to get more help and tell the truth. We are all going to tell the truth. No more secrets. And if you ever do anything like this again, your papa will beat you to a pulp—because he loves you."

Fred tearfully promised to stop lying and said that he would call his attorney the next morning to enter a guilty plea. Trust level being tentative, his parents requested that he come to my office to make the call, which he did.

After the trial, his family supported the judge's decision that Fred must serve a one-year jail sentence without possibility of parole, followed by a five-year probation during which he was required to have weekly therapy. Many of his sessions have included his siblings, parents, his present wife, and his ex-wife, who had left him because he had abused their daughter. History does repeat itself until we see ourselves clearly, gain the courage to tell the truth, and commit to change. It has been said that we remain as sick as our darkest secrets. Several years have passed and today, as my heart tunes in to this family's contribution to the cosmic symphony, I hear a harmonized chorus singing a glorious hallelujah!

Reflection Exercise

▶ How would your family of origin handle a serious crisis of exposure today?

▶ What "secrets" do you suspect might be revealed? What do you suspect others might be repressing that could emerge and free your family from pretense?

▶ What might come into the light if your holding tank were opened?

▶ Consider your parents' traits as objectively as possible. Make a list of their physical characteristics, positive and negative qualities, eccentricities, fears, likes and dislikes. Circle the ones you recognize in yourself.

▶ If you are adopted, this exercise can still be valid. Do this exercise for your birth parents, if you know them, and the parents who raised you.

▶ Now make a list of the ways you consider yourself to be unlike your parents and siblings. How did you come by or develop these traits? Was it from someone you have emulated, or some unique experience or accident that affected only you?

▶ What major social and cultural changes have occurred that could cause you to have values different from your parents?

NATURE AND NURTURE

THE LEADING CONTEMPORARY model of "how you become who you are" is that the genes of your birth parents combine in a complex, but always unique, configuration. After birth, you are immediately incorporated into a relationship web with others, who are also an integral part of a larger and more extended web of relationships. You become tied into a system of caregivers—usually defined as your family, whose stresses, coping styles, defense mechanisms, habits, and patterns continue to mold us. As this process continues, the interactions between them and you will change you to varying degrees, but your core nature remains uniquely who you are born to be. A contemporary philosopher, Sam Keen, explains that we are born with our own "hardware," then people around us begin to insert "software" to influence us to live by their authority.

Research by Dean Hamer, a contemporary molecular geneticist, and the increasing mass of research on identical twins raised apart, have proven that we are to a larger degree than we've previously realized, "hardwired" to be similar to our parents. Hamer's labora tories have isolated specific genes linked to the behaviors and personality traits of aggression, shyness, intelligence, novelty seeking, anxiety and worry, depression, desire, addictions, homosexuality, and even sleeping patterns. However, the real beauty of his work, *and the hope for us as human beings,* is that he is also proving that the *interplay* between the genetic hardwiring and the environmental soft wiring—nurturing, conditioning, and choices—is critical in determining who we turn out to be. Hamer states that giving children security, love, positive stimulation, and knowledge can be the difference between one's turning out to be a clever crook or an extraordinary scientist.[2]

In his book, *Living With Our Genes,* Hamer makes a strong case for allowing children to be the best they innately are, rather than trying to mold them into someone they are not. The bottom line is nature provides the genetic blueprint, but nurture, environmental influences, cultural and social expectations, and our personal choices shape and refine the final product. Michelangelo is a prime example. He was similar to his family in many ways, especially his father, but his unique difference was that he "fell in love" with marble. He made a personal choice to pursue that love. Anyone who has ever stood in the Sistine Chapel or viewed his David has felt the awe that moves us beyond the limitations we usually place on ourselves and others. His life, which continues through his magnificent art, attests to James Hillman's theory, as explained in his book, *The Soul's Code,*[3] of the soul's "daimon," a guide that leads our soul to its fulfillment.

Reflection Exercise

▶ Close your eyes, exhale slowly, and then allow an image of yourself to fill your mind's eye.

▶ Give this image of yourself permission to manifest its highest and best potential. What would that self be doing? (Assume that success is guaranteed.)

▶ How would you change what you are now doing?

▶ Would your family support you in accomplishing this?

▶ Why do you believe you are on this planet at this time, born into your family of origin?

▶ What have you learned from them about love?

▶ If you have children, why do you believe they are in your life?

▶ What kind of nurturing do they need from you to attain their highest potential? Consider that parenting our children can be the greatest mission and challenge any of us will ever have.

CRITICAL EARLY NURTURING

YOUR FIRST ENVIRONMENT and experience of nurture is the uterine home provided by your mother. You were connected to a supply of all the elements you needed to live and grow without consciously expending your own energy. Most psychologists believe that this represents the kind of attachment we all try—in vain—to reestablish for the rest of our physical lives. Infants and young children love out of their need to be attached to someone who will help them survive. As children, we will do anything to stay attached to our caregivers. We smile for them, imitate and emulate them, obey them, and believe what they tell us. Yet, we are often terrified that they may not love us enough to stay attached to us. For the most part, this is unconscious processing, but this fear dominates our early years of dependency. The ways we are treated by our initial caregivers—including how we are touched, looked at, talked to, attended to—become automatically our first definition of love, even if their treatment of us is not loving. As Sam Keen says: "If your mother burned the toast, then love means burned toast! It is as if the ways you were treated by your parents forms a grid in your minds by which you begin to measure yourself and assess your degree of lovability."

The primary state of love is attachment, and the primary response to love is positive attention giving. When an infant has a need, she makes a noise that will signal distress. If aid comes to relieve that distress, she feels content, secure, and reconnected. Love begins. Research with infants and young children supports the premise that it is of utmost importance that attention giving must be predictably present, so that the infant is not in doubt about her connection to love. If no aid comes, she begins to feel doubtful, fearful, insecure, and helpless. Interestingly, the infant who moves into helplessness does not continue to send out distress signals, but will become listless and passive. Apathy develops in this passive space.

A continued lack of response to the infant's signals eventually breaks down apathy, and the infant moves into a space of disconnection—separation—darkness. The darkness is soon filled with devaluing of self, depression, and fear. Devaluing of self leads to the devaluing of others, and the opportunity to develop empathy, which should be the next stage of love, is diminished. A poverty of soul—feeling unwanted, disconnected, and helpless to do anything about it—begins. Mother Theresa often stated: *"Loneliness and the feeling of being unwanted is the most terrible poverty."*

This state of poverty is a vacuum of numbness, nothingness, nonexistence. Nonexistence is the deepest fear in human nature. We humans will commit any act that will verify that we exist. This process of validating our existence continues to cycle throughout our lives. When we feel assured of our existence through the consistent and positive attention of someone who loves us, there is no need to initiate destructive behaviors. Infants who are ignored for lengthy periods of time, not consistently nurtured, will bang their heads against their cribs or bite themselves. The pain is assurance of life, which is preferred over feelings of nonbelonging that are too painful to bear. The hope of belonging to a nurturing other is lost. Despair moves in. In this place of despair, anything can happen. This is why children kill themselves—and others.

Love, pain, and fear become entwined and inseparable in the psyche of a child who must remain attached to a primary caregiver to survive. In 1997, a shocking true story came to light about a young boy who was born to a carnival-working mom in Texas. The boy was kept in a cage in the back of a truck and was fed garbage in a dog dish slid into his cage. His mother tried to put him up for sale when he was eighteen months old. Police intervened and the child was taken away from his mother. He was more like a wild animal than a child, yet he screamed for his mother, for she was his only source of survival. She was all he knew.

There are millions of children who have little chance to learn love because they were never consistently nurtured. Most parents tell their children that whatever they do to them is "in the name of love." Children who are abused "in the name of love" continue to believe that abuse and pain are aspects of love. Most people who have been abused by their primary caregivers seek out other abusers to "love" them. Abuse, with the pain that follows, is preferable to being totally ignored because the pain verifies existence. Our self-esteem, even as adults, remains highly correlated to the amount of positive attention we received from our parents when we were most vulnerable as infants and young children.

While visiting my mother, who now lives in the assisted-living quarters of a retirement center, I became aware that the woman in the next room called the aides about every fifteen minutes to ask them what time it was. One of the aides came into my mother's room to see if we had an extra clock we could lend to the woman. My mother responded that the woman had two clocks, but she hid them because it gave her an excuse to get someone's attention. It did not matter that the aides were irritated and cross with her. She was desperate to know that she still existed and could create a momentary connection by obtaining a brief response. Many, like this woman, carry the cry of little Emily in Thornton Wilder's *Our Town* somewhere in our psyches throughout our lives: "Mommy, mommy, please look at me as if you can really see me."

Reflection Exercise

This exercise requires that you stay centered in your present power, understanding that you have grown stronger as a result of enduring whatever hardships and difficulties life has dealt you. Everything that has ever happened to you is stored within your memory, although experiences too painful for your brain to assimilate at the time of the experience are deeply repressed. You must trust that if the experience itself did not destroy you, neither will the memory. Exhale deeply, breathing out any anxiety, and then allow yourself to slowly inhale until you feel calm and relaxed. Allow the years to melt away and give your brain permission to remember:

▶ How your mother looked at you.

▶ How your father looked at you.

▶ How any other significant caregivers looked at you.

▶ Did you feel seen as a small child?

▶ How did it feel to be held by your mother, or female caregiver? Your father, or male caregiver?

▶ To whom were you most connected as a young child?

▶ What do you remember about those connections?

▶ What is your earliest memory?

▶ What is your first memory of love?

MEMORIES AND EARLY DEFINITIONS OF LOVE

I HAVE SEARCHED my childhood memories in an effort to discover how I first experienced love and unconsciously created my early definition of what love means, which has changed and expanded throughout my life. I implore you to do the same, *for your story is more important for you than my story.* I share parts of my story as a guide shares a map, realizing that we are more alike than different at the deepest levels of our nature. Our nurturing (or nonnurturing) environments vary greatly, but our basic needs for positive attention and love are the same.

Via oral and recorded history of my first two years of life, I learned that my father was critically ill when I was just over a year old. He was taken to a large hospital in another town. Headlines in our local paper stated, "Popular Minister Near Death at Duke Hospital." My stoic mother would not have talked about my father's absence or illness because she truly believed that talking about anything negative made it more powerful, more real. She would not have talked about it because it involved a physical organ—in this case, my father's heart, but "nice women" just did not discuss body parts, even hearts. She would not have talked about it because she may not be able to uphold her stoic demeanor if she had tried to verbalize the truth. She would not have cried, for that would have indicated a weakness that she would not have wanted her baby daughter to see. It might also have indicated that she wasn't trusting enough in the love of God, or in the will of God, and then the church members might have found her lacking. Further complicating things for her, she was pregnant with my brother, who was born when I was fifteen months old. Her energy was spent in planning how to cope if she were widowed with two babies in the late 1930s, when mothers were expected to, and respected for, staying at home with their children.

However, that was not her fate. My father survived. He came home just before my brother was born. I immediately became "Daddy's girl," because the new baby needed his mother. Thus began my competition for mother's love. Since none of us ever receive all of the love we crave, we assume, unconsciously and at an early age, that love is somehow rationed and conditional, and that our share may run out unless we are "good," in whatever ways our parents or early caregivers define "good."

I am fairly certain that these early experiences of my father's disappearance, my brother's birth, and my mother's preoccupation with a new baby and a seriously ill husband, are somehow responsible for my issues around abandonment, jealousy, competition, and independence. "Love blocks" began early that caused me to hold enough of myself in reserve in any relationship so that I would never again experience such a depth of vulnerability. As an adult I've learned that holding back blocks the intimacy, trust, and vulnerability that are necessary ingredients of love. *It is interesting that adults seem to be able to enjoy intimacy to the same degree we are able to tolerate vulnerability.* All children are vulnerable and most are hurt; therefore, it requires courage to remain vulnerable as we grow older. We remain the most vulnerable to the people we love because they have the most power in our lives. While we are children, our parents are our omnipotent and omniscient gods, our heroes and heroines, and our lovers. This is a fact we as parents cannot afford to forget.

Reflection Exercise

► What are your "love blocks" (doubts that prevent you from trusting love)?

► Who, or what events, caused them?

► Do you still use your love blocks today to protect yourself from being vulnerable?

By the end of my third year, when Daddy would tuck me in each night, I can remember his whispering, "Good night, Sunshine, I love you." Love then came to mean someone's being there to give me a special bit of attention. When Daddy loved, he said so. He also swung me high in the backyard swing he'd made. We had fun together. Mother rarely said, "I love you," and even more rarely seemed to have fun, but she kept us clean, stayed with us, and fed us delicious meals. It took me years to comprehend that her love was a basic love necessary for Daddy, for me, and for my brother and sister (born when I was ten years old) to survive. Because she loved us enough to do the responsible nurturing and enough to put our needs and desires before her own, my father and we children could feel secure and free. Often when we are not loved in the specific ways we desire to be, the "fun" ways, we discount love from someone who may indeed love us from a different, perhaps deeper, perspective.

This becomes a problem of magnitude when parents of young children divorce. One parent usually has the larger responsibility of the daily dynamics and the "picky shit" stuff, which children take for granted. The other parent has weekend "fun" duty. Children—myself included—usually assume that the "fun" parent loves them more. This is rarely the case. With maturity, as we become more aware of what love requires, we see through new eyes many things that we could not see as children.

Reflection Exercise

▶ How did your mother or female caregiver show her love?

▶ How did your father or male caregiver show his love?

Your answers here will be your childhood definition of love.

SIBLING TANGLES

MY MOTHER'S LOVE included what she called "fairness." She went to great effort to divide everything fairly between my brother and me. Because World War II was in full swing, sugar was rationed and candy was a rare treat, sometimes used to entice us to take naps. If we napped "well" (stayed quiet and did not fight for an hour), and if I didn't suck my thumb, we might get to share a Baby Ruth candy bar, which was carefully divided and waiting for us on a small table. One particular day when I had napped well, I went to the table for my prize to discover that my brother had gotten there first and eaten both pieces of candy. I hit him and screamed for Mother, the fairness lady. When she came upon the scene of the crime, my brother began to cry and said I'd hit him. I screamed that he'd eaten my candy.

"Did not!"

"Did too!"

Thus the "fairness lady" had to make a loving decision, which for Mother meant she had to believe us both or punish us both. We were punished and there were no more Baby Ruths for a long while. I became confused about how honesty, fairness, and right or wrong, fit into this love thing.

I also began to dislike my brother, whom my parents kept telling me I loved. Did I?

What they were really saying was that I *should* love my little brother. Often I felt that Mother liked him better than she liked me. She was petite and pretty, and he looked like her. I looked more like our father, with his broad shoulders and large Roman nose. I can remember thinking that God had goofed us up in the factory, but that as we grew up, whomever was responsible for these mistakes would fix us so that I would begin to resemble Mother and he would change to look like Daddy. It never happened.

EMPATHY

THEN THE DAY came when my brother had to go to the hospital to have his tonsils taken out. My parents told him that he was going to a Halloween party, dressed him in a cute costume and mask, and carted him off to the hospital, where his Halloween mask was swapped for an ether mask. When he woke up in a strange place with his throat on fire, he was terrified. I felt terribly sorry for him. I loved him then and prayed that God would make him well. This is my first memory of feeling empathy, which is the second level of love following attachment.

Siblings more often than not share emotional ambivalence about each other, yet our sibling relationships are usually our longest lasting relationships and stand to teach us a great deal about ourselves and love. They usually survive the deaths of parents and, often, our spouses. Siblings remain in our lives after quarrels, fights, heartaches, and separations. They stand in the arena with us as we begin to battle with conflict, competition, jealousy, and friendship. My little brother was my best ally when I was angry with my parents, which I was, for having told him a lie about going to a party instead of the hospital. Siblings are possibly our best teachers of how filled with conflict love can be. We can hate them one moment and love them the next. This is true of all love, but a sibling relationship usually demonstrates it early and profoundly.

Reflection Exercise

- ▶ If you have siblings, list their names. (If you do not have siblings, list playmates or cousins you remember from childhood.)

- ▶ Jot down how you feel about each one today.

- ▶ Is this the same feeling you had for that sibling when you were a child? If not, how and why have your feelings changed?

- ▶ How close are you to each one today? Are you still fighting the same old fights?

- ▶ How could you improve your relationship with each sibling?

After reading the first edition of this book, my brother brought me a huge bag of Baby Ruth candy bars. We laughed and healed together. For total healing, there can only be forgiveness.

DUE TO BIRTH order, our innate differences, changes in the family dynamics, and financial, social, and cultural changes, no two siblings ever have the exact same parents. This often translates into conflicts with your siblings about your parents and childhood events. If possible, talk to your siblings about memories of your parents and family interactions. You will rarely agree on every detail, but each of you could be correct. Marian Sandmaier's book, *Original Kin,* is an invaluable resource for working through sibling issues.[4]

Most of us who have siblings wished at times during childhood that we were the only child, while most only children have wished for siblings. "Lonely onlies" used to get an overdose of bad press, but that has changed considerably during the latter half of the twentieth century. Research indicates that they may indeed receive more positive attention while growing up, and that the only real disadvantage is having the sole responsibility of looking after aging parents later in life.

TANGLES OF ILLUSION AND DOUBT

NO CHILD HAS ever had "perfect parents," and no parent has ever had "a perfect child." However, children tenaciously hold on to illusions of parental perfection. My parents' lying to my brother about his tonsillectomy is my first memory of having that illusion shattered. They claimed to have lied for his own good, and then said it had been my paternal grandmother's idea, which made me angry with her as well. This scenario was the beginning of my serious doubts about love.

Another childhood doubt about this love business comes from the infamous Biblical story of Abraham and Isaac, in which God tells Abraham to sacrifice his son, Isaac, to prove that his love for God is greater than his love for his son. I hated this story. It seemed as far from love as my occasional intense dislike of my brother. It also caused me to have a deep fear that God might choose to test my father in the same way, and that no lamb would appear before I was slaughtered. By age six, I was in serious intellectual and emotional love trouble. I didn't totally trust love, my parents, or God.

Reflection Exercise

▶ Have you thought of more "love blocks" you might still use today?

▶ What happened in your family to cause you to doubt love?

▶ How and when did you realize that your parents were not "perfect"? How did you cope with that realization?

▶ What illusions were woven into your family web?

▶ Do you still hold those same illusions? If not, how were they shattered?

One of the most harmful childhood illusions woven throughout my family web (the "Wall" web, as Wall is my maiden name) was the criterion held by my family for good and bad. People who professed to live by the Ten Commandments and went to Protestant churches on Sunday were "good" people. I didn't concern myself with "bad" people because I didn't believe I knew any. "Good children" were clean, never said four-letter words, were always polite to adults, but could argue and fight with other children. "Good families" tried to hide their problems from other families. The game was "Candyland"—always wear a smile in public. What the neighbors thought was more important than what was really going on within the family unit. "Good families" never got a divorce.

It was inconceivable to me that I would ever divorce, but I did—and so did both of my siblings. It was equally inconceivable that my brother, sister, or I would ever have the problems we have had throughout our lives. At least one of the three of us has violated every good principle in the "code" our parents tried to teach us.

Tightly woven throughout my "good" family web were high expectations of me, which were often stated as clichés: "Pretty is as pretty does" (Mother). "Don't be afraid to make a mistake, just be sure to make a new one every time" (Daddy). "Do what you know is right" (Mother). "Always put others first" (Both). "Don't talk until you have something to say" (Daddy). "Smile and the world smiles with you; weep and you weep alone" (Mother).

The more powerful messages were forcefully and subtly imposed through my parents' behavior: Keep negative thoughts and feelings repressed; you don't have a body, only a brain—use it; make things appear good and normal in this family, regardless of what's really going on; and, family secrets are sacred.

Reflection Exercise

▶ What messages were you given as a child about yourself?

▶ What expectations did your family have of you?

▶ What kind of image did your parents try to create? How did you fit into their image?

▶ What secrets did your family hold?

TANGLES OF SECRETS

SECRETS ARE USUALLY deeply embedded in a family's web. Some of the most destructive secrets are addictions, affairs, homosexuality, and mental illnesses. Secrets in these categories are called "private lies" by Frank Pittman, a renowned family therapist and author. "Private lies" are things we convince ourselves no one else knows, but usually someone knows, tells, and distorts. Often, these secrets are relived by the next generation, as if they are energized through repression. Since bodies tend to express what our minds repress, this is possible. Some of the most lethal secrets are genetic predispositions, which must be dealt with honestly or carriers will fall prey to disaster, like an unsuspecting mouse being stalked by a hungry cat.[5]

My paternal grandmother stayed with us for a short while before she died of cirrhosis of the liver. I was told that it was caused by eating too much pepper and spicy food. My paternal grandfather had died of the same "pepper disease" years earlier. As years passed, it slowly penetrated my brain that five of my father's siblings had problems with alcohol, so perhaps this "pepper disease" was what the rest of the world called alcoholism. This was only one of the shady secrets, which were kept to "protect the family image." Secrets and repressed negatives do not go away. They gain an insidious power that will corrupt someone, or several someones. They lose their negative, destructive power only when they are exposed to the light, discussed and dealt with in a positive way, in the sense that lighting one match will dissipate darkness.

Because the alcoholism was kept secret, we were not allowed to talk about it. Had we been allowed to ask questions, to openly discuss the problem and to educate ourselves about this disease, it is possible that several of the future alcoholics could have sought help earlier without shame and stigma. Few families escape being affected by alcoholism, yet very few families deal with it openly and constructively. I wonder how many fatal accidents could be prevented if parents had the courage to confront their drinking adolescents and enforce some rules for safety. Far too often the denial of the parents is greater than the denial of their children. And far too often, especially with alcoholism and other addictions, the parent(s) have passed the addiction on to the children. They blame the child rather than accepting their responsibility to clean up their own act. This can be emotionally, and even physically, deadly.

Homosexuality always used to be stuffed into the secret, or "private lie," box. Thanks to current wisdom, which allows us to understand that a percentage of the population arrives on the planet as homosexual, this is beginning to shift in contemporary culture. Many families have lost young adult homosexuals to suicide *because the fear of loss of love if people knew what most people know anyway was too much for them to bear.* The saddest part of this fear by the homosexual person is that it is based on their belief (and often direct experience) that love is conditional—for people to love me, I must be like the majority in my sexual preferences. The saddest part for the world is that most societies reinforce this fear by trying to make homosexuals feel ashamed and undeserving of love.

Our youngest daughter did not come out of the closet until she was in her thirties, after a stormy ten-year marriage had ended. There is no less love for her now than when she was married, but she feared there might be. Her coming-out process required tremendous courage and soul searching on her part, but the family is deeply grateful that she knows she is accepted, loved, and admired by each member of the family *as she really is.*

I believe that most parents do love their children unconditionally in their heart of hearts, but want so terribly for their children to "look good" that they throw in conditions to control their children's behavior. However, when we use love as a condition to control our children, they internalize *all* love as conditional. They then develop anxieties over losing love, such as: If I don't succeed, I won't be loved. Unless I perform well, my parents can't love me. If I don't measure up to their expectations, I'm unlovable.

Reflection Exercise

▶ On what conditions did you fear your parents' or caregivers' love was based?

▶ Did their behaviors ever confirm your fears?

▶ Do you use "conditions" to control people you love today?

Mental illnesses and emotional disorders are also often stuffed into "the secret box," making the person who has the illness feel that the family is ashamed of him. This can be especially tragic when the illness is genetic, as most addictions and mental and emotional disorders can be.

Polly was a student in a local college where I had been on the faculty and directed the counseling center. One day I received a frantic call from a college counselor saying that Polly was jumping around on desktops in a classroom, flapping her arms and cawing like a crow. Could I come immediately and try to talk to this "crazy" young woman? The counselor reported that the professor had dismissed the class, and everyone had left the room because they were afraid of Polly. I had worked with Polly and her family in therapy, and the college counselor was hoping I might be able to restore some order to the "hallowed halls," which were filled with curious students and faculty listening to Polly's cawing while she jumped around the room. I knew that Polly was a bipolar manic-depressive and probably had stopped taking her medication. I also knew that her parents would be mortified and probably would want her to drop out of college now that people knew she had a problem.

When I arrived with her medication, she stopped her inappropriate behavior, grinned at me, and said, "Wow, I guess I got their attention." Her distraught energy soon regrouped, she calmed down, and could admit that she was screaming for attention and help. When the tension and stress in her system became too much to bear, she "acted out" to get her needs met. Later that afternoon, settled at home with her parents, she told them that she was tired of "pretending to be normal." She knew she needed support from others and that she did not mind people knowing that she had an illness that needed to be controlled by medication. She explained that she'd rather people know the truth than think she was just a "weirdo." As long as her family lived in denial, then she could easily convince herself that she did not need her medication. She needed encouragement to take her medicine, and assurance that she would be loved and to know she need not feel ashamed of her illness.

After the crow incident, her parents agreed with her, and for the first time her father admitted that he had the same illness. Polly hugged him and expressed how thrilled she was to know that he was able to truly empathize with her. She had confided in an earlier therapy session that she suspected her father was manic-depressive, but he'd managed to cover up his real illness by becoming an alcoholic. He felt that being drunk was a notch above being "nuts." How sad that he had deprived himself and his daughter of a real loving connection over many years.

Today, Polly is grateful to have lithium and has formed a support group for others like herself, where they can openly share their honest feelings and encourage each other to continue with their medications. Her father comes to her group on a regular basis. Polly has a new boyfriend, to whom she's explained everything. She can trust him because she can trust herself and is no longer "pretending," or living with the fear that she'll have an episode and be deserted by him.

When there is awareness and open discussion, help is almost always available. The person with a mental or emotional illness is free to call on others for help without feeling ashamed or defensive. Most families are supportive when they are able to deal honestly and safely with whatever problems are present. The families caught up in protecting each member's image through lies and pretense will fall apart in the name of love, without realizing love cannot exist on lies. Conversations remain shallow and connections remain superficial, but no one dares to discuss "the problem" or dispel the lie, for fear an image will be tarnished or an illusion shattered.

Our darkest secrets and greatest illusions are usually formed around our deepest fears. The mentally ill force us to touch that part of ourselves that is not perfect—a bit crazy. Homosexuals remind us that there may be some unresolved aspect of sexuality within our psyches. Those who live out our most repressed fears threaten us at such a deep level that it is easier to shun them than to accept the aspect of ourselves that they threaten.

Reflection Exercise

▶ Which sentences in the above paragraph "trigger" your defenses? Why?

> ### *Reflection Exercise (continued)*
>
> ▶ How would your family be different if each person (yourself included) had always told the truth to the best of his or her ability?
>
> ▶ What damaged fences are you still trying to repair from your childhood?
>
> ▶ To whom do you need to tell the truth?
>
> ▶ Are you willing to initiate a change within yourself in order to initiate a positive change in your family? This is rarely easy, but always worth it!

Writing, but not necessarily mailing, letters (both positive and negative), poems, or eulogies is often an excellent way to cleanse our souls and create a more positive feeling within our hearts.

FOR EXAMPLE, THIS poem was written by my friend Charles James as he was driving home from the morgue, accompanied by the ashes of his mother:

Mother

It had to be raining chilling raw September
the day I drove north
to retrieve your ashes cremains he called them
mostly bones
Then we rode home alone your bones silent
yet persistently present
The wipers barely sufficient
That constant wash recalling all those baths showers all for
ashes
Wash wash wash
All that washing
Then the perfume always the perfume stockings high heels
Comfort was the sound of your washing machine
comfort the smell of your cherry pudding

comfort the taste of your scalloped potatoes
comfort the touch of fresh clean sheets
The wrinkle you never knew these touched me
and you never touched me until your clutch at ninety
"Don't go, please don't go."
And my, "If I don't leave, I can't come back."
and all the time the stars turned in our sky.
Love was my hope for us
Love was my ache for more love
my longing to belong
Love the weight of my failure
and all the time the stars turned in our sky
Touchlessness the incumbent
Trust the office seeker
fear and rebellion the campaign catalysts
Now the war over comes the counting of casualties
You I Dad Mary Louise
ahhh but the waves
How differently might I have touched had I been differently
touched
This is not blame blame is an endless regress
This is regret which the rain does not wash
only soaks it in
as the stars turn in their sky

THE TANGLED TRUTHS

CHARLIE'S MOTHER, LIKE most mothers, loved as best she could under the circumstances of her life when he was born. She, like you, and like all of us, was born to parents already tangled in the webs of their families and cultures. She needed to behave in the ways that would gain her parents' approval and love. The nature of parenting is to try to mold a child to fit into his surroundings with the least amount of disruption and pain. The sad truth is that this often denies the needs of a child to express who she really is and what she might need. There is a precarious balance between fitting into your individual mold and into the mold of your tribe.

Reflection Exercise

► Knowing whatever you know about your grandparents, how do you believe each of your parents were parented?

► What values have each of your parents tried to instill in you that were instilled in them by their parents?

► Have you fit easily into the mold cast for you?

► How have you changed the mold?

Living peacefully in our families often requires that we repress who we believe we are and therein lies the tangled truth. We are each the one and the many. We need to belong, to be accepted, and to feel loved, just as our parents and their parents did. In order to make this happen, we pretend, and damn the pretentious; we lie, and detest being lied to; we have secrets, and fear their discovery by others; we seek the truth, but are terrified of what we may find. We are living paradoxes. As children, we believe we are born to gods, but as we mature, we discover the flawed nature of those gods. To untangle this truth we must learn to understand ourselves. We must become conscious of our paradoxical nature and that of every other human being, including our parents and their parents. Becoming conscious, or waking up to carefully examine how we live love is one of the most important steps you will take toward achieving lasting love.

THREE

Are You Ready *to* Untangle Your Webs?

OH WHAT A TANGLED WEB WE WEAVE,
WHEN FIRST WE PRACTICE TO DECEIVE.
—SIR WALTER SCOTT

IT IS FASCINATING that spiders do not get tangled in their own webs. As a spider weaves her web, she secretes a sticky substance at intervals on the silken strands of the web to catch prey. Each time the sticky substance is deposited, it registers in the spider's brain on an internal cognitive map so she will forever after be able to avoid becoming stuck. These maps assure their salvation from their own traps. It is both our salvation and our shame that we are not equipped to avoid our own traps. It is our salvation in that we have to feel the pain of our tangled webs to "wake up," and be willing to work hard at changing a behavior. This is not fun, but seems to be a requirement for growth, due to innate stubbornness. Our lies, secrets, manipulations, and those of our families, do keep us "stuck," and tangled up, as Sir Walter Scott so aptly wrote over two centuries ago.

From the perspective of having within us "the stuff," the potential, to physically survive, we are like the spider, however, the single greatest difference is our primary need—physically and emotionally—to love and be loved. This need also becomes our greatest challenge due to the complexity of our intrinsic nature. Evelyn Underhill, a respected mystic and intuitive of the past century, explains this complexity well when she writes:

> The richness of the fully integrated human existence is that in swinging between the unseen and the seen, the social and the individual, incorporated and solitary must respond to the demands of our spiritual nature. Our social order will depend entirely on the place of the true spiritual forces of our individual consciousness and how we each live that in our daily experience.[1]

Love is the unseen primary emotion that connects us to our spiritual core. It has to be lived in our daily experience in order for us to maintain a stable psyche, a healthy body, and healthy relationships; therefore, unless we are aware of how we live love, we are unconsciously leaving the most important aspect of our lives to chance. To love consciously, it is necessary to wake up, or give ourselves permission to see ourselves, to know ourselves, as fully as possible. This is the first step in untangling ourselves from the conditional programs and negative patterns that can keep us stuck in unloving behaviors and relationships.

KNOW THYSELF: LEVELS OF CONSCIOUSNESS

ROBERTO ASSAGIOLI, AN Italian physician who worked with Freud and Jung, founded the therapeutic model of psychosynthesis, which offers me the best explanation of what composes you and me as human beings.[2] His model describes us as having a physical body, a mental body, and an emotional body, each controlled by many levels of consciousness. The first level is the lower consciousness, which directs our fundamental drives and primitive urges, and is intensely emotional. It drives us to feel things (about ourselves and others) like: I could kill you, I never want to see your face again, You are a horrible person. It also drives us to feel things like: I can't live without you, You are the most incredible person on this earth, You have to love me regardless of how I treat you. This level of primitive consciousness is programmed or conditioned early on by the ways our caregivers talked to us and treated us. When you are stuck in a tangle at this level, you will feel fearful, angry, and often depressed.

Reflection Exercise

▶ What do you most remember your caregivers saying to you about yourself?

▶ Write a list of what feels positive and one of what feels negative.

▶ Do you say those same things to your loved ones today?

MIDDLE CONSCIOUSNESS

THE NEXT LEVEL of consciousness is called the middle consciousness, which is more accessible to us than our lower consciousness. Memories are stored in this area and are easily recalled when triggered by a current event. When someone causes us pain that is similar to a past pain, a connection is made at this level of consciousness, which often causes us to overreact to the present situation. If we are tangled at this level, we will have a tendency to overreact, to repress our honest feelings, and to be overly sensitive and defensive.

HIGHER CONSCIOUSNESS

THE THIRD LEVEL is higher consciousness, which contains our potential to be the most and best of who we are. This higher level is our connection to love. The most illuminating aspect of our nature, according to Assagioli, is our connection to this level, for it allows us to be in touch with the original creative forces of goodness and love. Assagioli offers a view quite different from Freud's, which asserts that the original creative forces are totally selfish, and from Jung's, which asserts that we are always trying to balance good and evil. Assagioli believed that the forces of goodness and love are available to us throughout life, but that they become distorted by fear in early childhood. Fear is prevalent in childhood because we are deceived into thinking that love is conditional and that we may not be lovable unless we meet certain standards set by our caregivers. This affords caregivers of young children a powerful way to stay in control of a child's will, that aspect of each of us that gives us personal power and directs our integration as a functioning person. Our will gives us personal power and choice.

THE KEY: YOUR WILL

YOUR WILL IS your key to untangling the "sticky spots" of your webs *if you are willing to stay consciously aware of your feelings and behaviors, and are willing to change the ones that create negativity in your life and in the lives of the people to whom you are connected.* You do not have to automatically repeat your conditioning or your caregiver's negative patterns; however, you will unless you pay careful attention to how you feel and behave. A painful example of this phenomenon is, as a child, I hated that my mother often shook her finger at me when she was upset over my behavior. I would visualize biting off her index finger and often wished that she would cut if off by accident. I was definitely operating from lower consciousness. Over twenty-five years later, when my eldest son was three years old and pulled the release lever of the filled dirt collection bag on the vacuum while I was cleaning, my first reaction was to run at him shaking my finger in his face. My mother's finger became mine. I wanted to cut it off. I woke up. Awareness of negative behavior is necessary before you can choose to change.

The sad truth is that it is always easier to pay attention to others' behavior and try to change or control them than it is to turn that attention on yourself. The wonderful truth is that you can never totally control or change another's feelings or behaviors, because they also have a personal will. The important truth is that love can bridge the gap between opposing wills. Love allows the recognition of what needs to be changed.

Reflection Exercise

▶ List any patterns of your caregivers that you may be repeating.

▶ Circle any of these that perpetuate negativity in your life or in the lives of those you love.

You have the power to change these, if you employ your will and higher consciousness.

A MAN AT a recent book signing asked me why we human beings are so intent on controlling others. An important question with an important answer: Because we were controlled as children by our caregivers and often felt that our personal will was being thwarted, we spend the rest of our lives developing and testing the strength of our personal will. This is why tensions and conflicts are a necessary part of all relationships and are necessary for developing lasting love. I usually begin any organized group discussion on love by trying to assess how the members of the group think of love. I will ask them to complete the sentence "Love is." Invariably, women respond first with "pretty words," such as: caring, sharing, sensitive, trust, and fulfillment. Men are more prone to add words with more "umph," such as: confusing, difficult, frustrating, passionate, scary, and painful. One man responded, "Love is impossible!" The group laughed because we know that it is impossible for relationships to always flow smoothly, but we think they should. They should not. We would be bored and behave badly for the purpose of creating energy, tension, and passion. They cannot! Because we are a complex combination of all there is—the good, the bad, the wonderful, the horrible, the controlling, the selfish, the unselfish, the separate, the connected, the fearful, and the fearless. We are not able to live every moment of life in a state of higher consciousness. It has to be enough to know that it is accessible to us. We live from all three levels, regardless of our best intentions. The key is to recognize the level at which you are living at each moment. Becoming consciously aware of your feelings and behaviors is mandatory to untangling your webs.

The most destructive "sticky spots" in our webs are the ones woven by fear, which is the antithesis of love. The deep childhood fear of losing love forces children to develop defense mechanisms, which we will also use as adults if we continue to experience love as conditional, or as only existing when we are living up to someone's expectations.

DEFENSE MECHANISMS

CHILDREN HAVE THE right to deny the reality of what is too painful to bear, such as a lack of love from their caregivers or that their caregivers are abusive. They must develop defense mechanisms (sometimes referred to as psychological buffers) against painful realities that would otherwise crush their psyches. All children learn to lie, to project negative thoughts onto others, to exaggerate, to deny reality, and to creatively twist the truth to make themselves feel superior. Your defense mechanisms of childhood are necessary security blankets to protect you from fears, pains, guilt, and shame. When you become an adult, what served as a childhood security blanket can become a useless suit of armor in which you clank around, assuming you are still protecting yourself, when you are actually alienating yourself. *The healthiest adult is one who no longer has to rely on the defenses of childhood to deal with life, but can deal with reality—even the realities of pain and evil.*

Reflection Exercise

▶ How did you defend yourself from emotional pain as a child?

▶ How do you handle emotional pain today?

▶ Have you created a suit of armor from your childhood defense mechanisms? When are you prone to don your armor?

Reflection Exercise (continued)

▶ What kind of pain do you protect yourself from as an adult?

▶ Which defense mechanisms are you still prone to use?

A quick review of the most common defense mechanisms may be in order. Lying is the most prevalent for children and adults. At the deepest level, all defense mechanisms are aspects of lying to ourselves. Addictions and denial are close seconds. They keep us from dealing with reality and create a false sense of security, which robs us of personal power. Repression, the choice to forget what is too painful to remember, blocks from our consciousness feelings or thoughts we find unacceptable. Reaction formation is saying the exact opposite of what we are feeling in order to protect ourselves from a truth we are not ready to admit. Projection involves ignoring our dark side while we cast its shadow onto others. When anyone comes out with a statement, such as "I hate liars," beware. We all lie. Most of us know it, but the person who does not admit it is prone to have a severe problem. Sublimation is doing one thing to use energy we might really prefer to use doing something inappropriate. It's more appropriate to go for a walk than strike a child or a spouse. This is sometimes considered a healthy adult defense mechanism. However, after the excess negative energy is safely diminished, the healthy adult develops resources to express the anger appropriately. Regression is slipping back into behaviors of an earlier developmental stage that are no longer appropriate.

There are many other complex ways you may create to defend yourself from painful realities. But whatever mechanism you devise and use creates a false sense of self, which essentially becomes a block to love. Cultivating empathy and compassion require the ability to stand pain—your own and the pain of significant others in your life. Dealing with reality is often painful, but the truth is that the heart awakened to love is also opened to pain. In the final scenes of the beautiful movie *Shadowlands*, C. S. Lewis considers the difference between his denial of his mother's death when he was a young boy and his acceptance of his wife's untimely death of cancer in his adult life. He muses, "The boy chose the safety of fantasy. The man chooses suffering."

THERE IS A popular therapeutic saying that what you can feel, you can heal.[3] It is true that the only way out of pain and suffering is through it. Using any of the defense mechanisms—especially addictions—to avoid feeling what is natural and normal to feel eventuates in more tangles. Negative feelings are a natural and normal reaction to being hurt. The most painful hurt is the loss of love, but if you feel the hurt, express the anger, allow yourself to honestly evaluate your own behavior as well as the other person's, you will survive the pain, strengthen your will, and grow into a more emotionally mature person—ready for a healthier relationship. Denying the hurt and repressing the feeling will numb you, leaving you unable to feel love when it is offered again. One of the major dysfunctions of a family, or group, is to not allow children to express negative feelings. This causes a child to feel as if something is wrong with him, which begins to diminish self-love, and therefore diminishes the child's ability to love.

Reflection Exercise

▶ What did your family do with negative feelings?

▶ Were you taught how to deal with anger and pain constructively?

▶ What do you do with negative feelings today?

What must be understood is that denial and repression of negative feelings numb us to positive feelings as well. The danger of repressing our feelings is well illustrated by the therapy sessions I had with the Coxes and their son. The Cox family entered my office for a family therapy session—all smiles, with the father making a joke of how he'd missed a round of golf to support his nine-year-old son, Sammy.

He gave Sammy a thump on the head and told him that he was worth it. Sammy looked embarrassed, but avoided looking at his father. His mother flashed a big smile at his father. I felt as if I were about to play with paper dolls. Each person sat as far away from the others as possible. I decided to leave my chair and sit next to Sammy on the couch. Sammy's mother and father squirmed in their chairs. I remained silent. They remained silent. After several uncomfortable minutes, I commented that I imagined the father was sorry he was missing his golf game. Sammy laughed—a real laugh.

His father said, "No, I'm very happy to be here to help my son."

I commented that he didn't really look happy, as I noticed the smirk under his tight lips. Sammy and I laughed. The mother then told Sammy that she didn't see anything funny and that she felt he was acting out. Perfect serve. I hit the ball back into her court by asking if she thought that I was acting out as well.

She said, "Oh no, I guess you know what you are doing. I certainly don't understand why we have to be here at all, since it's Sammy who has the problem."

I asked Sammy, "So why are you here?"

He replied with the usual "I dunno," as he looked at his parents for an answer.

His father was becoming impatient and stated that he was very confused, since Sammy's teacher had them call me because she felt Sammy was very depressed and that I could help. I asked them all to come, which they did not understand, and were understanding even less now that they were present.

I replied that I really wanted to see how they interacted. Sammy laughed again.

"Oh, I've got it," I said, "you don't interact. You just act."

Mother looked angry, beneath her plastic smile.

Sammy said, "Bingo."

He and I started singing, "B-I-N-G-O, Bingo was his name-O."

It worked. His parents were furious, but did not say a word. The stage was set to get some honest feelings expressed. I gave them permission to express their feelings. That was all it took. Sammy got the thrill of his young life by watching his parents express honest frustration, confusion, anger, and pain. Their becoming honest gave him permission to be. It was a powerful session, ending with the four of us singing "B-I-N-G-O" together. It took several more sessions for them to understand how their repression had become depression, which was being absorbed by their son. Both parents were products of families that only allowed the expression of "nice." The father had overworked his way into numbness, while the mother had pretended her way to becoming the queen of charades.

They had been stuck in an emotional graveyard in which there can be no real relationships. The way to untangle their web was simply for someone to give them permission to express their honest emotions appropriately. Please give yourself permission to do the same. There can be no passion without the expression of feelings. There can be no lasting love without passion.

THE PROCESS OF UNTANGLING

UNTANGLING FROM STICKY places in your webs could be compared to climbing Mt. Everest with a partner of your choice, who is committed to making the climb with you. No one can go it alone. There are several important elements to this process:

▶ Become aware of the mountain and the challenges that will be encountered, with the critical awareness that some pain will be involved. You must carry in your mind and heart the knowledge that the summit offers a joyous climax, as well as a clear view of all there is. This requires believing that the process will be worth the risks and the determination of enduring hardships along the way.

▶ Assess your condition and get in shape, mentally, emotionally, and physically. This takes practice. In a relationship, you will need to practice listening, patience, and honesty. Honesty means giving up deceptions and defense mechanisms. It means standing naked and vulnerable to another human being, knowing that he or she has the power to hurt you and that you have the power to endure the pain. Your will, desire, and commitment to make every effort to stay connected to your higher consciousness will carry you through the process.

▶ Set priorities with your time and energy and use them wisely. Starting out too fast leads to an idealized fantasy that could cause a collision at some point.

▶ Evaluate at every turn and each stuck place. Don't blame the other for what you have both helped create. Take an honest look at how you may have sabotaged the process and take responsibility for your contributions to co-created negativity, knowing that negatives are an important part of any valuable learning experience.

▶ Study a map—before and during the experience. You must trust your intuition, but when feeling hopelessly lost, salvation can be found in a good guidebook. (Working through the reflection exercises in this book together will prove an invaluable source for building team strength.)

▶ Remain open-minded and openhearted throughout the journey.

▶ Respect yourself and your partner for the courage required to commit to the journey and appreciate each effort made to continue.

▶ Appreciate the positives along the way, which is as necessary as working on the negatives. It is easy to take the positives for granted or to diminish them when stuck in a negative spot. The positives strengthen and support you through the most difficult tangles.

▶ Feel all of your emotions and express them appropriately. This must be combined with giving your partner permission to do the same, while having empathy and compassion for what he or she is experiencing.

▶ Realize, above all, that the ultimate journey of life is the one taken to lasting love. The best things in life are not free, and if they were, we would not appreciate them.

RECOGNIZING THE POSITIVES

THERE IS REAL danger in focusing only on the negatives of your relationships. There will always, in every relationship, be some painful interactions, hurts, and distancing. There will be some tough times and tough lessons, for that is the nature of unique energies coming together to form relationships. Thankfully, all aspects of life in our families of origin do not entangle us. Many aspects strengthen and empower us—or we would not have survived. It is equally necessary to acknowledge and appreciate the positives that have allowed us to become who we choose to be at this point in our lives. Often, something that felt like a negative during childhood can in retrospect have a positive outcome. Sometimes a "no" to one of our childish whims feels mean to us at the time, but can eventually be seen as a loving act by our parents that saves us from harm. We all received the gift of life from our parents, and most of us received continuing gifts.

Reflection Exercise

► How have you been gifted by your parents?

► Draw a web that represents for you the one created by your parents.

► Illustrate in some way (perhaps with hearts or stars) the aspects of your family that were positive. There will be patterns, traditions, values, and experiences worthy of repeating.

► Do the same for the family in which you are presently living.

► How are the webs similar? How do they differ?

► How would each family define love?

Through your family you've learned values, have been given roots and wings, a definition of who you were and are, and a definition of love, which you are free to correct at any stage of your life. Most of our parents loved us as best they could *under the circumstances of their lives*. As you grow up, you have developed insights and abilities, have made choices and taken on responsibilities, which alter who you are and will be, and also tangle or help untangle the webs woven throughout your life. You can choose to stay stuck in old "sticky spots" and engage in parent bashing for the rest of your days—or you can forgive the negatives and be grateful for the positives, freeing your energy to love more honestly and fully. If you give yourself permission to see more clearly where you've been and commit to cleaning up the "sticky spots," you will be able to untangle yourself and live up to your highest potential as a loving person.

Reflection Exercise

▶ On a clean piece of paper, design the web in which you would like to spend the rest of your life.

▶ What do you need to change to make this happen? The power to do so is within you. It is the combination of your will and your connection to your higher consciousness.

A loving friend, Kathleen Payette, wrote this poem shortly after the birth of her first grandchild. It eloquently expresses the wish of a family committed to untangling webs and to the ultimate goal of standing together in lasting love:

Child of My Child

My eyes feast upon your precious face,
and I hold you close, intrepid voyager.
The universe beckons, your journey has begun
and well I know my time with you is brief.
The task before me then:
To walk with you through the threshold of today,
To send you joyfully into that future
where I shall not go.
To bless you with the love and wisdom
that was my own inheritance;
To endow you with trust and truth and wonder,
That with these tools you will forge
vision and purpose—and music
for your journey.
Tread the earth softly, child,
And may you be graced always with love.

FOUR

Are You Ready *to* Accept *that* All Things Connect *and* Are Bound Together?

WE ARE NOT MADE UP, AS WE ONCE SUPPOSED, OF PACKETS
OF OUR OWN PARTS, BUT WE ARE SHARED, RENTED, OCCUPIED,
AND CONNECTED TO ALL THERE IS, AND THIS IS
MORE COMPLEX THAN WE DARED DREAM.
—LEWIS THOMAS

AMERICAN INDIAN FAMILIES and tribes speak often about staying connected to their ancestors through stories, songs, and prayers. The words and music are woven into the basic fabric of their lives. Most cultures have special songs and stories that teach young children how all things are connected and how one thing leads to another. Many of us fondly remember being taught, and then teaching our children and grandchildren: *The itsy-bitsy spider went up the water spout, down comes the rain and washed spider out. Out came the sun and dried up all the rain, and the itsy-bitsy spider went up the spout again.* It reminds us in language familiar to every age that life is a combination of positive and negative exchanges.

Reflection Exercise

► What special songs, stories, or prayers were you taught as a young child that you still carry in your heart and soul?

► How do you feel when you remember them?

► Have you passed them on to others? Try sharing your childhood favorites with a young child.

Walking along the Ganges River in India amid crowds of native people performing their evening rituals. Missing my own family, I was overcome with nostalgia as I watched the Indian families saying their prayers, chanting together, placing tiny, lighted candles on leaves and sending them down the river to connect to deceased ancestors. I wanted to be part of one of their groups, but was aware that I stood apart. Lost in the beauty of the scene and in my loneliness, I was startled when a small dark hand touched me. A very young child had walked up to me in the dark and was motioning for me to join her and her mother, who was kneeling by the water. The mother had a baby swaddled in a shawl on her back. I sensed somehow that the father was deceased. They were sending him prayers, and offered me a candle and a leaf to join in their ceremony, which I willingly did. As we stood to wave to the disappearing boat leaves bearing their prayers and lights, the first evening star captured my attention. I began to softly sing, *Twinkle Twinkle Little Star,* one of my childhood favorites. The little girl and her mother soon joined in by humming the melody as I sang the words. A warm blanket of love, prayers, and music connected us under those stars that shine for each and everyone on our planet. Each night since that time, over ten years ago, when I see the evening star, I send that family a special prayer.

In his book *Wherever You Go, There You Are,* Jon Kabat-Zinn reminds us how interconnectedness works through the fable of the fox who drinks the milk from an old woman's pail while she is chopping wood. She cuts off his tail, which she promises to sew back on, *if* he gives her the milk back. He goes to a cow that promises to give him milk, *if* he brings her some green grass. When he goes to the field to get the grass, the field promises to give him grass, *if* he brings her water. And so it goes until he meets a kind miller, who gives the fox some grain to give to a hen, who then gives him an egg to give to a peddler, who in turn gives him a bead to give to the maiden, who offers him a jug to fetch the water to carry to the field. At the most superficial level, this tale ends happily when the fox gets his tail back because he could return the milk to the woman's pail. At a deeper level, however, the story has a happy ending because the miller chose to give the grain without asking for anything in return. He had learned kindness and generosity through someone's love. The moral lesson is that one small act of yours may have effects that are far greater than you can imagine.

I was graced with the love of my parents, who also loved each other. One of the greatest gifts any child can receive is to be raised by two parents who continue to love each other. Nonetheless, as I was sitting next to my mother on her bed in the nursing home where she has been dying by inches for the last two years, I feel restless. I wanted to take a walk, to get away—until I remembered her sitting beside me, reading me the fox fable when I was sick as a young child. Suddenly, I was overwhelmed by the wonders, the miracles, the cycles, and the connections we share. I know that her dying will not change what we've shared, except that I will not be able to physically touch her again. That thought makes my heart hurt. The dynamics of our connections throughout our sixty-three years together have shifted and changed, as they will continue to do, but the connection itself will live through eternity. Separateness is our greatest illusion. Connection is the only truth, one that our hearts understand even when our minds deny. My restlessness began to dissipate as I felt my heart's truth. I realized:

> I belong here sitting beside her, as she must have sat beside my
> crib,
> Or in a rocker nearby humming "rock-a-bye baby," to calm me,
> Hoping I would sleep, so she could sleep.
> Her belly already swollen with the fluids of new beginnings—the
> beginnings of my tiny baby brother.
> Her belly today swollen with the fluids of endings—her life's ending.
> And a powerful ending for me as well—to be in the world parentless.

Can that ever be, once we've been parented?
Do those voices ever stop echoing in our heads?
Good girl. . .Bad girl…You should. . .You should not.
I should be here now beside her with her white head bowed.
Is she praying?—Or sleeping?—Or already on another plane, in
   another world,
where I won't be beside her anymore?
Then, she could move within me, as I once moved within her,
within her body prepared for me, where all my needs were met
   by her.
I wonder what she might find within me—within my soul.
Will she shudder at the dark places
I can't hide anymore?

Reflection Exercise

▶ List the persons and other living things to whom
   you are most closely connected.

▶ Take a moment to feel each connection. Beside
   each name, write the dominant emotions you feel
   about the connection.

▶ Where in your body do you feel the sensations of
   each relationship?

▶ What fears (such as fear of loss or betrayal) do
   you have about each relationship?

▶ Make a wish for each. (Example: I wish my mother
   a peaceful death, with the full knowledge that she
   is loved and respected by all whose lives she has
   touched.)

CONNECTEDNESS: "THE HUMAN MOMENT"

A GROWING BODY of research is demonstrating that living in loving
connectedness is the key to emotional, psychological, and physical

health, yet with the rapid advancement of technology, we become more and more separated from "the human moment"—when two or more humans connect beyond the superficial. Beyond the superficial means heart to heart and at best, eye to eye.[1]

While phone conversations with and letters or E-mails to those we know can keep us connected, I am skeptical about Internet "chat room" meetings with individuals we have never met in person. We cannot truly know people we have not seen or touched. We often love a person's words although we know very little of the whole person, which leads to unrealistic fantasies. This dynamic is causing tragedy in the lives of many young and vulnerable people. Words can impress us, but our eyes are the windows to our souls. Words cannot cry and laugh with us, nor can they put their arms around us. Words do not cure loneliness. By contrast, a single eye-to-eye exchange can build a bridge of understanding without a word being spoken. It's easy for us to tell lies with words, but eyes tend to tell the truth.

Psychologists and physicians agree that loneliness is a primary underlying cause of much mental, emotional, and even physical, illness. So why do we systematically destroy our opportunities for human moments? It's easier and more convenient to tap at a keyboard than to commit to the hard work of developing and maintaining relationships. Like casual sex, "stranger chat" works in the short term. It fills our moments without filling our lives, or touching our souls.

As we become more invested in technological ways to pass our time, we forfeit our potential for lasting love. Being attached—connected—to another is the first requirement for love. Developing the ability to feel empathy, to share feelings with another is the second requirement. This is the point at which relating to and through technology compromises our ability to love others. I can get frustrated and angry with my computer, but it doesn't give a hoot—which makes me even angrier! I can enjoy a respite from emotional turmoil by playing a few quick games of Tetris or Solitaire on my PC, but that doesn't enhance my lovability or my ability to connect with others. The more I cut myself off from emotional connections and from my feelings, the less empathy I have for others. Tim, my husband, is an engineer and appreciates technology more than I, especially the efficiency it often offers; however, just this morning, as he was trying to connect to a person in a large corporation and had been put through several automated responses to his pressing numbers, he exploded, "How th' hell do you get a real person to talk to you on the telephone these days?"

Archbishop Desmond Tutu has stated that the fundamental law of human beings is interdependence: *"A person is a person through other persons."* The more people and human moments we eliminate from our lives, the less human we tend to become. The less human we become, the more our potential develops for harming ourselves—and others. Without developing feelings of empathy and concern for others, the darker parts of our being that encompass fear and hate are more likely to emerge.

ENERGY CONNECTIONS

LUDWIG VON BERTALANFFY, a contemporary biologist, has posited that living systems are open, organized wholes with flexible, ever-changing boundaries. We know that all living organisms emerge from energy and produce energy. Not only is each of us an energy system unto ourselves, but we are also simultaneously connected to all other energy systems in the universe. Information is constantly being exchanged through feedback loops of energy waves, both verbally and nonverbally.[2] This principle can be observed while watching mothers who carry their infants swaddled on their backs while they work, gently lift their infants away from them when the babies need to relieve themselves. Jean MacKellar, a researcher studying mother–child bonding in Uganda, once asked a young mother how she knew when to lift the child away from her body. MacKellar reported that the mother looked at her as if she were amazed by such a stupid question, and only replied, "How do you know when you need to go?"[3]

Each of us, like all living organisms, is in a perpetual state of changing and becoming; therefore, what we realize about ourselves is only a tiny part of our greater reality. This is best illustrated by one of Roberto Assagioli's favorite stories of a truth seeker who was searching for wholeness. The seeker was told by a voice from a well to go to three shops at a certain crossroad in the village. One shop sold wood, another sold pieces of metal, and the third had only strings of wire. The seeker was baffled and irritated. He returned to the well to demand an explanation. The voice in the well replied, "You will understand in the future."

Years later, as he was walking in the moonlight, he heard the hauntingly beautiful music of a sitar. Profoundly moved, he sought the source of the music. When he beheld the player and the instrument, he was overcome with joy, for he realized the sitar was made of wood, pieces of metal, and wire strings, such as he had seen in the shops years before, that he assumed were of no significance. He immediately understood the truth: *that we are always given everything we need for wholeness, but our task is to assemble and use it in a meaningful way.* Things that seem quite insignificant when we perceive them as separate fragments become whole when we are able to grasp how everything comes together. This is true for our individual selves, our families, our tribes, our world family, and for the opportunities we each have during a lifetime.[4]

The preceding concepts are reinforced through numerous studies of the effects of prayer on healing. Larry Dossey, a physician and author, has shown us that praying can, and often does, bring about significant changes in a variety of living beings—from grass seeds to humans. Prayers can heal. It does not seem to matter whether the supplicant knows or has ever had any contact with the person—or other organic system—for which he is praying. The energy of prayer transcends space, time, and knowledge. Health has been improved in many of the systems for which the prayers were offered. The ramifications of this are incredible when we consider the ways in which our energies connect. The thoughts and feelings—either positive or negative—we produce and send out to others can affect almost any aspect of our life, or the lives of other living systems.

In a scientific study at San Francisco General Hospital conducted by cardiologist Raymond Byrd involving 393 coronary care patients, prayer groups in various sections of the country were asked to pray for patients assigned to a "treatment" group. An equal number of patients were assigned to a "control" group, for which no prayers were requested. Other than being prayed for, the two groups received the same treatment. Neither physicians, nurses, nor patients knew who was being prayed for. Byrd discovered that the prayed-for patients had significantly more positive health outcomes than those not prayed for. Prayers from groups who lived great distances away were as effective as prayers from the groups living in close proximity to the hospital. This essentially means that the energy of praying does not qualify as conventional physical energy, which weakens over distance. The effects of the prayers were immediate, regardless of the distance.[5]

To try to understand this phenomenon, physicians and physicists turn to quantum physics, which deals with subatomic particles, the smallest known dimensions of the physical world. There have been many experiments in this field that indicate that if two subatomic particles are separated, a change in one correlates with a change in the other, which means they are never separated. In his latest book, *How To Know God,* Deepak Chopra offers us a model to understand the intricate and complex ways everything affects everything else and how prayers can heal. He posits that everything simultaneously exists on three different levels of reality. The only obvious level or dimension of reality to most human beings is our material reality, which is recognized by our brains as the physical dimension of form—things we can see, touch, taste, smell, and feel.

Prayer is a quantum event, and because quantum events connect the material to the virtual, the physical is immediately affected. Transformation, healing, and love are each miracles, which attest to our connection to the energy source of all creation.[6]

The next dimension is quantum reality, where physical form is actually composed of packets of subatomic particles, without recognizable form, only vibrations of particles. At this level, there is no past, present, or future. Everything that has ever happened, or will ever happen, is happening all the time. This level is chaos beyond what our brains can process, therefore our brains have organized it perceptually through our senses and assigned beginnings and endings to what is actually ongoing transformation. This quantum level is the dimension of mind, intuition, psychic ability, and prayer. It is a transition zone that connects everything to the third level of virtual reality.

Virtual reality possesses the power of action without the agency of matter or time. It could be referred to as the "throne of the Absolute," which holds the emptiness and fullness of all life. It is the power point of light from whence creation began and through which everything exists. It's the level of the spirit. Because all life operates on these three dimensions, there is an interrelatedness, a wholeness, which keeps everything connected to everything on all levels.

Reflection Exercise

► If you have any doubts about your energy connections, try staring at the back of someone's head while you are in a group. Usually, within less than a minute, the person will turn toward you.

► Have you found yourself thinking of a friend, who shortly thereafter contacted you and said, "I was just thinking of you?"

► If you pray, what results have you noticed, or heard about from others for whom you have prayed?

The exploration of the subatomic world by contemporary physicists and scientists has made us aware that no single phenomenon ever exists in isolation. While each of us is a unique whole unto ourselves, we are concurrently an integral part of larger wholes—our families, our communities, our towns, our countries, our planet, and the universe. Noting that "uni" means one and "verse" refers to song, Ken Wilbur, in his latest book, *A Brief History of Everything,* encourages us to conceptualize our universe as "one song." It is beyond our ability to comprehend the power of this song or the magnitude of our connections because we are an integral part of them.[7]

THE SYNCHRONICITY OF CONNECTIONS

CALL IT COINCIDENCE, synchronicity, or simply "happenstance," the following personal story forces me to stop and consider how interconnected our lives must be. A few years ago, Tim and I were hiking out in a desolate canyon area of Arizona. We had not seen another human for hours, and it felt as though we were alone on an unknown planet composed of slate and orange rock with a barely visible sandy path weaving around and over the rocks. Just as we were considering turning back, we noticed movement farther down the trail. It appeared to be a large dog or wolf, and a man walking several yards behind. Propelled by a mysterious force, we silently moved toward the approaching pair.

As the distance between us diminished, we saw a straggly German shepherd and an elderly man, who seemed as startled as we were to meet someone on this trail. We exchanged greetings, continued a few steps, then Tim and I stopped. Something felt incomplete. The stranger must have shared this feeling, for he also stopped and turned to face us. After chatting a few moments about the beauty and solitude of the area, he introduced himself as a hermit who had moved to this desolate place fifty years earlier, after a woman had broken his heart. He claimed that he'd sworn off love and with it, the human race. For some reason I can't explain, I asked where this woman lived. He replied that he wasn't sure anymore, but that she used to live in a little college town in upstate New York, called Elmira. Tim and I gasped. We live in Horseheads, New York, a small town connected to Elmira. I was on the faculty of Elmira College.

There was a pregnant pause. Then I asked the inevitable: "What is her name?"

The name he gave sounded familiar. I asked for his address and told him that with his permission, I would try to locate her. He chuckled and nodded, adding that she might be dead for all he knew. After placing a few phone calls when we returned home, I discovered that she was very much alive and was, in fact, a close friend of two of my friends, who knew she had never married, but had stayed at home to care for her invalid father. The father had passed away years before. I relayed this information to her former beau. Within months, she moved to Arizona to join her soon to be ex-hermit. They spent their twilight years happily together in a retirement community. Coincidence? I don't think so. I believe this was the work of a Master Weaver, who designed and wove its elements into a web that connects us in improbable ways. There is a popular saying that coincidence is only the Absolute's way of remaining anonymous.

Reflection Exercise

▶ Reflect on situations in your life that defy
  probability, but have significantly affected your
  life or the lives of others. You may discover that a
  few experiences that felt coincidental initially
  have had a monumental impact on aspects of
  your life—as well as on the lives of others.

▶ Return to your list of connections in the previous
  exercise. Consider how your life has interacted
  with, and affects, each of them.

▶ Extend the list to others whom you know you
  have influenced in some way.

▶ Include groups as well, such as students or clients.
  Be aware that when you cast a vote in any type of
  election, you are influencing lives.

THE VAST WEB OF INTERCONNECTIONS

WHEN FRANCES, A sad-faced, slightly hunched woman, walked hes-
itantly into my office several years ago, I smiled and asked if she'd
filled out the new-client intake form given to her. In response, she
began a stream of high-pitched chatter about her too-busy, stressed-
out life. She catalogued art and artifacts for a large nearby university,
she told me. What interested me more than her chattering, however,
was the big pasted-on smile that seemed totally incongruous with her
dull eyes. I took a risk and interrupted her. "You seem depressed and
lonely," I ventured. "It feels important for me to ask you not to mask
your true feelings in therapy, or you will waste my time and your
money." Her face relaxed and I saw the beginnings of a sincere smile
of gratitude—and relief. I ventured further. "Why not tell me about
your relationships?"

  She burst into sobs. Between gasps for air, she spluttered, "I don't
have any. My mother lived with me until she died three years ago. Not
one soul has been in my house since then. I don't have any living relatives. I'm an only child and my mother was an only child. My father

died when I was nine years old. I scream at the walls in my house to try to make an echo so I can hear a voice."

Deeply moved, I reached for her hand, which was trembling. We cried together for a few moments. Then she surprised me with, "I feel better. Should I go home now?"

I responded that I'd like for her to stay. Now, she seemed surprised, and as the sobs started again, she explained that her mother had always sent her away when she cried. She had learned not to cry in front of people. She had not shed a tear at her mother's funeral, but after the burial, had thrown herself onto the grave and clawed at the dirt like an animal, until a kind caretaker told her he had to close the gates to the cemetery. She felt so desperately alone that she asked him if he would come home with her. He had looked so shocked that in the three years since, she had never asked anyone to do anything for or with her. I felt overwhelmed by the depth of her loneliness and by the depth of the courage she had mustered to call for a therapy appointment.

Later that evening, I was called to the hospital to be with a client family grouped around the dying father's bedside. While standing with them, I noticed that on the other side of the room an elderly, Eastern European–looking male patient who seemed to be watching everything happen on our side of the room. Soon a nurse came in and asked the family to leave while she made their father more comfortable. As she drew the curtain around his bed, I decided to speak with his roommate. The roommate admitted that he loved sharing a room with Charlie because Charlie had lots of company while he had none. He was especially sad that Charlie was dying because he'd mentally adopted Charlie's family as his own. I decided to be his company until Charlie's family returned to the room.

I asked him if he wanted to share his story. He explained that he had shown some artistic talent when he was a young student in Poland in the 1930s, which spurred his family to send him to America to become a famous painter. The plan was for him to become rich and famous so he could then bring his family over to this land of opportunity. Chuckling, he said, "I did become a painter—of houses, and barns, and window sills! Because I was always saving my money to bring my family over, I never married. I don't have a family here, and now I don't have one there either." The smile left his face, and he sighed, "Most of them died in the war and I've lost touch with any that may still be alive."

For the second time that day, I felt my heart crack. Charlie only lived a few more days, but I also continued to visit Manfred, his Polish roommate. By the time Frances returned for her next appointment, I had hatched a wild scheme. Because I noticed that she had made some progress in reaching out to colleagues at work and seemed somewhat hopeful about life in general, I dared to suggest that she accompany me on my next visit to Manfred. I saw the terror on her face, but allowed her to sit with it until it passed. She expressed extreme reluctance until I explained that Manfred was literally going to die of loneliness, and that I thought she might actually enjoy talking to him about art. Unbeknownst to me until that evening, her father's family had also come from Poland.

Over the next few months, she and Manfred became special friends, even discovering that they were fourth cousins. They were concerned that this distant blood connection might prevent their obtaining a marriage license, but since both were past childbearing age, it was not an issue. Frances retired. They are happily traveling all over the country and abroad, visiting museums. Manfred is painting again—not houses, this time.

I received a card from them recently with this note by Stan Dale on the front:

> The only way we are ever going to ensure peace on this planet is to adopt the entire world as "our family." We are going to have to hug them, and kiss them. And dance and play with them. And we are going to have to sit and talk and walk and cry with them. Because when we do, we'll be able to see that, indeed, everyone is beautiful, and we all complement each other beautifully, and we would be poorer without each other.

Demographers have determined that each person on the planet is at least a sixteenth cousin to each other person. Scary or comforting? Perhaps both. The critical point is that we each belong to a family—a world family that is connected at a deeper level than most of us ever consider. Although we do not fully understand the types of energy that keep us connected, the connections are real nonetheless.

REAL LOVE CONNECTIONS

"WHAT IS REAL?" asked the Velveteen Rabbit of the Skin Horse in Margery Williams' *The Velveteen Rabbit.*

> "Real isn't how you are made," replied the Skin Horse. "It's a thing that happens to you. When a child loves you for a long, long time, not just to play with, but really loves you, then you become real."
> "Does it hurt?" asked the Rabbit.
> "Sometimes," said the Skin Horse, for he was always truthful. "When you are real, you don't mind being hurt."
> "Does it happen all at once, like being wound up—or bit by bit?"
> "It doesn't happen all at once," said the Skin Horse. "You become. It takes a long time. That's why it doesn't happen often to people who break easily, or have sharp edges, or who have to be carefully kept. Generally, by the time you are real, most of your hair has been loved off, and your eyes drop out and you get loose in the joints and very shabby. But these things don't matter at all, because once you are real you can't be ugly, except to people who don't understand."[8]

In this beautiful love story of a boy and his toys, the Skin Horse depicts many of the ways our culture seems to have gone wrong with real loving connections. Instead of giving our time and energy to sharing ourselves with those we love, we tend to put our emphasis on staying young and attractive and on accumulating and achieving to impress other people.

Reflection Exercise

▶ How do you try to make your self lovable?

▶ What qualities attract you to another?

▶ What would change if you lived by the wisdom of the Skin Horse?

ILLUSIONS HIDE CONNECTIONS

ILLUSIONS ARE THE belief systems we hold about ourselves, others, things, and situations based on the way we think things *should* be. They limit us to what we feel we are able to comprehend and control—to some extent. They limit our maturity and psychological growth when we hold onto them tenaciously, which we often do in order to enhance our illusion of control and security—or of love.

In *The Star Thrower*, scientist and naturalist Loren Eiseley relates a fascinating experience through which he received an unexpected lesson from an orb spider. He was in a long gulch looking for fossils when he came eye to eye with the huge yellow and black spider spinning her web among the tall spears of buffalo grass. He realized that this web was her entire universe and that her senses did not extend beyond the delicate structure she had established. When he poked the web gently with a pencil, it began to vibrate until it was a blur as the spider prepared for the struggle that would entrap her victim. His pencil point was an intrusion into her world without precedent; therefore, she had no way to integrate it into her limited universe. There was no awareness beyond her spider web universe. He was struck with the realization that he did not exist in her universe, but that he could destroy her and her universe with his pencil.[9] Most of us try to live like the orb spider in our own self-centered universe, over which we delude ourselves into thinking we have complete control.

Forty years ago, when I was attending the University of North Carolina, I believed that I had a corner on truth until a certain teacher literally blew apart that illusion. I entered a Philosophy of Religion course feeling secure in my knowledge of the Bible and confident that I knew the theories of other major religions. What that meant was that I could discuss the basic ideologies of other religions as they related to my particular Christian belief system, which I then considered to be the *ultimate truth*. How embarrassing at this stage of my life to have to admit that I was proud of my closed mind at that time. Because I had made superior grades on all the tests thus far, I fully expected that I would ace the final exam and the course.

Final grades were posted. I had been given a final grade of just above passing. After recovering from the initial shock, I decided that my grade had to be an error and went to find the professor, confident that he would correct *his* mistake. He did not seem surprised to see me. When I stated my reason for coming, he responded, "I wanted to fail you because my primary objective in teaching this course was to open your mind to the possibilities of many truths. You came into this course with your little Christian belief system all tidied up as if you could wrap it in a hankie and carry it around in your pocket, and you never even took it out to examine it. You have possibly learned some facts, but you've miserably failed to open your mind."

I felt the ring of truth in his words. I literally began to shake from their impact, as my faith in what I'd been taught to believe about religion and myself began to unravel. Perhaps for the first time in my entire life, I asked a few intelligent questions from a place of sincere *unknowing*. I've remained in that place a good deal of the time since. The last thing my professor asked me to do was to read Dostoevski's *Brothers Karamazov* and come back for a discussion, after which he might consider changing my grade. The novel compelled me to examine and challenge every religious concept I'd held onto as a security line. Just like Loren Eisley's orb spider, I did not consider that there could possibly be a system or web more meaningful than the one I had spun. As a child I was more open to other possibilities—ergo, my yellow spider fantasies, but as a young adult struggling to find a way of faith to sustain me through temptations, I had made a steadfast and ultimately blind commitment to Christianity.

Reflection Exercise

▶ What illusions do you hold on to about yourself that could be preventing your becoming more "real," and more lovable?

▶ What illusions do you project on to others that either limit or enhance your connection to them? (For example: My colleague is so smart that I couldn't ever talk to him because I'm so stupid.)

The difficulty of giving up illusions is well illustrated in the relationship of Don and Jane, who came to me for marital therapy. Don grew up in a family with a domineering father, of whom he was afraid as a child and refused to associate with as a young man. He identified more with his mother and became her confidant as they shared their feelings about what a terrible father and husband he was. Don only dated women considerably older than he, and assiduously avoided sexual activity. He claimed that he was not gay, although he admitted that many of his girlfriends had accused him of being so. His mother had subtly built and shared the illusion that men are beasts—especially if they want sex.

Jane had been raised in an almost identical situation with the genders reversed. She had fought with her mother most of her life and had never enjoyed being with her. Instead, she had become her father's confidante, as they shared stories about what a horrible mother and wife she was, one who often sexually rejected Jane's father. When Jane was in college, she had become her father's sexual playmate. They shared the illusion that it was okay as long as there was no actual intercourse.

Don meets Jane. She is older by eight years. She is excited by Don's stories of his horrid father, just as she'd become excited by her father's stories of her horrid mother. In her deeper psyche, she knew her father had abused her, but she had repressed the anger to share closeness with him. Don's expressions of anger at his father were a release for some of her own repressed feelings, which was an unconscious turn-on for her. Don was turned on by her treating him as if he were her child, for he could feel the same kind of love he felt from his mother. They had no intercourse during their courtship, which seemed natural to both of them. But when they continued to have little sexual connection during the first three years of their marriage, Jane became sexually frustrated and had an affair with an older male colleague from her office. Don was devastated; his illusion that men are beasts was reinforced. They came to me for therapy.

Initially, neither wanted the marriage to end and could not get beyond their childhood illusions. After two years of intense therapy, they realized that their marriage was only a continuation of their childhoods. Jane's father and Don's mother had created destructive illusions to selfishly hoard each child's love. Jane and Don had to learn to see through new eyes to understand what they needed as adults to have healthy intimate relationships. They realized that they were not healthy for each other and agreed to divorce.

Although they are each married to other partners, they have remained close friends. Jane married an older man, and Don married a younger man. His mother's convincing him that all men were beasts had previously prevented him from following his natural sexual preference of loving another man. It is often easier to live as if our illusions are true than to deal with truth. Agreeing with his mother's illusion about men was certainly easier than dealing with his homosexuality until his unhappiness in a heterosexual marriage forced him to face his personal truth. At a deeper psychological level, Don's mother could have suspected her son's homosexuality and purposefully sucked him into a "man-hating" illusion to try to prevent his ever living as a gay man. We build illusions to hide from truths that seem too painful to face. However, truth will eventually emerge, for that is the nature of truth.

We seem to need our illusions to convince ourselves that we fit in, especially when we are afraid that we may not, if the truth be known. The flip side of the same dynamic is equally true: We also need to feel we are unique and different. We create ways to identify ourselves as separate and different, while craving to be intimately connected. The truth is that we are intimately connected and that each of us is also unique; therefore, our fears are often our most destructive illusions. This is powerfully illustrated by Anthony de Mello in his poem, *The Truth Shop*:[10]

I could hardly believe my eyes when I saw the name of the shop: *The Truth Shop.* The saleswoman was very polite. "What type of truth did I wish to purchase, partial or whole?"

"The whole truth, of course." No deceptions for me, no defenses, no rationalizations. I wanted my truth unadulterated. She waved me on to the other side of the store.

The salesman there pointed to the price tag. "The price is very high, sir," he said.

"What is it?" I asked, determined to get the whole truth, no matter what it cost.

"Your security, sir," he answered.

I walked away with a heavy heart. I still need the safety of my unquestioned beliefs

THE GREATEST ILLUSION

THE GREATEST ILLUSION of all is that any one of us can live independent of connection to others. When we try to separate ourselves from the whole and attempt to live outside a cooperative model of sharing, love begins to die. The illusion of separateness is the first stage of "no-love." No-love feeds the illusion of separateness and differences, which becomes the breeding ground of hate, fear, mental illness, war, and evil. This was powerfully driven home in a nearby community this past year when two local teenage girls were kidnapped, raped, and brutally murdered by a neighbor. The murderer was a Vietnam veteran. He was described as a man always alone. He had been abandoned as an infant and was raised in foster homes. He was separated from love throughout his life. He could only connect in rage. We all avoided him—left him alone. He committed suicide in prison prior to his trial. Most of us who knew him felt relieved.

As long as we do not try to understand why this horrific crime could have happened, we set the stage for more crimes of this sort to happen. Regardless of how strongly I would like to deny any responsibility for crimes of this sort, I know that I do have a responsibility to behave compassionately toward all other beings, including this man. The Dalai Lama defines compassion as "open-hearted." This is ultimate love—to remain openhearted to everyone.

The extent to which we live with closed hearts and minds, as though we are not interrelated, we create the space of no-love, in which crime happens. We forget that the nature of love requires it be given away to increase. We forget the meaning of "uni-verse." We forget that we are bound together. How and why do we forget?

A POSSIBLE ANSWER FROM MY YELLOW SPIDER

OFTEN IN MY childhood, the chilly winds of doubt blew apart my warm illusions of a safe and loving world. Singing *"Jesus loves the little children, all the children of the world, red and yellow, black and white, they are precious in his sight"* in Sunday school would not rest easy in my mind when I heard the news of wars and could see prejudice all around me. Why did coloreds have to use a water fountain different from whites, or sit in the back of the bus? To protect myself from the uncomfortable doubts these questions raised, I would retreat to my yellow spider fantasy. In my childhood imagination, "the creation story" continued like this:

> My spider had created her little people from her energy. They shared the same original web, but she never dreamed her web would become so tangled. She began to question whether she had made a huge mistake when she separated people by colors and allowed each color group to have its own section of the web. She had noticed that each group developed its unique ways of doing things, but she knew they shared more similarities than differences. She had intended for love to be the glue that held the entire web together, but she'd not given love a color. Each group certainly noticed the color differences between themselves and other groups. It upset her terribly that the yellow people did not seem to like the red people, and vice versa. Each group began to design its own section of the web so that other groups could not enter. They created boundaries and borders, and then fought over where they had been placed.
>
> When the people began to focus on differences, they became afraid that different might mean better or stronger. This led to their becoming afraid of what they perceived as different. Fear began to weave itself through the heart of the web. The fear pushed out love and the heart of the web became dark and cold. Fear caused many bad things to happen. People began to compete for space, food, and love, things there would have been plenty of had they shared, but they chose to hoard.
>
> The spider crawled off into the dark void to think things over. Perhaps distance would give her a clearer perspective on how to untangle the mess her dream had become. However, she marked her trail with a tiny yellow strand of web, just in case any of the people tried to find her. They would have to take a journey if they wished to reconnect. Since each person possessed a bit of her energy inside of him or her, it would be possible for him or her to reconnect by taking an inward journey as well. But she left that for them to figure out for themselves—what she called a gift of "free will." From her new space far outside the original web, she chose to simply watch the people and allow them to do whatever they could to work out their problems.

She watched as the people continued to weave webs that would keep different groups separated. Next, they wove webs that would separate families within groups. Then, as they competed for love, fearing there may not be enough to share, they wove webs that would separate people within families. Alas, the saddest moment came when the spider realized that the people were leaving love out of the designs they were weaving because they had discovered powers more recognizable than love. They designed physical power, and gave it the color purple. Big people could dominate small people with physical power. They designed intellectual power and colored it bright blue. Smart people could dominate and manipulate less smart people with intellectual power. They designed financial power, and gave it a green color, signifying envy. Rich people could dominate and control poor people with financial power. They designed sexual and seductive power, and colored it red. Beautiful and sexy people had the power to cause others to feel ugly and undesirable.

Their competitive games began to consume huge amounts of time, energy, and money. They began to call them "wars." Men could become heroes through war, and women worshipped heroes. With a heavy heart, the yellow spider crawled farther and farther away, knowing that without love, the entire web would be destroyed. Since she had given the people free will, all she could do was continue to send loving energy towards the web, with the hope that people would eventually feel enough love to seek a path back to loving connections.

Color is immoral when it causes prejudice between groups of human beings. We remain more alike than different. We have used color to distinguish groups, to create an illusion of differentness when the truth is sameness. Color bias is formed through our perceptions.

We have designated white a superior color from our need to compete for a superior position, when the truth is, there is no lasting superior position.

Regardless of how it all began, it is clear that when we decided to compete for, rather than cooperatively share, our resources and to value money and power over love, the fear of scarcity became our modus operandi and the "other"—anyone or group we perceive as different—became the enemy. We've allowed this fear to dominate our lives to the point that we have forgotten the truth: that we are inextricably interrelated particles of energy. When I use my energy to hurt another, I've forgotten what I learned in childhood about connections and consequences of connections—that the hurt will eventually come back to me. All behaviors, and often thoughts, have consequences. We reap what we sow. We have choices about how to use our energy. At an elemental level, life is energy management, and controlling our energy is a real challenge. Energy is energy, neither positive nor negative until it is channeled into producing a negative or positive act.

Reflection Exercise

▶ Make a list of the last ten things you have done today.

▶ What are the most likely consequences of each action?

▶ Evaluate whether you added positive or negative energy to the world through each behavior.

Bo Lozoff, founder of the Prison Ashram Project in Durham, North Carolina, which has restored hope and meaningfulness to thousands of lives, recommends that we consciously ask ourselves the purpose of each of our specific behaviors. Is it to share, to give, to help, to learn? Or is it to compete for attention, to grab something for ourselves in an effort to satisfy our insatiable egos? We must become aware of how our behaviors are affecting not only our lives, but also the lives of others, the planet we call home, and the larger universe. We know that every drop of water in the ocean is affected each time a wave rolls onto the beach, but we often forget how powerful each of our acts and thoughts can be.[11]

With each choice we make, we add to the constructive or destructive energy around us. If we deny our power and try to see ourselves as separate, we tend to increase the power of the destructive forces, which are constantly operating in opposition to life-enhancing forces.

We know that energy never dies, but is only transformed. This means that each of us can change negative into positive energy, and that each of us will live forever *in some form*. Through the meticulous scientific research and writings of psychiatrist Brian Weiss, M.D., we gain valuable insight into the possibilities of past lives and their affects on our present lives.[12] This adds magnitudes of possibility and complication to our ability to manage our energy—unless we accept how powerfully influential we are as individuals and accept our personal responsibility to use our power constructively and cooperatively. There will always be forms of competition, but there can be cooperative competition, such as healthy games and athletic events, after which competing parties shake hands in friendship. The key is to use competition as an incentive for growth for all competitors, and not as "killing fields."

In the jungles of Brazil there is a tribe of people, the Canela, who believe that the key to survival is sharing. They share everything: food, bodies, and homes. No one goes hungry as long as there is food. No one is left with unfulfilled needs if she makes the need known, which she is expected to do, as everything is openly discussed in tribal meetings. Their ultimate goal is peace, not justice. They remain united in peace unless jealousy over a sexual partner causes strife. When this happens the entire community comes together to discuss the problem and resolve it without fighting. The problem is often acted out in dramatic presentation so even the children can understand the dynamics of what has happened and participate in the resolution. There are no secrets. There are no wars. Every child is loved and raised by the entire village. What would happen if we could manage our lives like the Canela just within our family units? Granted our sexual mores and taboos would prohibit some of the Canela's behaviors, but perhaps it would serve us well to adopt the basic ethos that sharing *is* survival. Our ultimate survival as a family on planet Earth requires that we share more and fight less.

An old Ethiopian proverb states, "When spider webs unite, they can tie up a lion." If we unite in cooperative sharing, we could end abuse, poverty, and war. It cannot happen, however, until each one of us recognizes the good in ourselves and in each other person. I am no longer naive or idealistic enough to believe that this will happen during my lifetime. But I remain hopeful enough that if each of us makes an effort to assume responsibility for the consequences of what we think and do, we will be a step closer to living in a safer, more peaceful world.

Perhaps we Westerners could learn something from the peoples of India and other parts of Asia, who greet each other with the expression *Namaste,* which means: "I honor the place in you in which the entire universe dwells. I honor the place in you which is of love, of truth, of light, and of peace. When you are in that place in you, and I am in that place in me, *we are one.*"

Namaste.

FIVE

Are You Ready *to* Remember Your Love Teachers?

*FOR ONE HUMAN BEING TO LOVE ANOTHER IS PERHAPS
THE MOST DIFFICULT TASK OF ALL, THE EPITOME, THE ULTIMATE TEST.
IT IS THAT STRIVING FOR WHICH ALL OTHER STRIVING
IS MERELY PREPARATION.*
—RAINER MARIA RILKE

IN HIS MEMOIR, *Time Regained*, Marcel Proust writes: "Falling in love is like falling under an evil spell in a fairy-tale against which one is powerless until the enchantment has passed." At this point in the book, he is madly, deeply, passionately in love with Albertine. But later in the book, he writes: "Now I no longer love her. It's as if I became a different person who did not love her. Or did she become a different person whom I could not love? It leaves me quite unmoved, indifferent. I simply ceased to love her."

He is essentially saying: I am no longer energized by being with this woman—or by thinking about her. And he is essentially asking: What happens over time to that kind of passionate energy?

Hundreds of times, over the past twenty years, I've heard almost identical words from a husband or wife in my therapy office. Husbands tend to say something like, "I don't know what happened, but one day I looked at her, and wondered, what am I doing with this blob? I was in love with her once—but she was thinner then."

More often than not, this is said by a balding man who is also carrying extra pounds around his middle. Unless, that is, he's already having an affair with someone who is younger and thinner than himself. If this is the case, he has usually joined a health club, started jogging, invested in the latest new technique to grow hair, and missed many dinners at home.

I know a man who ate two dinners every night for six months to keep both his wife and his mistress from suspecting his infidelity. He'd told his mistress he had separated from his wife and told his wife that he absolutely was not having an affair and had become ingenious with his excuses of working out of town. Gaining weight finally forced him into therapy. When he realized his marriage did not stand a chance of survival as long as he continued to put all of his positive energy into the other relationship, he withdrew from both, put his energy into losing weight and getting his head on straight. Eventually, he asked if he could bring his wife into therapy with him, an idea that I wholeheartedly supported, *if* he would commit to being faithful to her during the course of the therapy. He did. They learned to create a safe place in which they could express their honest thoughts, feelings, and desires. He now claims that he must have been temporarily insane to have had an affair, for what he really wanted and needed was a healthier marriage. He learned that when he interacted with his wife in the same loving manner he had interacted with his mistress, his wife responded in kind, and he felt passionately loved.

A wife once came for an initial therapy session and began with, "My husband has become so critical and seems to delight in making me feel bad about myself. He must think that giving me a compliment would cost him a million dollars, because he has not given me one in years." After identifying his critical nature as their number one problem, she continues to criticize him, telling me with relish every negative thing he's said or done since the day they met—twenty-two years ago. I asked her when she had last complimented him. She blushed, without replying.

My intuition prompted me to inquire as to whether she had recently met someone who lavished her with compliments, since she had stayed with her insensitive husband for twenty-two years without coming for therapy. She had. What she really wanted was my permission to leave her husband. I assured her that she did not have to have permission, but that long-term marriages ended with less devastation if the couple came together for "separation" therapy. They did. He confessed that he wanted out of the marriage as much as she. They completed their marriage during hours of honest dialogue and were able to divorce as friends. When there is no positive passionate connection within a relationship and no desire to recommit energy into revitalizing the connection, it is time to consider an ending.

What happens to our perception of love as things change over time? The same thing that has happened over and over again when we assume that being struck by cupid's magic arrow is all we need to guarantee eternal bliss. All of us have witnessed couples who begin a relationship deeply in love, but over time, experience a painful deterioration that collapses the relationship, leaving two bewildered and wounded people, who cry out, "But we were so in love." Perhaps you have experienced this bewildering disappointment yourself.

The reality of "lasting love" requires more of us than the beginning of love might lead us to believe. Continuing to live in love with another individual is possible, but it requires that we sufficiently know and appreciate another person—warts and all—enough to maintain a genuine emotional, sexual, and spiritual connection. It requires that we grow up and grow with another toward a mutual goal of sharing our true selves with each other. Because our culture worships instant gratification, we often give up too easily and quickly on love. True love is never "instant." How have our ideas become so convoluted that we expect infatuation, sexual passion, and the act of marriage to be the only requirements for a lifetime of intimate fulfillment? It's as though once we legalize love through marriage, our nonloving behaviors gain an arena in which they play themselves out.

A Partial Answer: The Fairy Tale World

MY GENERATION WAS raised on fairy tales of love, and my children on Walt Disney's version of those fairy tales:

One day a handsome Prince came to the forest and saw Snow White. Charmed with her beauty, he kissed her. At last Snow White awoke! The Seven Dwarfs danced with joy, and the Prince carried her off to his castle in the clouds.

MY FAVORITE WAS always Hans Christian Anderson's *The Shepherdess and the Chimney Sweep*, in which two porcelain figurines survive hardships and tragedy, dramatically proclaiming their love throughout. After almost losing each other several times, they end up happily side by side on their shelf. My father would read this in a syrupy voice. And then his voice would lower as he read the last line: *So the porcelain people were left together, and they loved each other— till they broke into pieces.* At this point, he would burst out laughing. I would laugh, also—because he laughed. Finally, one night I asked, "Daddy, why is that funny?"

He smiled, kissed me good night, and looked at me gently. "I'm afraid someday you will know," was all he said.

I would love to rewrite many of those tales: *Thus the tall, skinny prince and the slightly overweight princess lowered their expectations of bliss and lived a reasonably happy life, with the normal ups and downs that life has in store for each of us. They taught each other to understand what real love requires, and decided to stand together in loving commitment, forgiving each other often, and saying "I'm sorry," when necessary.*

Reflection Exercise

▶ What were your earliest fantasies of "romantic love"?

▶ What fed your fantasies? (Songs, fairy tales, movies, TV, books, listening to the "love stories" of older siblings or adults.)

▶ Remember your way back to your first feelings of romantic love.

ONLY PUPPY LOVE?

IT HAPPENED THE first time when I was ten years old. Billy Harris had just moved in next door to my friend, Patsy. She had been my very best friend since first grade, and we spent the majority of our after-school time playing in a large playhouse her grandfather had built in her backyard. He had also built a large wooden seesaw behind the playhouse in a field of high grass. In this overgrown grass were nasty stinging nettles, which we Southern kids called "stingy-nettles."

One day, while we were ensconced in the playhouse, we noticed a new kid in the backyard next door. The house had been empty for a few weeks, and we had been excited over the possibility of a new playmate moving in. But this kid was a boy. We both had younger brothers, and considered boys in general to be brats. Still, out of politeness, I felt we should ask him over. I remembered the seesaw, forgot the nettles, and invited him to seesaw. He did not say a word. He simply walked over and got on one end, while I got on the other. We seesawed until his mother called him. He jumped off his end of the board, dumping me into the nettles. I fell—both literally and fig-uratively. His mother ran over to see if I were hurt. Billy told her, "She's stinging, but she's not even crying. She's nice." I remember feeling proud of myself and promising that I would never cry in front of a boy—regardless of how badly I might be stinging. Little did I know! What I did know was that I couldn't wait to see if Billy Harris would be in my class the next day at school. He was! School became more exciting.

That "fall" lasted for the next several years. Billy was the first boy I kissed, and to this day, I can see the freckles across his nose, which he would wrinkle up when I kissed him. While playing spin the bot-tle, he told me I should close my eyes, but I wondered whether he was closing his, so I usually peeked. He did close his eyes, unless he thought mine were open, then he'd open his, and the giggles would begin. We both were in the band, and on the way home from school we'd carry each other's instruments. The inconvenient fact that I played the clarinet and he played the trombone didn't matter. Noth-ing was too heavy to bear as long as I could walk home with Billy. As the years passed, we lost touch, but the name Billy has always made my heart flutter. People may call it puppy love, yet romance casts a powerful spell at any age—with a few "stingy nettles" to warn us of things to come.

Until I began to understand a fuller definition of love, I considered Billy my first love.

THE ROOTS OF ROMANTIC LOVE:
WHY BILLY HARRIS?

OUR BRAINS, PROGRAMMED by our experiences, are our most powerful love organs. I believed I'd learned quite a bit about love by the time I'd survived a divorce, ending a thirteen-year marriage, then had a heart-wrenching affair, and finally remarried four years later. Three years into the second marriage, I knew it was in dire straits, and concluded that I must have a LQ (Love Quotient) of minus zilch! Seeking to learn why I kept missing the boat, I traveled across the country to attend a workshop on love with Jacob Needleman, one of the wisest people I've ever met, and a Professor of Philosophy at San Francisco State University. His opening question got my attention big time: "Can anyone deny that our American culture is starved for a new understanding of love—of what it means to live together and not give up?"

By the end of two hours, I was aware that Billy Harris had not been my first love, after all. Like most Americans, I had been so caught up in fantasies of romantic love, that I had separated it from the context of real love. I'd never seriously considered why Billy, or any other specific person, had become the object of my affection. My brain assumed that chemistry, proximity, and fate all played a hand. While this was true to some degree, the stage was set for Billy's entrance into my life because of the "program" installed in my brain through experience with my previous loves: especially my parents, siblings, grandparents, and friends. The program was also influenced by my physical, social, and psychological development, and by the stories, books, and films of the culture. However, my mind had constructed a barrier that divided my first recognizable romantic feelings from all previous love experiences. Most of us construct this barrier, which is a healthy, positive one when it comes to energy management. A lack of this necessary boundary between adults and children can lead to emotional and sexual abuse.

Our parents, or other early primary caregivers, are always the original authors of our relationships, just as their parents were the authors of theirs. We must be assured of their commitment to our welfare to survive childhood without deep emotional wounds and to be able to give and receive love in our adult lives. However, every adult is a member of the "walking wounded," to some degree. None of us have ever experienced all of the parental love we desired, or needed to feel adored. This is not to cast stones at our parents, nor at ourselves as parents. I was wounded by some of the ways in which my parents tried to love me, and I, in turn, have wounded my children. This is rarely intentionally done. It happens because we are still working out and working through what loving involves. Bob Hoffman, the founder of The Quadrinity Process,[1] writes in *No One is to Blame:* "No one is to blame, but everyone is guilty." We always hurt those we love. But when we are committed to maintaining a loving connection, we do not hurt them intentionally or maliciously. Moreover, we must forgive, and be forgiven, over and over again.

Those of us conceived in love by parents who loved us reliably and appropriately are indeed blessed. Their words and behaviors imprint a pattern deep in our subconscious to which we will refer and defer for the remainder of our lives. These patterns carry energy that is always seeking a match—that is, we hope to connect to an energy system like the one we participated in with our first love teachers. Not only do we seek to match that energy pattern, but we also harbor the hope of healing whatever wounds we still carry from our early childhood. Unconsciously, we want someone like a parent, who will evoke feelings of passionate love and simultaneously be able to heal our emotional wounds. Quite a tall order!

I've had more than one woman in therapy tell me that she needed to find a man who made her feel the way her father made her feel. Re-creating that particular energy connection allowed her to feel loved. One female client actually divorced a caring, good husband because, as she explained, "I just never feel the way with him that I felt with my father, who really loved me—although my father was an alcoholic, and I don't want another man with that problem, but my father was such fun. He was really hilarious when he was drunk. Now, take my husband, he didn't drink at all, and sometimes I'd try to get him to have some wine with me, thinking that then we could have more fun. I must have been totally insane!"

Something about Billy Harris's energy field matched that of my father's, which I understand as an adult, but was unconsciously sucked into as a ten-year-old yearning to have a boyfriend. One of my deepest childhood wounds was that neither of my parents was big on compliments. Overhearing Billy tell his mother that I was nice and courageous for not crying initiated me into the beginnings of romantic love. I made the immediate assumption that he could heal my wound of never feeling quite good enough, which he did for a short while—until he began to pay more attention to football than to me. My heart ached in the same way it ached when my father seemed more interested in his church congregation than in me.

It is quite a common occurrence for couples who have lived together for a time to make remarks such as: "You're just like my father, who always put my mother down," or "You're just like my mother, always nagging and whining," or "You're so damn controlling, just like my. . . ." Does this sound familiar?

Harville Hendrix, founder of IMAGO Relationship Therapy, explains that each of us carries a fantasy partner constructed in our unconscious minds based on those we loved as a child. This fantasy guides our search for a love partner. Most therapists who work with relationships accept this theory that there is a deeply embedded—but hidden from direct awareness—pattern of what we consider to be love based not only on the ways our caregivers treated us, *but also on the ways they treated each other.*

More often than not, we will find someone to match the energy of the parent who wounded us most, the one from whom we still long to obtain something we did not receive and continue to need. The situation becomes extremely complex since this new love person, our IMAGO match, like the parent, probably isn't any more capable of meeting our particular need than the parent. We may have given up trying to change our parents, or having our needs fulfilled by our parents, but the new person in our life presents a whole new opportunity. It becomes an exciting and challenging quest—the quest for the mythical mate. It always has an intensely stimulating beginning, and often an intensely distressing ending. However, when we become aware of the deeper roots of romantic love, we can free ourselves from the webs that have kept us trapped into repeating destructive patterns. IMAGO Relationship Therapy offers courses throughout the world to teach couples how to heal each other's childhood wounds within the context of their relationship.[2]

Whichever fates conspire to teach us love lessons arranged for me to have another instant fall later in life, after I'd become somewhat more educated than I was when I fell off the seesaw. This man and I simply passed in a hallway where we both worked. It was as if the world stopped spinning. When we made eye contact, my legs turned to rubber, and I could feel myself flush. We'd never seen each other before, although we'd each heard about the other through professional contacts. After passing him that day, I made a conscious decision to avoid him, for I had heard the warning bells. Fate was kind for a while. My husband's company moved us to Paris, France, which required that I leave my job. I left willingly without knowing much about this other man, except that he was very like my father. He had the same family background, the same profession, played the same sports, read the same books, and had many physical similarities. He even smoked a pipe, like my father. The main difference was that he lavished me with compliments, unlike my father. Freud would love this.

After some years passed, this man and I found ourselves again in the same professional environment. This time the spell was cast with an intensity that carried us beyond reason. Our energy connected at every level. I believed I had finally *realized* my *idealized* fantasy person— except he was already married, and therefore unavailable—just as my father had been. When the relationship ended, I fell apart! The price of our relationship was high for both of us—and for our spouses. Tim and I had legally separated, but had miraculously remained supportive friends. It will take me the rest of this lifetime, or longer, to put this relationship in a peaceful place in my psyche. C. S. Lewis has said, "Experience can be a brutal teacher, but we learn, by God, we learn."

I learned that I would never grow up as a lover unless I were willing to give up the father fantasy and work at building a healthy relationship with someone available to me. Tim, as my friend, was my best candidate. He is not at all like my father, but interestingly enough, he shares many of my mother's traits, including a reluctance to give compliments! I've learned to ask when I need one. We did participate in an IMAGO Relationship Therapy weekend course and learned how to help each other heal many of our childhood wounds. We have become love teachers to each other.

Recently Bill Harris and I became reacquainted. When I first heard his voice on the phone, I was shocked at how much his adult voice sounded like my father's voice. When we have conversations, we tend to talk for hours, and I feel a genuine love for him. But my sexual energy is committed to my husband. It is a conscious decision, one that Bill, Tim, and I honor. Feelings for people we've loved do not go away. They just move to a quieter place in our minds and hearts. The energy changes, but never dies.

Reflection Exercise

▶ What did you enjoy most about your mother or female caregiver?

▶ What do you most need from her now?

▶ How did she wound you?

▶ What did you most enjoy about your father or male caregiver?

▶ What do you most need from him now?

▶ How did he wound you?

▶ How do you believe your parents would answer these same questions about their parents? (If it is possible, this can be a powerful conversation with your parents.)

▶ Now take a more careful look at your first romantic involvements.

▶ Does the theory of seeking a parental figure to help heal your childhood wounds hold true for you? If so, list the ways. If not, list the ways your involvements have been different.

MORE POSSIBILITIES

A FEW YEARS ago, I visited a family in India, where most marriages of young adults are arranged by their parents. It is standard practice for the parents of an eligible young woman to advertise her virtues in the newspaper. One morning I noticed the youngest son, Bobby, who had just completed medical school, studying the personal ads in the New Delhi Daily News. I asked him what he hoped to find. "A wife," he replied. I laughed. Quite sincerely, he asked, "Why do you laugh? It makes much more sense to me to find a compatible wife with the personality characteristics, family status, education, and culture I want to share with a partner. I plan to be a successful doctor. I don't have time to fall in love with someone who gazes at me seductively, takes me for all I've got, then leaves me for the next guy she wants to seduce. To be so technically advanced, you Americans have made no emotional progress at all. I believe our way is more truly loving than yours."

Today, Bobby is one of three seemingly happily married, successful sons in this family. The last photo I received showed a family gathering of Mama, Papa, three sons, three daughters-in-law, and nine children, all with glowing faces, admiring Bobby's new daughter. There seem to be no walls or gaps between the people in the photograph. I cannot remember when I've last seen an American extended family photograph like this one. In such photos in our culture, at least one of the adult children would be with a second, third, or fourth spouse. What secrets do they have that we have not yet discovered, or have just forgotten?

I am not advocating parentally arranged marriages or seeking partners through classified ads, but I am questioning why we, who profess to believe in love matches, have an over 50 percent divorce rate, which soars to 60 percent for second marriages, and over 70 percent for third marriages. While trekking in Bhutan this past spring, our group was invited to the home of a lovely Bhutanese couple, who had a twenty-year-old daughter. A member of our group asked her how she felt about her parents choosing her future spouse. She replied without hesitation, "Oh, I think my parents will do a much better job of finding me a good husband than I could do."

Several members of our party immediately began to suggest that she spend some time with an attractive bachelor who was traveling with us. I felt embarrassed, along with this young woman and our bachelor companion, that we Westerners could not simply accept the ways of her culture.

As Dr. Needleman suggests, our American culture is so busy seeking instant passion that we do not want to take time to seriously define the kind of love that can last. We become attracted to someone because we feel "turned on" by his energy. It could be the way he smiled at us in a special moment when we needed a bit of special attention. The smile becomes a conversation, either in reality, or in our fantasy, where instant romance *initially* dwells. We feel that we've fallen in love—hoping to ride off into the sunset and live happily forever after.

Reflection Exercise

▶ List all the people for whom you have "fallen." For each person on your list, ask yourself: Did the relationship begin as "instant" love—or love at first sight?

▶ How long did it last? What precipitated the ending?

▶ How well did you know the person in the beginning—and by the end?

▶ Have you ever had blind dates arranged for you by someone, who knew you and the other party? What happened?

I am not trying to discredit all relationships based on "instant love"; for it is possible for instant loves to become lasting and rewarding relationships when both parties make a commitment to staying together. Such has been the case of my dear friends, Suzanne and George Moffat. Suzanne captures her first reaction to meeting George, her husband of over thirty years in this poem.

Meeting

Whoo—oooo—oooooo
A faraway whistle of impending change
Fast approaches the gates of my heart,
The station of my soul,
Railroad crossing, Look out for the cars,

I stop—look—listen.
Heart longing for heart home
Soul longing for soul home
I watch,
Breathless—
And here it comes! Clickety-clack, clickety-clack,
The beat of the track
Irresistible.
A choo-choo train of instant inner insight:
This is the one! This is the one! This is the one!
Brooking no left brain argument
Just repeating in the deep subterranean self
Pulsing in the beat of the blood-rich brain:
This is the one! This is the one!
Don't miss the train!
Whoo—oooo—OOoooooooooo

PAST-LIFE RELATIONSHIPS

AT THE OTHER end of the continuum from instant love, there is an ancient theory that we have all had past lives, which could have left us—or the essence of us, our souls—with "unfinished business" with another's soul. There is a rapidly accumulating amount of scientific research, beyond the religious ideas of reincarnation, indicating that our souls do have more than one physical lifetime. Through past-life regression therapy, Dr. Brian Weiss, a certified and qualified psychiatrist, has explored this idea of having an intense relationship in one lifetime that ended with important issues unresolved.[3] Frequently he has helped couples solve severe and chronic problems through hypnotic regression into past lifetimes they may have experienced together, thereby exposing the root of the problem.

Sue and Al, a client couple of mine, were locked into a more than stormy marriage. They claimed to have fallen in love at first sight. She even reported that she had seen him in a dream three days prior to actually meeting him. They married three weeks after they met and had their initial grand fight on the first night of their honeymoon. She had gone into a jealous rage over the way a waitress had flirted with him. He had blown up when he felt she had over-tipped the bellhop. They had continued to fight for the next four years, usually over sexual issues and fears of infidelity. Rarely did they make it through a therapy appointment without one of them threatening to leave. During a particularly explosive session, she did leave, but discovered he had the car keys in his pocket. Since she had declared that she would never speak to him again, she went out to the highway, stuck out her thumb, and tried to hitchhike home. Luckily, Al was the one to pick her up. They called the next day to inform me that they were through as a couple, but each wanted to continue individual therapy. I confess I felt relieved to have a respite from refereeing their joint sessions.

However, I sensed such powerful energy between them that I knew they belonged together—at least until they learned whatever they were together to learn, or to complete. Since I had recently been trained and certified as a past-life regression therapist by Dr. Weiss, I asked Al if he would be willing to try this type of therapy. He was receptive to the idea. Sue was jealous that he would have the first session and wanted to come with him. I was reluctant, but he was pleased and wanted her there. She promised to sit quietly across the room and not interfere. Under hypnosis, when instructed to go as far back in time as he could to his first memory of interacting with Sue, he began to recount how they had met as slaves to an Egyptian nobleman's family. They were deeply in love, a state not sanctioned by the nobleman, who caught them enjoying a sexual act. As punishment, they were forced to fornicate with others in the household in front of each other. Afterward, they were brutally tortured. Al died from the wounds inflicted. The nobleman had then taken Sue into his harem, where she lived in misery until she took poison to end her life. By the end of recounting this ordeal, Al was sobbing and crying out in an Arabic-sounding language for Sue's life to be spared.

When brought back into present time, to the room where Sue was quietly crying, he reached for her and held her as if she were his entire life. That was the first of many such sessions. They are still together, have two children, and still have passionate arguments. I imagine they will stay passionately together for many years. Research conducted and presented by John Gottman, Ph.D., a renowned family therapist, in his latest book, *Why Marriages Succeed or Fail,* indicates that couples who fight well, even if the fights are volatile, learn how to resolve their conflicts and tend to have marriages that are as stable as marriages with less volatility.[4]

Reflection Exercise

▶ Have you ever met someone and felt that you've known her or him well in another time and place, but are not able to recall the where or when? List any such experiences.

▶ Have you met a person that you feel you have previously seen in a dream?

▶ If you've had past-life regression therapy sessions, what did you learn about yourself and your relationships? What did you learn about love?

My second instant "fall" definitely had the energy of a past-life experience. There was a strong and immediate attraction, and also a warning to avoid this person, which I did not cognitively understand. In a regression session with Dr. Weiss to help me resolve some lingering issues around this complicated relationship, I was able to access a distant memory of this man's owning me. It was a lifetime spent in ancient Greece. My lover had kept me in a beautiful white palatial dwelling, but would never allow me to leave the surrounding gardens. He was good to me, but the confinement became unbearable, and I eventually escaped. I spent the rest of that lifetime as a vagabond hiding from him, aware that he still owned me. Perhaps he and I will work out our issues next time around.

After this experience and the insights I gained, it was easy for me to confront several of the issues that complicated our relationship in this lifetime. I learned that passionate connections could surface at any time, but that a healthy loving relationship requires more than a passionate connection. No truer words were ever spoken about affairs than in the movie version of *The Bridges of Madison County,* when she explains to her lover why she cannot leave her husband and children:

"What we have had cannot last if we try to live together and what I have here in my home cannot last if I leave." Timing and the circumstances of our present lives are important. Rarely is lasting love built on wrecking other people's lives.

Some argue that if one "falls in love" while still married to someone whom he no longer loves, he should have a chance to be happy with the new person. A sage psychoanalyst, Dr. Harbans Nagpal of Paris, France, once told me, "After listening to people's stories for over thirty years, I've learned that certain skills are required to share life with a person, and when we master those skills, and are mature enough to live intimately with another, we probably could live with any person we have loved." I disagreed with him at the time, but today I think there is some truth to his observation. In any case, switching partners never automatically creates nirvana. When changing the circumstances of our lives as established prior to a new relationship creates an overwhelming amount of negative energy for everyone affected by such a change, that same degree of negative energy seems to infiltrate the new relationship. Dr. Gottman's research strongly indicates that the positive energy in a relationship must outweigh the negative by five to one for the relationship to remain a source of contentment for each partner.[5]

THE CHEMISTRY COMPONENT

PHEROMONES ARE CHEMICAL substances produced by animal bodies that serve as a sexual stimulus to other animals of the same species. There is an existing theory that we humans are subject to the same stimulus-response situation. It is not unusual to have an individual say, "I don't have any idea why I fell for this person. One moment, one glance, and I was a goner. We have nothing in common, but I'm obsessed with thoughts about her."

A growing body of research indicates that what we call romantic love is a mixture of our evolutionary roots, brain imprints, and biological secretions. Close to four million years ago, in the fertile valleys of Africa, when humans began to stand erect, affording full visibility of each other, anthropologists believe sparks of passion began to pass between people as they gazed at each other. The brain is flooded by phenylethylamine (PEA) and natural amphetamines, which produce feelings of euphoria. The pituitary gland then secretes oxytocin, which anthropologist Helen Fisher in *Anatomy of Love* refers to as "the cuddle chemical." This chemical attracts a love object, not necessarily of the opposite sex, for the reaction is equally as strong between homosexual lovers as heterosexual lovers. The big question regarding this chemical reaction is how nature selects who triggers the reaction in whom? The most viable answers seem to be the unconscious pattern based on the ways we were loved by early caregivers, or perhaps past-life relationships. Another major component of the equation is the level of our personal needs for love and intimacy at a given time.[6]

A male client once asked me in all seriousness if I knew a brain surgeon who might consider giving him a prefrontal lobotomy to get a particular woman, with whom he had to work closely in a professional laboratory, out of his head. He said, "I swear she's put a curse on me. I get close to her and feel faint. Logically, I know that continuing an intimate relationship with her will destroy everything that's always been important to me, but when I'm not with her, I want her with me. I can't stand her being with anyone else. Am I sick or insane?" After his wife died of cancer two years later, he married the woman who "possessed" him. The marriage lasted six months. The "cuddle chemical" seems to last from six months to four years. It can be reignited at any time after a conscious decision is made to stand in love, but the natural life of the phenomenon is short lived.

My analysis of this client's situation is that he had built up such unrealistic fantasies in his mind about how marvelous their relationship could be that when he was with his lover day in and day out, there was no way she could possibly live up to his expectations. The same held true for her expectations of him, as her expectations were based mostly on his professional behavior. She discovered that he was not always the same benevolent provider at home that he was at work. When someone is not fully available, we convince ourselves it is "safe" to build fantasy relationships around him. It is similar to building a dream castle, but moving into it often causes the walls to tumble down. If this situation sounds familiar, or if you catch yourself building such fantasies around persons you consider "safe," consider talking it over with a good friend, or making a therapy appointment.

THE FIVE PASSIONATE STAGES OF LIFE

THE KEY PHRASE in Dr. Nagpal's statement about living with another person is "when we are mature enough." Aye, there's the rub. How do we know when we are sufficiently mature enough to stand in love with another? The best model I've studied for understanding our "love quotient" is presented by Sam Keen, a friend and contemporary philosopher, in his book *The Passionate Life*. Keen constructs a life-map that traces the evolution of erotic, intimate love throughout the course of an ideal lifetime. He arbitrarily divides our intimate love development into five stages: the child, the rebel, the adult, the out-law, and the lover.[7]

THE CHILD'S BEING: STAGE 1

ACCORDING TO KEEN, the child's being is dependent and unself-conscious. The primary motivation of love is bonding with the matrix and being encompassed by the patrix, which includes being initiated into the taboos, oughts, and rites of the family and tribe. When this is done in a healthy manner, the child develops suitable dependency, basic trust, openness, wonder, obedience, curiosity, and the enjoy-ment of intimacy from being appropriately adored and held by child-hood caregivers.

If you pass through childhood without developing these qualities via interactions with your love-teachers, you tend to remain childish to the degree that bonding, initiation, trust, intimacy, and playfulness are either deficient or excessive. This childishness often leads to your being overly possessive or hungering obsessively for approval. Such could be the case with Al and Sue, regardless of their past-life expe-riences. One possibility does not discount the other. My husband, Tim, and I represent excessive and deficient childhood modes, respectively. Since my parents did not believe in open adoration and did believe that compliments would make me vain, I seem to have a need for approval that can become annoying to my husband. By con-trast, his parents showered him with compliments, openly adored him, and were convinced that he could do no wrong. Consequently, he could care less about other people's approval, which can be frightening for me! I cringe with fears of rejection and disapproval when he freely expresses whatever comes to his mind in public situations.

> ### Reflection Exercise
>
> ▶ Return to your list of childhood love-teachers. Consider the manner in which you did, or did not, develop these qualities: dependency, trust, openness, wonder, obedience, curiosity, and enjoyment of intimacy.
>
> ▶ How do any of these issues affect your present relationships?

THE REBEL TEMPERAMENT: STAGE 2

KEEN'S SECOND STAGE is that of the rebel, who defies authority and establishes identification with a peer group, which replaces identification with parents. The rebel temperament is independent and self-conscious, seeking new ideals and choosing new heroes and heroines. In this stage, which ideally occurs in adolescence, you tend to idealize and adore your boyfriends and girlfriends, driven by rich fantasies of what romantic love offers. The healthy rebel learns to doubt, criticize conventional wisdom, establish healthy boundaries, express anger appropriately, and maintain friendships.

My adolescence was one divided between healthy and not so healthy. On the healthy side, I was committed to my swimming career and to my boyfriend, Bud, who was also a swimmer. Bud was not an instant love. We fell in slow motion through sharing time and interests. I was attracted to his personality, wit, nice physique, and the fact that he took swimming as seriously as I did. Our energies were consumed by swimming, academics, and chaperoned school activities. We had healthy fun and were good friends. We've remained friends throughout our lives. When we were sixteen, my younger sister informed me that if I didn't marry him, she was going to. She did. When they became reacquainted as adults, their relationship had the "cuddle chemical" needed to bond them sexually as life partners.

On the less than healthy side, I never rebelled during adolescence when it would have been appropriate and could have been done with my parents standing close enough to bail me out of trouble. I idealized them, followed their rules, and never wanted to disappoint them. At a much deeper level, I was still stuck in trying to prove that I was worthy of the love they rarely expressed. My father withdrew his physical affection when I reached puberty, as many fathers do; my mother had never been verbally or physically affectionate toward family members.

Those who do not successfully complete this stage tend to stay lost in fantasies, become adult playboys and playgirls, who tend to have affairs rather than work at developing lasting love. They remain incurable romantics and become angry when reality rarely matches their expectations. Usually they tend to blame their disappointment on their partner. I've worked for several years with a woman in her forties who has been married five times. Each man had glaring personality and character deficiencies, yet her idealization of them prevented her from seeing their limitations until after she'd waltzed down the aisle. Her father was an alcoholic and, during her adolescence, her mother divorced him. She loved both her parents, but tried to rescue and look after her father when her mother rejected him. She's continued this pattern through five relationships, but to her credit, she is presently unmarried and looking after herself.

Since I did not have a healthy rebellious side to my adolescence, I remained at the child's being stage until I was well into my thirties, married, and the mother of four children. My most important love teacher was my first husband, Wayne. Our love story began during our college years, with three years of dating, necking, and heavy petting. He is one of the kindest men on earth and was my first sexual partner—but not until our wedding night. I could not break my parents' rules—yet!

I confess that had I made it through my rebellion prior to this marriage, we might still be together. But because I was "erotically" developmentally delayed, I became bored and started breaking my husband's rules. I went back to college to take graduate courses, and found that I delighted in having some single friends, meeting career women, and not always coming straight home after class. Wayne would be justifiably furious, and I, unjustifiably, would act like the antagonistic adolescent, putting him in the role of the rigid father. I forced the deterioration of the relationship, which resulted in the break-up of the marriage. I also walked out of the church, which was a long overdue rebellion against my parents, and moved, with our children from Greensboro, North Carolina, to Atlanta, Georgia, where I returned to graduate school. It was not a pretty time, filled with struggles to keep food on the table, be a decent mother, which, at times, I was not, keep my grades up, and have some fun. Had I this lifetime to live over, I would be an outrageous adolescent during my teenage years, when it is safer and more appropriate. Fewer people I love would have been wounded by my rebel temperament.

Reflection Exercise

▶ Who were (or are) your love teachers during your rebel stage?

▶ Have you learned to set healthy boundaries, maintain friendships, and express anger appropriately?

▶ How are your present relationships affected by your development during this stage?

THE ADULT PERSONALITY: STAGE 3

AFTER COMPLETING THE work of the rebel, according to Keen, we move into emotional adulthood, wherein we seek the stability of membership in our community. We usually take marriage vows, create a home and family, and invest energy into raising our young or making other contributions to society. The healthy adult personality demonstrates responsibility, gains the ability to delay gratification in order to give to others, becomes more predictable and consistent, obeys laws, and respects authority when it is just and reasonable.

Four reckless years after leaving my first marriage, I reentered the adult stage more prepared to deal with its demands. I married Tim, gained two stepchildren, took a full-time job teaching in a local college, and settled into a less rebellious lifestyle. Tim and I are more high-energy compatible, which has made this marriage more interesting—and more challenging. By the time we met, we'd broken all the rules and were ready to try being grown-up and more responsible. It was easier this time around, until his career threw us a curve.

Reflection Exercise

▶ Who are (or were) your love teachers during your adult stage?

▶ How are you conforming, or did you conform, to your community's expectations?

▶ What are you learning, or have you learned, about love at this stage?

▶ What is your next desire?

THE OUTLAW SELF: STAGE 4

THE OUTLAW SELF seeks autonomy and independence, but not at the expense of severing our intimate connections. The tasks of this stage are to reown our shadow, or the darker side of our nature, without seeing ourself as evil; to gain the courage to give up illusions and defense mechanisms, which leads to being more honest with ourselves and others; to accept our freedom to be who we choose to be; and to attain wisdom. This correlates with Carl Jung's idea that we do not develop the capacity to understand who we are as a unique individual or to reflect on the deeper meanings of life until we are past age forty—and have experienced a few dark nights of the soul, a basic requirement for wisdom.

When Tim's career required that we move to Paris, our lives turned upside down and inside out. A total cultural and social change can play havoc with any developmental stage—and, in our case, it definitely did! In retrospect I realize that Paris was a love teacher, but the kind of teacher one hopes not to encounter more than once in a lifetime. To lose our sense of place, of belonging, and of expectation threw us into being outlaws without the cultural limitations of our past. We both behaved more recklessly than was healthy for our relationship, or for our children. Looking back, it is nothing short of a miracle that we have survived as partners. Staying together required that we reevaluate everything about ourselves and our relationship.

Reflection Exercise

▶ Who were (are) your love teachers during your outlaw stage?

▶ Do you feel free to be yourself and express your honest opinions?

▶ Do you know with whom you would most enjoy sharing the rest of your life?

▶ What do you most need to accomplish that could increase your self-respect and self-love?

▶ What emotional or psychological wounds still need to be healed in your life?

▶ What masks do you still wear? When? With whom?

▶ What do you still need to prove to yourself? To others?

Tim and I are still supporting each other through this stage. Our years in Paris afforded us many dark nights of the soul—nights of tears and painful confrontations, days of doubt and decision-making, and many hours of therapy. To come through this stage successfully, each of us must be willing to clean the lies from our psyches and accept the consequences of our behaviors. During this stage we seek passionate connection, balance, and wholeness. We are no longer afraid to love, and we understand more deeply what love requires of us. We are ready to ask ourselves whether the people whom we claim to love actually feel loved by us. If not, we are willing to work at changing our unloving behaviors.

Reflection Exercise

▶ Do the people you claim to love feel loved by you? Ask them.

▶ Are you willing to make sacrifices to heal their wounds and help them feel more loved? This does not mean sacrificing your happiness, but it often does mean changing some habits, becoming less self-involved, and making every effort not to control or manipulate others. It means being honest and forgiving.

THE LOVER'S SPIRIT: STAGE 5

THE FINAL PASSIONATE stage of life is that of the interdependent lover, in which we trust ourselves to love and be loved without the neurotic interfering with the erotic. At this stage we have developed empathy and are moving into compassion, which encompasses the ability to accept differences without trying to control or manipulate for change. We choose to be loyal through the bad times, and to make allowances for weaknesses, for we know there is no perfection. The ultimate goal of this stage is to stand in love, no longer questioning or trying to dodge the requirements. It does not mean foregoing passion, for the joy of sharing life physically, emotionally, sexually, and spiritually over years of supporting each other through fears, hopes, broken dreams, and realized dreams rewards us with an unsurpassed depth of passion. Psychologist and author Leo Buscaglia wrote that lasting love is the deepest level of friendship that has captured passion. This feels true. Constant passion does not drive us to sexual union as often as in the early years, but it still happens often enough for each of us to feel desired and appreciated.

Most of us never achieve consistent mastery of this fifth stage. If we did, we would live in a far more peaceful world, with less divorce, fewer crimes, and happier homes. Yet, it is a goal that I know is attainable because I am blessed to know a few people who have lived at this level of love: my maternal grandparents, and as a result of their influence, my parents. Tim and I visit this stage for extended periods of time, but, so far, have not been able to make it our permanent residence. On our twenty-fifth wedding anniversary, I wrote the following verse for him:

> Love begins with bells ringing
> And sometimes, over time
> Their music can be difficult to hear.
> But at this time
> Over a long, long time,
> Their symphony is
> Deep and clear.

It seems likely that with each new relationship, we move briefly back through each of these five stages. The good news is that once we have totally achieved the goals of any given stage, we do not have to spend significant time at the earlier stages. However, as Katherine Anne Porter has written, *Love must be learned, and learned again and again; there is no end to it.*

Reflection Exercise

▶ As you look over your list of love teachers, ask yourself: At what stage is each relationship? Or at which stage did the relationship end?

▶ Overall, at what stage do you consider yourself to be now—child, rebel, adult, outlaw, or lover?

▶ How could you advance to the next stage in your present intimate relationship?

TRUE LOVE STORIES

TIM AND I have had the pleasure of knowing a couple who met in an orphanage when they were preschool children and became instant best friends. They held hands as children, married without ever dating anyone else, raised three children, and are continuing to hold hands now that she is a victim of Alzheimer's disease. Their love is still palpable and still touches the hearts of all who come into their presence. It could be that they are completing the business of many previous lifetimes. It could be good luck. It could be that they learned the value of love at a very early age and chose to love each other no matter what life threw at them. Having had conversations with each of them about their life together, I know it has not always been easy. Strong-willed people, they have faced and made it through many challenges. As the end of their life together is approaching, it is a precious experience to see that their respect, admiration, and passion for each other remain intact.

The last wedding at which my father officiated was that of my eldest daughter, Karen, his first granddaughter, and Saadin, who is Ecuadorian. He added a thought to their ceremony that remains constantly in my mind—and theirs:

> "Love is content with the present, hopes for the future, and doesn't brood over the past. It involves the day-in, day-out chronicles of irritations, problems, compromises, disappointments, victories, and common goals. It requires standing together through victories and defeats."

Karen and Saadin's marriage is an intercultural one, which always adds extra stress and challenges. They lost their first son, a devastating experience that can rip hearts open beyond repair. But they now have three children and remain a happy, deeply loving family. It is a joy to be with them and their children, who are definitely among my most important love teachers. While with Karen and Saadin, I observe that they face the same conflicts in their relationship that most of us do: disagreements, different emotional reactions to situations, conflicts with busy and complicated schedules, and the added burden of cultural differences around holidays and special events.

What they do differently from many couples is set aside special times almost every day to talk to each other. One listens while the other is speaking. Every phone conversation ends with, "I love you." They compliment each other often, and defend each other if the children, or anyone else, makes a negative comment about the other. They never put each other down or try to make the other feel inferior.

In all intimate relationships, difficulties are inevitable. Fears and defensiveness will rear their powerful heads, arguments and fights will happen, and the relationship will be threatened by various changes. Those like Karen and Saadin, who make their relationship thrive, develop and utilize effective ways to cope with these negatives. In short-term relationships and in affairs, it is far easier to overlook the negatives since the "picky shit" of living through daily dynamics does not interfere. It is far more difficult to overlook problems in a committed marriage, but as we come to understand that negatives are a part of love, as my father stated during my daughter's wedding, and not an excuse to end our relationships, we free ourselves to move into more advanced stages of love.

This is not to say that all relationships should last. There may be such an accumulation of negatives with so few positives that to continue a relationship is not constructive to either partner, or to their children. When this is the case, it seems best to end the relationship and move into the more advanced stages of love with someone who is able to cocreate more positive energy. Whether or not we feel energized by a relationship is a key component in assessing its health. When a relationship saps our positive energy and disallows natural spontaneity, it is time to assess the value of the relationship.

One of the most difficult relationship situations to assess is when one of the partners is an active alcoholic or drug addict. Most addicts love their drug or habit more than they are capable of loving a human being—including themselves. However, there are treatment centers and programs to help break addictions, and there are loving ways to get an addict into treatment. Often a major problem is that the addict's partner is a major enabler, or lives in major denial. When the partner begins to realize that she also needs help and has become a partner in a destructive death trap, there is hope for change, and for love to be restored.

Reflection Exercise

▶ Review your list of love teachers. On a scale of
1–10, rate how energized you felt, or feel, in that
relationship.

▶ Jot down what you think the ratio of positive to
negative energy might be in each relationship.

▶ Which relationships drained, or might be draining,
your energy?

▶ Which relationships continue to energize you?

▶ List things you could do in each of your present
relationships that could generate more positive
energy in each.

▶ Do any of your relationships need to end? If so,
how can you say good-bye without destructive
consequences?

▶ If you are trying to have an intimate relationship
with an active addict, seek help immediately.

Let's revisit Suzanne and George, the whooo—-oooo coming down
the track. Here is another poem, *Incumbent Love,* written by Suzanne
after many years with George:

Shakespeare sings
Incipient love—
Our Romeo so quickly flares,
His Juliet takes fire!
Fourth of July burns oh! So bright
In razzle-dazzle-pop!—then dies
As do these two.
We'll never know if love they had
or simply teen-age crush—
That longing, longing, "can't have" love
That changes names so fast—
Ah, Rosaline! Oh, Juliet!

For me, I'll take incumbent love
That lasts and lasts and lasts,
And weaves between our every part,
Fills every cranny of our hearts, and more!
Thanksgiving Day's *our* holiday—
That filling, filling "can have" love
Whose names are writ in stone.
The fullness of eternal Ah's
The grace of constant Oh's!

Theirs continues to be an energized relationship. They share many interests and enjoy doing things together. They each give one hundred percent without keeping score. This does not guarantee constant "harmony on the pond," as they have sailed through their fair share of rough waters, but it has allowed them to advance to being true lovers. They compromise, but do so from a place of love and validation of each other, rather than one filled with lingering resentments. They allow for appropriate spaces in their relationship to replenish individual wholeness. This dynamic is crucial as we age together. It ensures that you and your partner are complete as individuals, and therefore have more to offer each other, keeping your relationship interesting and energized.

WHAT REALLY MATTERS?

GAIL GODWIN'S *THE Good Husband* is a poignant love story in which the woman, an English professor, is dying of cancer. Her friend Alice comes to visit her close to the end of her life and asks her: "And what does matter?"

"Things you've loved. People . . . some you've never met. Ideas. You love certain ideas. What finally matters. . . ." Her voice sank again.

"What? What matters?" Alice was embarrassed by the sound of desperation in her own voice.

"Ordering your loves." Magda replied.

"Ordering . . . ?"

"Not like you order somebody around. The other kind....putting in order. I wrote a paper on it once. Published somewhere....I forget."

Her yellow hand made a pounce and claimed Alice's again. "But, mark my word, it will be the big question on the Final Exam."[8]

I am sure this is true. If we have lasting love in our lives, it can make up for a great many things we lack. But if we do not have love, no matter what else we have, it is never enough to hold the dark at bay.

SIX

Are You Ready *to* End *the* Wars?

THE RAINBOW

IF THERE ARE POTS OF GOLD THEY ARE PAILS
OF HONEY OF EXPERIENCE
HANGING FROM THE SHOULDERS OF THE RAINBOW.
BUT THE THING THAT IS BOW-LEGGED
AND CAN'T PUT ITS FEET TOGETHER
IS THE RAINBOW.
BECAUSE ONE FOOT IS THE HEART OF A MAN
AND THE OTHER IS THE HEART OF A WOMAN
AND THESE TWO, AS YOU KNOW, NEVER MEET.
SAVE THEY LEAP
HIGH—
OH HEARTS, LEAP HIGH!
THEY THEN TOUCH IN MID-HEAVEN LIKE AN ACROBAT,
AND MAKE A RAINBOW.
—D. H. LAWRENCE

OUR PRESENT CULTURE seems so intent on dissolving differences, rather than appreciating them, that I fear we have forgotten the requirements for creating rainbows. Sunshine and raindrops are different. Colors are different. Males and females are different. You and I are different. Differences create curiosity, mystery, attraction, balance, beauty, and love. Differences also create tension, antagonism, revulsion, hate, and fear. When you accept, appreciate, and work with differences, you are able to respect and love. When you fear and are threatened by differences you flee or fight.

John Gray's *Men are from Mars, Women are from Venus* begins with an appropriate metaphorical story of how the men from Mars viewed the women on Venus through a telescope. They were intrigued by how unusual and beautiful these beings looked from afar, so they decided to go investigate. The men traveled through space to meet the women, respected and appreciated their differences, fell in love, and had happy relationships—until they decided to relocate to Earth. There, amnesia set in. Women and men forgot that they were from different planets. The greatest love affair and the longest war have been going on ever since.[1]

I got up especially early one morning recently to get a jump-start on the day. I was busy fixing breakfast, packing my husband a lunch to take with him to the airport, where he planned to work on our airplane. I was feeling excited that he would be gone all day and I could be totally free to write. My mind was lost in reconstructing a paragraph for this book, as my body was bending down to get a lunch bag from a low cabinet. He tiptoed up behind me, reached underneath and around me, and gave me a hug. Startled, I screamed and stood up quickly, knocking him off balance. Annoyed, I chastised him for interrupting my flow. I blurted out, "Damn it, I hate it when you sneak up on me like that, especially when I'm busy fixing your breakfast and lunch."

"Then I'll fix my own damn breakfast and lunch," he quickly retorted. We soon had the beginning of World War III in our kitchen. He accused me of being as cuddly as a porcupine and I accused him of being as sensitive to my needs as a turnip. We ate breakfast in chilly silence. When he left for the airport, I felt ashamed and knew that he felt angry. I realized that I'd hurt his feelings, but I also felt irritated that he had scared me. He soon called on his cell phone to tell me to be careful if I planned to drive, as there was black ice on the roads. I recognized this travel advisory was his way of making up. I thanked him and asked if we could talk about the morning incident. I felt him freeze up, just as I was melting. I was feeling a need to explain, while he was feeling a strong urge to forget the whole thing—retreat into his cave, as Martians do, according to Gray. He mumbled a feeble "I love you," and hung up. I squeaked out, "Me too," but I was on the verge of tears, arising from frustration over our different-ness.

Reflection Exercise

▶ How do you see yourself as different from someone you love?

▶ How do these differences affect your relationship?

▶ What traits do you and your significant other have in common?

▶ What do you enjoy most about each other?

▶ What causes the most frustration to each of you in the relationship?

▶ How do you work with your differences?

HE AND SHE OR S/HE?

IT IS NO longer relevant or appropriate to argue that one gender is superior to another. What is clear is that each gender has its fair share of strengths and weaknesses. It is a biological given that all embryos would become female fetuses without the intervention of the famous "Y" chromosome, contributed by the male sex partner, which turns an embryo's unisex gonads into testes, which produce testosterone: ergo, the fetus becomes male.

This is not to say that females are nature's choice, but it does indicate that we each begin as tiny unisex embryos, then nature assures that we are divided into two genders: male and female. Because we are thus divided, each gender comes with identifying characteristics, but the differentiation process does not prohibit females from having some masculine traits or males from having some feminine traits. It does not prohibit males from being sexually attracted to other males, or females from being sexually attracted to other females, but it does prohibit same-gender couples from reproducing their species. For this primary reason, there is a biological difference between males and females, which is here to stay.

Of greater importance, there are more differences among the sexes than between them.

Although males tend to have broader shoulders and females faster fingers, I have broad shoulders, inherited from my father, and slower fingers than my brother. Typing was more difficult for me than advanced algebra in high school. Our piano teacher encouraged my parents to put the money spent for my lessons into developing my brother's talent and suggested that I find something else to fill my time. In high school, he became a successful musician, and I a nationally competitive swimming star. I doubt that anyone has ever considered me ultra-feminine, but I am a female. I am in love with my husband, a male, who has faster fingers than I, and our shoulders are equally broad for our respective body frames. Males are credited with having superior quantitative abilities beginning in adolescence, when testosterone kicks in big time; however, there were three girls— including me—in our high school trigonometry class, and all three of us were in the upper third of the class. This could be attributed to study habits, but I doubt it. The top student in my creative writing class was male, even though females tend to score higher on verbal creativity tests. The point is that our unique genetic combinations make each of us different in ways that far exceed the differences between genders.[2]

Reflection Exercise

▶ Could it be that we tend to exaggerate the differences between genders mainly because most cultures have divided work into women's jobs and men's jobs?

▶ Why is gender usually the first question people ask about when an infant is born?

▶ List your most obvious traits. Do you consider your traits primarily masculine, feminine, or unisex?

Back to the morning "war in the kitchen" incident: As tears of frustration were forming over my confusion about my reactive behavior, I remembered the hurt look on his face when I had shunned him. I bawled. But now the tears were from a deeper and less selfish place. I realized that he needed love and understanding just as much as I, although we may express our similar need in different ways. Because the masculine brain is more compartmentalized than the integrated feminine brain, he is more focused on taking direct action to accomplish a goal than in talking about his needs—or mine. His ability to take action quickly has saved my life more than once when we were in perilous situations, and I was grateful. I remain grateful that our underlying needs for sharing our lives motivate us to accept our differences *most* of the time.

I was the one who owed him an apology. When I brought the incident up that evening at dinner, he'd forgotten all about it. I'd thought about it for hours. Just another difference—not a matter of right versus wrong or good versus bad. It's simply a matter of different, without which our relationship would lack the necessary tension for growth. Growth is stretching, reaching to unite or bond with a catalyst that will eventuate change. Tension is a necessary part of the process. When I stay stuck in "my way," I miss an opportunity for developing and growing as a lover—the promise and reward of our differences.

Reflection Exercise

▶ How often do you stay stuck in your ways of thinking or behaving?

▶ How important is it to be right?

▶ How important is it to be happy?

▶ How might your relationship change if you gave your partner's point of view equal consideration to your own? How might you grow as a lover?

I've often heard it said that most of us would rather be right than happy. There is probably a great deal of truth in this. Most of us, regardless of gender, feel rewarded when we have the last word. Wayne Dyer claims that the most validating words we can say to any-one are: *"You are right about that."* Men, in general, seem to need this validation more than women, while women, in general, seem more willing to acquiesce, which may be a cultural phenomenon rather than a natural innate one.

However, there do seem to be innate gender psychological differ-ences that cause differences in social behaviors. In a recent experi-ment, social psychologists placed a dead bird by a playground fence to observe reactions of elementary schoolchildren. The young girls tended to express sorrow for the bird and many wanted to bury it. The boys suggested stomping it to see what would happen or throwing it to see if dead birds could still fly.

Complex differences in social and psychological behaviors cannot be denied since the case of Canadian David Rimer, born male, have come to light. Due to a botched-up circumcision, he was surgically altered in early infancy and raised as a female named Joan. He never fit in socially and was uncomfortable using female rest rooms. He became so miserably unhappy at school that his parents had him home-schooled. By age fourteen, he became suicidal. Desperate to keep him alive, his father told him his gender truth. David then made his own decision to be surgically corrected, and today is a happily married father of three.

The male brain is physically more compartmentalized than the female brain due to the fact that there are not as many connections between areas as there are *within* areas. This enhances most men's ability to: focus on one thing at a time, pay attention to detail, sidestep distractions, move logically from category to category, and organize data logically and quickly. These abilities allow men to lie with less conflict than most women experience when we tell lies. Males are quite able to put a wife in one mental compartment and a mistress in another. Whatever is not being focused on can be easily dismissed, as if they have a special garbage disposal unit in which information they choose to ignore can be deposited without leaving any residue.

On the other hand, the female brain is more integrated, with con-necting synapses between areas; therefore, we need to reconcile dif-ferences, pay attention to many things at one time, and have a great deal of conflict when we try to lie. We process every angle of every problem and learn to manipulate data for effect—or the way we believe it may affect another. We never totally dispose of any information, even the "garbage." We have the ability to retrieve it ad infinitum—or ad nauseum. Having listened to literally thousands of arguments between males and females during my years as a marriage therapist, it never ceases to amaze me how we women can pull out every piece of dirty laundry we have ever seen, while the men look as if they've never seen a stitch of it. One husband interrupted his wife by saying, "I thought we gave that one to Good Will years ago."

His wife stopped, reflected, and responded, "You probably did. I should have."

He had initiated the perfect intervention to get her to focus on the present. Ending wars and growing into love rarely happens when we stay focused on the past. Because we females don't forget easily, especially things that contain emotional content, it makes forgiveness more complicated for us, even when it might serve us well to forgive and forget. Emotional content might be the key to this difference, for in general, women have a wider range of emotional reactions than men.

COMPLEMENTARITY

COMPLEMENTARITY, ACCORDING TO Webster's Dictionary, is "the interrelationship or completion or perfection brought about by the interrelationship of one or more units supplementing, being dependent upon, or standing in polar position to another unit, or units." This is evident in every aspect of nature: Positive/Negative, Dark/Light, Hot/Cold, Good/Evil, Serenity/Rage, Health/Disease, Love/Fear, Male/Female. These combinations are viewed as opposites, but each represents the two ends of a continuum. Along each continuum, there are degrees of interaction, which form different progressions toward each end. Cold meets hot forming warm or cool, depending on which direction on the continuum the energy is moving. This is equally true with human traits and characteristics.

It is the tension, the energy, created by the opposing forces that allows for the existence of life. We observe these tensions in the weather, in all sources of power, and we feel them within ourselves, even though we often deny them. The continuation of life is totally dependent upon males and females supplementing each other, perfecting each other, being attracted to each other, to be able to bond in sexual union. I believe that the perfecting of ourselves also demands that we learn to live in peace with differences: between genders, within genders, between ourselves and others, and within ourselves. There is no perfection, no wholeness, and no energy without differences.

> *Echoes of happiness rang throughout the universe, when male first met female and life began. It was deemed that one cannot be without the other; human life is impossible without the rhythms and cycles in both man and woman.*
> —Veronica Velarde Tiller, Apache (inscribed on the wall of The Museum of Indian Arts and Culture, Sante Fe, New Mexico)

Regardless of differences or similarities, each of us is born from the body of a mother whose love we need. Due to the prenatal connection to the female body, there is a stronger *initial* need to remain connected to a nurturing female, but an infant needs to be exposed to both male and female energy and nurturing to experience the integration of these polarities. This need continues throughout our lives for the two energies complement each other into wholeness. Male and female energy seek and find each other under all possible circumstances.

DIFFERENT-NESS

STEPHEN, MY SECOND born son, came into the world different. He was a nervous baby and required much more attention than his older brother. The pediatrician assured us that he was within normal ranges of development, so we tried not to be overly concerned, but noticed that he sat too close to the television, held picture books close to his face, and bumped into things often. As soon as he was old enough, almost three, I had his eyes checked and, not surprisingly, he needed glasses. The first thing he asked as we left the optician's office with his new spectacles was, "Oh, are those leaves? Mommy, I can see leaves moving on the trees." The realization of how limited his world had been because of his nearsightedness was my first insight into how most of us, who are fortunate to be "normal," are not even aware of the coping skills that must be developed by those who are "different."

During the next year, I noticed that if he were pedaling his tricycle, he would stop steering and run into things. He did not seem to be able to combine two separate motor skills, although he could perform one thing at a time. He could throw a ball well, but was not able to catch one, a more complex action. His coordination and timing were off. His speech was not as clear as most other three-year-olds. I felt a gnawing concern that professional help would be required for him to be able to have a "normal" life. At that time, the early 1960s, there were no educational programs for "the exceptional child," unless the child was mentally limited, which he did not seem to be. His memory was exceptional. He loved books and his thinking processes seemed well organized unless he were emotionally stressed, which he often was because he was frequently teased by his brother and other children for being awkward and because his speech sounded different.

Under emotional stress, he would disintegrate more rapidly than seemed normal. We finally located a pediatric clinic, where he was diagnosed as "different" enough to qualify for recently developed programs for "slow learners" who had relatively high IQs. His medical label was "Strauss syndrome," which means that his synapses do not respond in even, normal rhythms. He was placed in a school for children with cerebral palsy, where he could receive speech and occupational therapy. Strangely, he was "different" here as well, because he was physically and verbally higher functioning than most of the other students.

One day when I picked him up from school, he was sobbing. I felt terrified as to what could have happened. The only reason he could give me for his distress was that everyone called him "different." Banging his head against the wall, he cried, "I don't want to be different anymore. Mommy, what's wrong with me?" I felt like a cored apple—empty and helpless to make things better for my child. All I knew to do was tell him how much we loved him, that he was fine just as he was, but that he was going to have to work harder than most children to do many of the things he wanted to do. He had already learned this, but it certainly didn't feel fair, a concept he was not able to verbalize, but obviously could intensely feel.

As he grew into young manhood, his pain was increased by social rejections from women his age. At age thirty, he announced that he was going to the Philippines to find himself a wife who wouldn't make fun of the way he talked and who could love him with his disabilities. I panicked. My fears that he would be badly hurt, even killed, were immense. I begged, cried, and pleaded with him to look harder for the right partner closer to home. I tried to arrange dates with several young women I hoped would be suitable, but most of my attempts were disastrous. He purchased a booklet featuring young women in the Philippines who were interested in marrying American men, and selected a few with whom he began corresponding. In his letters he was totally honest about his disabilities and his reasons for looking outside America for a wife. A young woman named Evelyn became his favorite pen pal. He and Evelyn continued writing, and then began talking on the phone. Finally the day I feared would arrive did. He was flying to the Philippines to meet her and possibly get married. I was sick with concern for his safety, but he would not be deterred and did not want anyone to accompany him.

He called several weeks later to announce that he and Evelyn were getting married. Her family accepted him and had no objections to his disabilities. On the contrary, they made him feel respected and adored in a way that he had never experienced in our culture. He was a hero to them because he offered their daughter a better life than she had had in the Philippines.

He is physically a tall and large man, so he was different from most of the small Philippine men in a positive way that gained him great respect in their culture. Her family and friends feted them with parties and gave them a big wedding. Evelyn's eleven brothers and sisters were attendants. His calls home were filled with excitement and plans to bring his new wife to the United States. Evelyn called to tell us how much she appreciated and loved our son. He told us that he felt complete, whole, for the first time in his life. They have now been married ten years. It has not been easy, but they have persevered, working through cultural barriers and many differences. Her skills and abilities complement his. She is an extremely fast learner and well coordinated. She has a secure job and has helped him considerably in his business, which allows them to financially help her family in the Philippines. Together they seem to have perfected each other.

Stephen's life has been filled with overcoming handicaps due to his differences from the majority. He and Evelyn have taught our entire family a deeper respect for differences and more about love than we could have ever known without Stephen's being different. I've learned, above all, to trust that each of us has a sense of what we need to complete ourselves as lovers. And that mothers do not always know best.

It is my experience and clinical observation that we each seek a lover who is strong in the areas in which we may consider ourselves to be weak. It's as if we have an innate sense of the type of person we need to complement ourselves into a stronger whole unit than we can be alone. Trust this sense within yourself. Your own intuitive sense of what you need for completion is more accurate than anyone else's sense of what you need.

Reflection Exercise

- ▶ How do you and your partner complement each other?

- ▶ How do or did your parents complement each other?

- ▶ How did they influence your ideas about males and females?

- ▶ If you do not have a partner, where are you looking?

- ▶ What are your expectations of a partner or lover? How tolerant are you of differences?

If you are without a love partner, you may be looking in the wrong places, or you may expect perfection in another. My father once accused me of this, but warned me that my time would be best spent working on perfecting myself, knowing that would be an impossible task. The feeling of touching perfection usually does not happen until love weaves its mysterious web to capture and complete us through complementarity.

VULNERABILITY AND INTIMACY

WHAT INTERFERES MOST with our innate sense of what we need to be "perfected" is our fear of being vulnerable to someone who is different from us. The paradox is that some difference is required for the tension or energy of attraction to happen; yet the fear of the unknown or the different is our greatest fear. This fear is so deeply embedded that we often give ourself permission only to see similarities when we are initially attracted to someone. Listen to new lovers. Their most common comments are: "We're so much alike. We were meant to be. We're soul mates. We enjoy all the same things." This is always short-lived, for the more time we spend with anyone, the more we discover we are not exactly like any other person. When we discover the differences that always exist, we often move into control or "change you" modes. When both partners do this, competition and power struggles play havoc with our emotions. The warm "cuddle chemical" seems to freeze up. Our fears of intimacy begin to freeze love out of our life.

Because our culture considers fearful males less masculine, and often labels little boys who admit to being afraid "sissies," men tend to hide their fears to protect their masculine image. The unfortunate result is that in this complex process, their vulnerability also freezes. Without a willingness to be vulnerable, there is no true intimacy. Many males, and some females, forge a suit of armor around themselves to protect their vulnerable emotions, but instead, it prevents love and intimacy from entering their hearts. Our suits of armor are forged of repressed anger from hurts inflicted by others, often in the name of love, and of our fears of being hurt again. We harbor fears of pain, of loss, of exposure: "If I allow this person to see the real me, he might find I'm not a nice person, or that I once kicked my dog, or that I have some real problems, or that I wear padded bras, or that my penis is not very large." The thing we should most fear is the voice of doubt and fear within us that tries to convince us that we are unlovable.

Reflection Exercise

▶ Do you believe you are lovable?

▶ How do you protect yourself from real intimacy?

Intimacy involves exposing your vulnerable spots, which cannot happen if the fear of appearing vulnerable prevents you from revealing who you really are. This is brilliantly depicted in the film *Analyze This,* in which Billy Crystal, as a psychiatrist, dissolves Robert DeNiro, a macho mafia boss, into tears of unresolved grief over his father's death. DeNiro, who now believes he is seen as a sissy, gives up his powerful position and becomes a lovable person.

Robert Fisher, a successful writer of television comedies and Broadway shows, weaves a lighthearted—but *profoundly psychologically true*—tale called *The Knight in Rusty Armor,* about a knight who is seeking love in all the wrong ways—mostly by trying to impress.

One day, Juliet confronted her husband, "I think you love your armor more than you love me."

"That's not true," answered the knight. "Didn't I love you enough to rescue you from that dragon and set you up in this classy castle with wall-to-wall stones?"

"What you loved," said Juliet, peering through his visor so that she could see his eyes, "was the idea of rescuing me. You really didn't love me then, and you don't love me now."

"I do love you," insisted the knight, hugging her clumsily in his cold, stiff armor and nearly breaking her ribs.

"Then take off that armor so that I can see who you really are!" she demanded.

"I can't take it off. I have to be ready to mount my horse and ride off in any direction," explained the knight.[3]

Juliet declares that she will ride out of his life unless he can rid himself of his armor, so the poor confused knight goes on the most perilous mission of his life—to rescue himself and find the meaning of love. He discovers that to succeed on this mission, he must give up his fear of vulnerability, his anger—which feeds his self-righteousness—and his pride. This mission is required of each of us who have donned armor to protect ourselves and impress others, for that is not the way to sustain lasting love.

Women, who have been given more cultural permission to express fears and vulnerabilities, tend to give men double messages regarding their vulnerability. We often demand that they be more sensitive to our needs, while simultaneously insisting that they be unafraid and strong to protect us. This point was well illustrated in a *New Yorker* cartoon. Suzy is telling Harold good night on her doorstep. She tells him she's had a lovely evening and really appreciated his empathy and would love to go out with him again, *if he were not such a wimp.*

Freud claimed that males would do anything females wanted, if they could only figure out what it is that women want. This may sound patronizing on a superficial level, but having listened carefully to men's confusion about this for many years, I believe his point should be well taken. It is well established that women are better equipped to live fuller lives without men than men are able to without women. Men know they want sex, love, nurturing, and adoration from women. It seems that we women may want different things from men according to our individual needs and preferences, yet we do not need them in the ways they tend to need us. In most cultures, women have more permission to give each other nurturing than men have been given. Freud was well aware of this, as are most men.

On the other hand, men have certainly been given more permission to express anger, which women have been denied, or we are labeled "bitches." Women have often tried to use men to express our anger for us, which many men enjoy doing. The problem is that it never works. Our anger stays repressed and we become depressed.

Since World War II, females have proven that we are capable of doing most things that were previously considered masculine work and activities. Women are in every branch of the military and competing in every sport. What does this really mean when we consider male and female as separate units created to form a sexual balance in the universe? It was depicted in a shocking and terrifying way in the movie *The General's Daughter*. The daughter wanted to emulate her father, as many of us do. She joined the army and could outperform most of the men in her regiment. They hated her for having better skills at war games than they. It was as if she robbed them of what they most respected in themselves. They in turn used the violence required to be good soldiers against her. She became the enemy they were trained to kill. Rather than kill, they brutally raped her and became the enemy she was determined to destroy. They taught her that she could not destroy them with brute force, as they had destroyed her image of herself. She solicited her father's help, hoping that his position and the depth of anger *she needed for him to express on her behalf* would deprive these men of their careers and their power. The General, her father, was not strong enough emotionally to do what she had hoped he might. He did not love her as much as he loved his position of power.

Her unresolved anger at the brutes who had raped her transferred to her father, whom she had once adored. She repressed it, using the fury it generated within her to become the whore of the military post. She lost her ability to love—herself or others. She paid with her life.

We train the military to kill, which demands reducing their sensitivity. If we females want to be trained to kill, we must thoroughly understand the requirements. Reducing our sensitivity in an effort to prove we can do everything men are trained to do will not create a more loving world. Expecting men to express our anger creates an angrier world. We need to devise ways to express our anger appropriately without destroying our ability to love. If we commit ourselves to efforts of peace through our innate superior abilities to integrate and negotiate, as Madeline Albright has done, I believe we might make a positive difference without destroying the balanced wholeness. I am not saying that women should not participate in the military, but I am saying that we must understand the price we pay for such choices.

Most of us will do almost anything to attract love, but we have become so tangled in destructive power webs, that we have forgotten the requirements for love. Some women let themselves become victims to attract rescuers and even worse, some become prey to attract predators. This stems from a deep fear that we are the weaker gender and need a "brute" for protection. Male predators are men without love. They are sick with anger and rage, and rather than appear vulnerable, become brutes to appear strong. Angry women often become self-loathing and depressed. They become women without love. These two polarities seek each other and destroy each other. Sadly, children who have been the victims of abusive parents, or who were the victims of brutes—of either gender—usually become abusive brutes themselves, or their prey.

Reflection Exercise

► Why do you believe it is more culturally acceptable for girls to be "tomboys" than for boys to be "sissies"? How would you define a "sissy?"

► If you are a woman, do you ever feign weakness to capture a man's attention?

► If you are a man, do you pretend to be stronger than you feel to impress a woman?

► For both genders: Have you ever given yourself permission to be totally vulnerable to another? If so, what happened?

► For both genders: How do you feel when a man cries in your presence? How has it affected your feelings about the man? How does it affect your feelings about yourself?

► For both genders: How do you feel when you see a policewoman carrying a gun? How has it affected your feelings about the woman? How does it affect your feelings about yourself?

After watching *The General's Daughter,* I was terribly shaken. My husband said, "It was only a movie. Don't let it get to you. It isn't a true story." His comment pierced the core of my soul. I was painfully aware that the exact story of the movie may not have happened, but the deeper story happens hundreds of times a day in our world, in which men and women compete with each other in destructive ways. As long as you feel you have to prove superiority, you will be at war.

On several occasions, physicians have asked me to be present when they have to tell a person that their love partner is terminally

ill. When a man is given this news, he usually moves first into questioning the doctor's judgment, and then into denial. When a female
is given this news, she always begins to cry, although she may question and deny to some extent. Yet, regardless of gender, the minute we
are out of the doctor's or patient's presence, the person has fallen into
my arms and sobbed. We are all vulnerable and suffer equally when
our hearts are broken. It is way past time for us to give males permission to express their fears and shed their tears. A man needs to
feel he will not lose respect or love to give himself this permission.
Women need to create a safe space in which boys and men can
express their vulnerability without the fear of losing our respect or
love. Men must create a safe place where girls and women can
express their anger without losing our self-respect or love, or the
respect and love of men.

POWER DIFFERENTIAL

LOVE AND RELATIONSHIPS should not be about power over others,
but about empowerment—of yourself, as well as of your partner. We
have lived in a masculine-powered society for several thousand years
with males in the more visible positions, controlling more money and
making the majority of decisions that affect the general welfare.
There are literally thousands of books on this topic, so I see no need
to repeat the obvious. I highly recommend *The Longest War* by Carol
Tavris and Carole Offir, if you want to pursue an interest in sex differences and similarities and in male supremacy. I am curious as to
why this has been the case when, in fact, females begin and end life
as the sturdier sex. Female infants have fewer birth defects and
childhood diseases of all types, and have longer lives than males.
There are always exceptions, but when evaluated as a group, the
above statement is indeed true. Interestingly, as more women move
into positions of external power, as defined by our culture, we are
closing the longevity gap by dying earlier.[4]

Every male is born to a female, whose love he needs and craves
and whose rejection he fears. Women tend to forget this reality
because most cultures have valued males' ability to make money over
females' ability to make love. Little girls tend to play games that

require cooperation and an integration of skills, including nurturing skills. Boys tend to play power games that have a competitive base and terminate with winners and losers. This does not mean that girls do not engage in power games and that boys are not capable of cooperative sharing. It does mean that most cultures encourage this division because, in our deepest psyches, we know that there must be a balance of cooperation and competition, of male and female energy, and of love and ambition.

When you value the "outside" power of whomever is working outside the home to bring in the money *over* the "inside" power of whomever is at home raising the children, you have bought into destructive competition between money and love. Women have proven that we can and do have "outside" power and some men have proven that they indeed have "inside" power, but we have yet to work out a cooperative way that respects the complementarity of both ways equally. When we empower money and "outside" more than love and "inside," we are committing love murder. We are dooming the human race to wars over symbols of wealth—such as money and possessions. *This false belief that money is more valuable than love will destroy our ability to cocreate lasting love.*

Reflection Exercise

▶ Who worked outside and who worked inside the home when you were a child?

▶ If both parents worked outside the home, did they share the work inside the home equally?

▶ Which parent (or caregiver) did you respect the most?

▶ Which one did you find yourself trying to emulate?

▶ What were your parents' messages to you about females? What were their messages about males?

▶ How did these messages affect your ideas about yourself?

> *Reflection Exercise (continued)*
>
> ▶ Have you and your partner been able to share and
> balance your workloads with equal respect for the
> work and for each other?

EXPECTATIONS AND RESPECT

NOT MANY THERAPY sessions surprise me to the point that I begin
to question every expectation I've held about role and gender behavior. The following one did, although I'd worked individually with, and
respected, each member of this family. The mother was a strong professional and the instigator of the therapy sessions, as women usually
are. The father was also a strong professional. Their daughter, Jan,
was beautiful, talented, popular, and a recognized leader in her high
school. They seemed to have their act together as a family; chores
were fairly divided at home so that each took an active and responsible part in home life.

But there had been an incident that was tearing them apart. The
father had abused the daughter by touching her breast in her bedroom while saying good night. I listened to each person's point of view
of the incident. The daughter was justifiably hurt and confused.
The mother was furious. The father was ashamed. The daughter
requested this particular session. She wanted each parent to listen to
her feelings, and then try to work out a way they could go on with
their lives. She knew her mother wanted to take the case to child pro-
tective services and have her father removed from their home. She
said she would agree to this unless her father could respect her
boundaries. She and her mother had tried to talk this through, but
she felt that her mother's anger at her father prevented her from even
considering an alternative to having him removed from the home.

The daughter asked that her mother come into the session room
with her first because she wanted to save her emotional energy to deal
with her father. She also wanted her mother's support in negotiating
ways they could stay together as a family. Much to my surprise, the
mother refused to listen and told her daughter the marriage was over
and she'd best understand that. Jan then threw a grenade. "You know
Mom, I think I'm being used as a way for you to get him out of your

life. I do love him and he is my father. He did a "no-no"—a bad one. I never want him in my bedroom again unless I'm wide awake and give him permission to come in. I think I can work that out with him."

Her mother was irate, stated that the discussion was over and that she would not even consider forgiving him and wanted him out immediately. She left the room. Jan asked me why her mother always seemed to take the moral high ground and tried to make her father look like a bad guy. She added softly, "I think I'm beginning to understand that he may have turned to me for the love he needs that she may not give him."

I reminded her that his behavior was still very inappropriate and that he must respect her boundaries. I chose to keep my mouth shut about her mother's behavior, but my eyes had been opened. We invited her father into the room. He took one look at his daughter, asked her if he could give her a hug, saying he would understand if she said no, which she did. He bit his lip, saying that he would accept that. Then he began, "Jan, the fact that I touched your breast was wrong. I know that and I am ashamed." Tears began to stream down his face. "I love you and I never meant to hurt you. I sometimes feel that I am dying for love and have lost the ability to find it. I came in your bedroom just to hug you good night. You were already asleep and your pajama top was open almost exposing your beautiful budding breast. I thought it was the most gorgeous thing, and I wanted to touch it, like a curious little boy. When you woke up, I was so ashamed of my weakness. I pray that someday you can forgive me."

She was silent. So was I. I didn't trust myself to speak for I knew I was watching a man perform open-heart surgery on himself. It was very painful for all of us.

He continued. "I know your mother cannot ever forgive me, and I will not ask her again. But you, I need your love and respect more than I've ever needed anything. If I've lost my right to that, I'll have to accept my loss, and that will be a punishment worse than anything the courts could impose." He dissolved into tears. She allowed him to cry, and then she broke, reached for him and rocked him in her arms as if he were her child.

"I love you, too, Dad, but you've got to grow up and find a woman your age who can share your love. And you are never again allowed in my bedroom without asking my permission."

By this time, the mother was pounding on the door, asking if she could come back in. We agreed that she could. She looked the situation over, let out a "harrumph," and closed the door on us. We three burst out laughing. The father and daughter continued in therapy. The mother filed for divorce, which was granted. Jan spends time with each parent and continues to love each one. Each has remarried and seems happy with their partners. I continue to hear from Jan, who reports that her father has never invaded her privacy again. She recently said, "They both needed love, but not from each other. I guess I'm a composite of both of them. Funny, I think most of my outer strength comes from my mother, but there's an inner strength that comes from my father. It has to do with seeing things through eyes of love rather than with my critical eye. Isn't this the opposite of the way it's supposed to be?"

I've spent years reviewing the lessons this family taught me about expectations, the ways males and females try to get their love needs fulfilled, the complicated dynamics of forgiveness, and respect. The father lost his self-respect because he violated boundaries. His daughter helped him restore his respect through her forgiveness. The mother could not forgive him out of her love for her daughter, and lack of love for her husband. I learned that gender expectations are the result of tangled cultural webs that have zilch to do with the reality of any individual person. You must be willing to be vulnerable and be able to forgive to know lasting love.

Reflection Exercise

▶ With whom do you most identify in the above case?

▶ What did you want to happen? How do you feel about what did happen?

▶ Have you blocked love from your life by holding on to inappropriate gender expectations?

▶ What is required for you to forgive someone who may have hurt you?

▶ Do you find it easier to forgive people of your same gender? Why?

WHOLE POWER

MEN KNOW THAT they need love and nurturing from females who must first love and respect themselves. Women sometimes need the extra muscle power and the ability to forget what is best forgotten from men, who are willing to be vulnerable if we women will help create a safe place where vulnerability can happen. Each gender contributes unique skills to create a balanced whole. Women do not need to become more like men to have power. Although the idea of penis envy has been out there since Freud, it is a fact that men have been mortally afraid of the biological power of women's bodies since the beginning of recorded gender history. It could be called "Venus envy," a term coined by writer Rita Mae Brown.[5] Male dominance of the church was founded upon this fact, which has had tragic results for both genders, as well as for the church. King Henry II imprisoned his wife, Eleanor of Aquitaine, because he knew she was more powerful than he in every way. Human nature drives us to oppress what we fear.

Male dominance has been changing during recent decades due to the power of the feminist movement. It could well now be time to drop our crusade for feminist causes and join with men for humanist causes, recognizing that the power differential is a perceived one that we have allowed to dominate our culture for far too long. *Women and men are equally powerful. This must be accepted by both genders if we truly want to end the longest war.* Each gender, as an aggregate, has skills and traits to complement the other into wholeness and within every relationship; each person offers skills and traits to grow the other.

Harville Hendrix, the founder of IMAGO Relationship Therapy, maintains that every relationship is composed of a turtle and a hailstorm, and that there is no foregone conclusion about which gender will play which role. When there is a problem, the turtle will withdraw from conflict while the hailstorm will beat upon the turtle's shell to get him to come out and deal with the problem. This causes the turtle to further retreat, which, of course, causes the hailstorm to hammer with greater determination. The hailstorm *appears* to have the most power, but in truth, each possesses equal power and no one wins. It is a futile competition. Often, one will give up. If the hailstorm gives up and the turtle's head comes out expecting peace, he may find the war begins again. On the other hand, the hailstorm may have truly given up, and we might find that the two will switch roles temporarily.[6] The only way there can be real peace is for both to find the courage to meet in the middle and hear the other's experience of the problem. For this to happen, you must be willing to let go of your needs to be stronger or weaker, right or wrong, superior or inferior. You have to understand that you contain the potential to be any, or all, of the above.

Let's revisit the knight in his not-yet-rusty armor, whose first encounter on his journey toward love was with Merlin, who tells him he was not really brave at all, but very afraid, which is why he put on the armor in the first place. After some time with Merlin, the knight realizes that this is true—and the truth hurts. The knight cries, causing his armor to begin to rust. Merlin explains that to get rid of his armor, he must visit three castles. First, the castle of silence, where the knight must learn to listen to his heart, which is breaking from the weight of the pain he has caused others by not listening to them. He cries again, and the rust begins to weaken his armor. Next, he visits the castle of knowledge, for knowledge is the torch by which he must find his way. Here, he learns that he cannot love others because he does not love himself. His need to impress others has only been his way to prove to himself that he was worthy of love, but he truly did not believe it. In fact, he stayed so busy trying to prove his worth that he had no time left to feel love. More tears. More rust. Less armor.

He finally comes to the castle of will and daring, inhabited by the fiercest dragon he has ever encountered: the dragon of fear and doubt. After doing battle with the dragon, the knight realizes that he doesn't need to feel fear and doubt as long as he has truth, self-knowledge, and self-love. The last hurdle of his journey is to reach the summit of the mountain of truth. When he is almost to the top, his path is blocked by a huge boulder with the inscription *Though this universe I own, I possess not a thing, for I cannot know the unknown if only to the known I cling.* The poor knight realizes that he has always clung to his own perception of truth, his own needs, and his own beliefs. He has never opened his mind or heart to the unknown, the different from himself. He competed with those different things to prove that he was right. He never had the courage to trust the other, the different, the unknown. All of a sudden, he knows that he must let go of the rock, which he knows, and fall into the unknown.

As he falls, he begins to feel free. His willingness to embrace and trust the unknown has set him free. At last he can cry tears, joyful tears, from his heart, which is filling with love. His armor dissolves. No longer does he need the shining reflection of his armor, for now he has a radiant inner light, the light of truth and love. He is one with the universe and has nothing to fear. Fear is only an illusion of different-ness. The truth is we are all the same when we choose to open our minds and hearts to compassion and love.

While this chapter has focused primarily on differences between and within genders, the ideas can be applied to differences between races, classes, colors, abilities, and sexual preferences. William James, who's considered the founder of psychology, stated that most of us are only rearranging our prejudices when we claim to be thinking. I contend that we must give up our prejudices if we hope to survive. Until we are willing to see "the other"—anyone different from ourselves—as a potential friend, who is just as in need of love as we are, we are doomed to competitive power struggles that only lead to death and destruction.

After visiting the Holocaust Museum, a high school student wrote:

> There are many lessons to be learned from this history.
> The most important lesson is power is not an excuse for ignorance.
> Someone should not be condemned because they aren't the same as you, and they should not have to suffer because of someone else's ignorance.
> Maybe there would not be so much tragedy if more people took a stand against violence.

Not only do we need to take a stand against violence, we need to make every effort to understand what has precipitated the violence. It is almost always a fear of differences, which is another way of expressing ignorance and a lack of love. Violence never leads to love. It only creates more fear, which in turn creates more violence. More love and less fear is the only possible way to end violence.

This is poignantly driven home in the movie *Dead Man Walking*, when Sister Helen Prejean, played by Susan Sarandon, says to Poncelet, a rapist and murderer who is strapped to the table, awaiting execution by lethal injection, "I will be the face of love for you." Without a face of love, it is almost impossible to face life—or death. Without a face of love in our lives, our fear of no love drives us into the darkest and most evil aspect of human nature—our power to harm ourselves and others. Men are often praised for exhibiting and wielding this power. War is the prime example. No one wins a war. Wars will never end until we can accept differences for what they are—the perceptions that make a rainbow possible.

While visiting my daughter's family in Ecuador, my granddaughter Nina was reading one of her Bruce Coville books.[7] She came to a paragraph that stopped her short, and said to me, "Grandma, pay attention to this. I mean really pay attention. Bruce Coville says that the reason we Earth people don't know about the aliens from other solar systems is that they do not want to know us, because we haven't learned to live at peace with the people like us here on our own planet, so they don't want us messing up everything else in the universe. They know that until we learn to get along with different people, you know, like boys and girls, and other colors, we'd never be able to get along with aliens, who might really be different."

She had my attention. "Well, Nina, I think he may be right. What do you think?"

"Hmmm, I think I'd better stop fighting with Matthew." Matthew is her younger brother. She got the point. I picked up the book after she'd fallen asleep and read it from cover to cover. It held several profound truths, the greatest of which is that until we can learn to respect, rather than fear, differences in others, we will never attain the only power that can save us—the power of love.

In the touching film *Notting Hill,* Julia Roberts, playing a wealthy film star, stands before Hugh Grant, portraying a modest bookstore proprietor, and says, "I'm just a girl standing before a boy and asking if you could love me." At first, he turns her down, believing that the gap between their financial statuses and stations in life is just too broad to cross. Then he reconsiders, recognizing his most vulnerable self within her most vulnerable self. When we open our hearts to allow our most vulnerable loving self to be exposed to the same in any other person, miracles happen.

Although each of us is uniquely different, each of us has within us the same vulnerable child, perhaps in different clothing—a male child, a female child, a white child, a black child, a Jewish child, a German child, an Islamic child, a Christian child—standing before the world and crying, "Can you love me?"

SEVEN

Are You Ready *to* Open Your Heart *to the* Healing Power *of* Love?

LOVE IS A FEELING THAT EMANATES FROM THE HEART
AND EXTENDS THROUGH THE BLOOD
TO EVERY CELL OF THE BODY.
—ALEXANDER LOWEN

FEELING LOST IN one of the darkest periods of my life, I was seriously considering if it were possible to commit suicide with grace. My first husband and I had separated. I'd moved with my four children to an old farm outside the city to escape from the upper-middle-class neighborhood where a "scarlet A" had been painfully stitched across my forehead. My own carelessly sewn stitches were the deepest and most painful, for I had been inappropriately involved with a neighbor's husband. My shame was overwhelming. My grief and guilt over the price my children were paying for my transgressions was next to unbearable. They never complained about being uprooted and made to change important aspects of their lives. They still trusted me, and that was terrifying. It forced me to realize that our children believe we are gods, even when our behaviors are gauche, immature, and selfish.

I could see no way to get my life back on a decent track. I wanted to run and never stop, but I knew they would run after me. I was scaring myself by staring at knives and bottles of pills. Visions of what the children would do if they came home to either of those scenes stopped me from acting. My physical, mental, and emotional energy felt as if it were being sucked into a black hole.

On an unusually chilly March morning, preparing breakfast, packing lunches, getting three of the children to the school bus stop, and delivering the youngest to kindergarten had drained me. Everything in the house needed attention, but I had no energy left to organize into constructive action. I looked past the mess of cereal bowls on the table and last night's dinner dishes piled in the kitchen sink. I could only gaze out the window and pray someone out there would save me, or show me a way out of the larger mess I'd made of life. I was no longer sure that there was anyone out there, although prior to this time, I'd been sure there was a God, or some kind of spiritual being to whom I could turn for support. I was losing my grip on everything. Especially love. After all, what had felt like love had triggered the entire catastrophe.

Absentmindedly looking out the window, I began to notice that the ground still held a few patches of old snow. A giant oak tree was directly in my gaze, with dirty snow clinging to the hollows between its protruding roots. A ray of sun struck a particular patch of snow and caught my attention. Peeping up through the glistening snow, I saw the bowed yellow, purple, and green bud of spring's first violet.

My heart swelled with gratitude. The message of hope was instant and powerful. New energy began to stir from the depths of my being and flow through my mind and body. I felt alive for the first time in months. Tears that had been frozen by my fear and numbness began to overflow. A tiny voice from my soul whispered "thank you" to the violet. The tiny bud seemed to nod in response: "We'll make it."

A line I'd heard on a tape by Thich Nhat Hanh, a Vietnamese Zen master and peace activist, "The rhythm of my heart is the birth and death of all that is alive," passed through my mind with a magnitude of new meaning.

After crying a few minutes, I used my renewed energy to wash dishes, clean the kitchen counters, and even the floor! The sun cast a stream of light through the window. Its warm healing rays were healing me back into a wholeness I'd forgotten existed.

HEALING IS WHOLENESS

ACCORDING TO DEAN Ornish, M.D., who was recognized by *Life Magazine* as one of the fifty most influential members of our generation for his contributions to preventative medicine, there is a vast difference between curing and healing. Curing is measured by the degree of improvement toward health from a physical, mental, or emotional disease. The word "heal" derives from a Saxon word meaning "whole," and always has carried a connotation of spiritual wholeness. Healing is the process of becoming whole. Healing may occur when there is no cure for a terminal physiological disease. In other words, we are capable of becoming whole, of reaching a place of deep spiritual peace, when curing may not be an alternative. Wholeness is an honest place of peace and love. Ornish stated that he knew of no factor in medicine that has a greater impact on our quality of life, incidence of illness, and premature death from all causes than the healing power of love and intimacy.[1]

Ann Marie is a dear friend of mine who has bone cancer and is mostly restricted to a wheelchair. She is well loved by many friends, her children, grandchildren, and her dear husband, who is in more pain watching her deteriorate than she is in the midst of the disease's ravaging effects on her body. She recently shared with me that she felt closer to God than she's ever dreamed possible, for she knew with all of her being that the spirit of God was with her every moment. A joyous radiance emanated from her face as we both cried. I knew she was more whole than I. She must have sensed my thoughts, for she softly laughed and said, "I have a feeling that you really do understand, but I know it sounds crazy to anyone who looks at me today. Yet, I am whole in a way I never was when I *appeared* healthy to most people."

Reflection Exercise

▶ How, physically, mentally, and emotionally, healthy are you today?

▶ How spiritually whole are you today?

▶ What is your daily plan for physical health?

Reflection Exercise (continued)

▶ What is your daily plan for mental and emotional health?

▶ What is your daily plan for spiritual wholeness?

Curing is wonderful when it happens, and God knows each of us who knows Ann Marie is praying for a cure so that her life can continue. We want her grandchildren to know her as the vibrant and healthy person she's been. Her husband and I rant and rave about the unfairness of the situation. His faith is strong that she will recover from the cancer, yet his pain over the possibility that she may not stops him in his tracks. When he left the room during one of my recent visits, she whispered, "Poor Luigino, denial is the only way he can cope with this now, but I know God has a continuing wonderful life planned for him when I'll be in Heaven cheering him on."

I wanted to tell her that she may end up right here with him and they will continue to have a wonderful life together, but she looked at me with such love that held a superior knowledge and wholeness to mine that I kept quiet. She will be whole, regardless of her cancer and regardless of what happens to her body, for she knows that wholeness is not physical. Physical health can be taken away from you at any moment of your life, but wholeness is a gift of love, something that cannot be destroyed by disease.

The fact that I allowed the ending of an illicit relationship to drain my emotional and physical energy attests to my lack of wholeness at the aforementioned time. Like the knight in rusty armor, I was looking for love in the wrong places. Love is always present, but if we don't recognize real love, then we'll wear ourselves out searching for that indefinable, elusive something. We are often afraid to love—to be vulnerable—because we fear the loss of love, which is an illusion at best. We cannot lose love, if we understand the *whole* concept of real love, which has nothing to do with lust and everything to do with feeling our connection to the universal life-force.

The survival through the winter of that tiny violet reminded me that spring always comes when we open our hearts to the wonders of nature and to the beauty of the cyclic processes of wholeness. I knew in an instant that each of us is a powerful part of a grander whole. I had been blinded to this by narrowing love down to a lustful relationship.

After applying my renewed energy to cleaning my kitchen, I called my dearest friend, Carol. She stood by me through my catastrophic involvement and had tried to warn me that I was headed for disaster. I called to tell her that she had been right and I had been wrong. We laughed and cried together. Later she came out for a walk in the woods, where signs of spring seemed to greet us all along the path. Afterward, we shared a bottle of wine to celebrate my healing back into real love—the love of a true friend, of nature, and of the awesome mystery of connections to all there is.

Author May Sarton, in describing a dear friend, wrote: "She became for me an island of light, fun, and wisdom, where I could run with my discoveries and torments and hopes at any time of day and find welcome." Carol has been, and remains, this kind of friend in my life. This kind of friendship offers deep healing love. It is the ideal cornerstone for any love relationship.

THE PALLIATIVE PATH

PALLIATIVE IS A term often used in the medical world to describe something that is an excuse for a cure, but does not really cure. A palliative treatment might cloak or disguise a disease, but is not able to abate the seriousness of the disease. Affairs (defined as sexual relationships between two people, at least one of whom is still engaged in another *supposedly* committed relationship) often palliate loneliness and a lack of love. Affairs never cure these situations. They are disguises or excuses for real love. They offer flamboyant emotional ups and downs—like a wild ride on a roller coaster, during which you ecstatically rise to the crest of a high track and then are sure you will die on the next descent. Affairs usually happen when you are bored with life in general, or are lonely and need an emotional fix. They never heal our hearts, but they can allow the individuals involved to feel cured of emotional loneliness for the duration of the good times; however, the bad times will be lurking in the shadows—always! This is not to say that all affairs end up as disasters, but it is to say that there will be disasters before an affair can grow into the kind of relationship that could heal you into the wholeness of lasting love.

No whole person has an affair. I know this because I was an

unhealed "hole" (antonym to whole) for a long time. A whole person loves and respects himself enough to end one relationship before beginning another. However, there are many "hole" persons who believe that changing partners will heal them into wholeness. Never happened, never will! There is a saying I have taped to the refrigerator to keep me aware: *It is not easy to find happiness within ourselves, but it is not possible to find it elsewhere.*

Most affairs are escape routes for escape artists, or emotional cowards, who lack the courage to deal honestly with whatever might be wrong with their marriages. Many use the excuse that their marriage can't change and they deserve to be happy. What they are often saying is: "I'm not willing to change and I'm not willing to be honest with my partner." Surgery is usually required before healing can begin. The operation can take several forms: ocular, to remove the blinding cataracts that prevent the person from seeing reality; open-heart, to literally open the heart to the pain that she is causing, but seems unable to feel; or brain, to remove the massive tumor that has blocked emotional truth and courage.

Actor Robin Williams claims that the reason men have affairs is that God gave them a brain and a penis, but only enough blood to run one at a time. As trite as this may sound, after listening to hundreds of men's stories, I think there is a grain of truth in his comment. Many men would agree with him. At a primordial biological level, this is why most men fear the biological seductive power of the female body. I know several married men who live as "paragons of virtue," respecting every letter of the law, until a female offers to share her body. The equation that follows usually works for both genders: weakness → pleasure → guilt → pain → crisis → major decisions → more pain.

Reflection Exercise

▶ Remember yourself back through any affairs you may have had.

▶ Who was hurt? What did you learn?

▶ If you have not had an affair, have you been tempted? What are your feelings about resisting the act?

Married for nineteen years with two teenaged sons, Dick and Arlene had a lovely home in the suburbs and seemed to be an ideal family. He was a top executive and she was a respected community activist. Their image was of vast importance to them. They never argued. They always wore smiles in concordance with their fine upscale clothing. They only discussed daily dynamics, schedules, and "the boys." They took their marriage for granted and never considered that it might not continue. This was quite strange, considering he was involved in his fourth affair and she had become a closet alcoholic. They invested endless energy in keeping up appearances. They invested no energy in becoming intimate life partners.

Dick had a rude awakening when he discovered that he had contracted a sexually transmitted disease, which was beginning to cause considerable discomfort. He knew he was in big trouble unless he could infect Arlene, so that when treatment was required, they would appear equally guilty to the family physician. She was thrilled when he became amorous and obliviously became prey to his wretched scheme. Their physician was not so easily seduced. He opened a can of worms with his questions about their sex life. Arlene removed her blinders, though it devastated her ego. However, with her ego out of the way, she freed the abundant energy that had been supporting it and reinvested it into making an honest assessment of her marriage, and her life. Putting her pride aside, she attended AA meetings and stopped drinking. She demanded that Dick leave their neat little nest. When he refused, she threw everything he owned into the front yard for all the neighbors to see. The two sons were shocked, but at a deeper level, they were proud of their mother's newly discovered honesty, courage, and energy. It gave them permission to be honest as well. Gradually, the three of them learned to laugh and cry together.

Dick went away to lick his wounds, thinking he would have no problem finding a new playmate. It didn't work. He became more and more depressed, especially as he watched Arlene and the boys thrive. They seemed to be a whole family without him, which he could not fathom. After experiencing a few panic attacks, he realized he needed psychological help, which he had always considered the refuge of weak people. He walked into my office looking like a lost dog that had not been fed for months. He described his success in business, his once happy home life, and then complained that his wife had changed into someone he did not know.

"Oh, I see. Did you know her before this change?" I inquired. He looked startled, but something seemed to click.

After a few thoughtful moments, he answered, "Maybe not."

We were on our way to healing a hole so deep and wide that it had swallowed up the real person. Over time, Dick learned that his affairs, lies, and addiction to images needed to be discarded if he truly wanted to be healed. He cried tears that had been held back for decades. Months later, we invited Arlene into a session to meet this changed man, to whom she was still legally married. She was dubious and fearful that he might have only conjured up a revamped, more appealing image that could trap her again. It took months of honest conversations for him to prove that this was not the case. She refused to sleep with him until she felt she could trust him as a friend.

They are presently growing together as friends in love. They have given up palliative cures for real healing. This process always requires painful soul searching, honesty, forgiveness, vulnerability, courage, and self-love. Arlene could not love herself as an alcoholic and Dick could not love himself as a womanizer.

Reflection Exercise

▶ What do you desire from friendship?

▶ Is your lover a friend as well as a sexual partner? Are you a friend to your sexual partner?

▶ Do you tend to change to accommodate your sexual partners more than your friends? If so, how?

▶ In which relationship are you the most honest? Why?

▶ In which relationship are you the most comfortable? Why?

▶ In which do you feel the most loved and accepted? Why?

▶ Do you love and respect yourself? Why or why not?

SELF-LOVE

BECAUSE YOU CANNOT give to others what you do not possess, you must love and respect yourself to give love and respect to others. Self-love is not self-involvement, nor narcissism. It is not selfish, nor conceited. During the seventies, the "me decade," it became obvious that doing everything my way was a dead end, lonely street. Many became so lost in the search for themselves—frequently on drugs—that they've never found their way back to whomever they might have been had they maintained self-respect and a reality-based definition of self-love. One of my close friends during this crazy time said one day, "God knows, I'm so tired of trying to find *my thing,* which supposedly is the path to happiness. The search is depressing me." Depression seemed to be the result of those idealized, self-involved years. Self-involvement transforms into selfishness and alienation. Self-love, rooted in self-respect, extends outward to others, for that is the nature of real love.

Christopher Reeve is the epitome of someone who has true self-love. After playing Superman, the hero who could accomplish any physical feat, he has now lost most of his physical abilities through a spinal cord injury. Christopher and his wife, Dana, who continues to love him and stay by his side, have founded an association for research to aid victims of spinal cord injuries. They have not allowed his disabilities to hinder their love for themselves, for each other, or for mankind. Without the armor of his "superman" image, today he is more loved and more respected, for he has proven that physical disability does not destroy our capacity for spiritual wholeness.

Following such a debilitating accident, many of us would become self-pitying and self-absorbed, trying to milk love from others. That is not the way love works. When you pity yourself, others begin to pity you. When you become self-absorbed, others stay away as if you wore a "keep out" sign across your chest. Self-love is a primary ingredient for loving others. The catch is that it is extremely difficult to love yourself and to believe you deserve to be treated with love and respect, unless you have been treated in a loving and respectful way by someone who values you. In the best of worlds, this process always begins through the love you received from your primary caregivers.

But we do not live in the best of worlds and the sad truth is that our country is filled with adults who were not sufficiently loved as children to be able to love themselves as adults, or raise children who love themselves. Therefore, if this applies to you, you must develop the ability to begin loving yourself as an adult. You need to weave a web of love around yourself that will begin to heal and strengthen you. A college student of mine came to this realization in a class on love and relationships, expressing it in this poem.

Spiderwebbed

Entwined, my being,
tangled, my life.
I weave the patterns,
so elaborately interlaced, so intricate.

I am the fly,
the captured prisoner.
Laboring, trying to resist, then,
fatigued by struggle, submission.

I am the spider,
my legs stretched in abundant directions.
With no compassion I devour.
With enduring energies I liberate.

Spiderwebbed.
So elaborately interlaced, so intricate,
I weave the patterns.

During her therapy appointment, a bright adolescent female with a complicated history of eating disorders and suicide attempts stated, "I'm finally beginning to understand something my sister told me that she learned during her therapy with you: that when I begin to love myself enough to take care of myself properly, peace follows. Life becomes so much simpler and healthier. I have to stop manipulating others for attention and love, and nurture myself instead of punishing myself all the time to punish them."

This young woman and both of her sisters had gone to some dangerous extremes to challenge their father to rearrange his priorities and their mother to become more assertive about her own needs. The oldest sister had been hospitalized several times for anorexia and the middle one had a serious problem with bulimia. Theirs is a complex story that poignantly illustrates several truths about self-love and healing into wholeness. These parents love their children, but the father works out of town during the week and comes home only on weekends. He was fathered by an absent father and terribly resented it, but was unconsciously repeating his father's behaviors.

The mother was fathered by a very dominant man who did not allow his will to be questioned by anyone, especially his wife, my client's grandmother. My client's mother was repeating her mother's behaviors, although as a child she was determined not to do so. Luckily, the three sisters were more determined to change things than their parents had been; however, they went to drastic measures to do so. They resented their father's appearance on weekends to rule the roost. They also resented their mother's allowing him to do this. Their resentment blocked their feeling loved by either parent. The entire family was "spiderwebbed."

It seemed to them that their father only cared about making money and being in control, while their mother only cared about keeping him happy, regardless of her own needs. Eating disorders are the perfect weapons for children and adolescents to express anger, which they may be afraid to express overtly, at their parents. All parents notice when their offspring stop eating. It threatens the very core of our concept of nurturing; therefore, the offspring get attention. Usually this attention is negative, but even negative attention is empowering. These girls needed power to be able to change the system. They got it—but at a tremendous price to their health, and to their parents' wallets.

When the parents came into therapy and became aware of how they were repeating the negative parenting they had received, they woke up. The waking up process required hours of painful, honest confrontation and intense moments of unleashing fury that had been stored for years. It required that each person in the system stop harming himself to manipulate the others for attention and love. It required giving up some beliefs about themselves and their family. It required that each person take some responsibility for changing himself, with the support of the others, but not through the victimization of the others.

They set new priorities. The father began to spend more fun time with his daughters and became less demanding and controlling. He learned to listen and became more attuned to their needs. The mother began to speak up when she disagreed with her husband and began to ask that some of her personal needs be met. The girls developed a new appreciation for her, and for themselves as women. As the members of this family learned to take more loving care of themselves, they became free to love each other. They are having fun together, communicating, arguing in more open and constructive ways, expressing what they feel and stating their needs. Through developing self-love, each has become part of a whole loving unit.

As we mature, we tend to treat ourselves the same way we were treated by our early caregivers. We repeat many of their behavior patterns in an unconscious effort to stay united with them. This can keep us trapped in the webs that were woven around us in childhood, although as we mature we develop the capacity to weave our own patterns. What many of us do not develop is the awareness that we have the ability to change things, if we are willing to "see" what needs changing. One of the most accurate indicators that you need to change something in your life is the degree to which you, as an adult, nurture yourself, and the extent to which you balance self-love with love for others.

Reflection Exercise

► How are you presently treating yourself?

► Do you take proper care of your body? Do you feed yourself nutritiously and appropriately?

► Do you use food to gratify needs other than hunger rather than asking for what you really need?

► Do you drive yourself to please others and feel guilty when you ask for what you want?

► Do you ever consider what you want or need?

Love and need are not the same phenomenon. We tend to confuse them when our need capacity becomes greater than our love capacity. When you hurt yourself by denying and\or repressing your needs, you feel resentful and create negative energy, which becomes a part of you, and then spreads to others. This process seems to become a reactive chain that perpetuates itself for generations. Whatever is sown shall be reaped. This is not a new idea, but one that is easy to ignore because it is overwhelming in its truth. You must see the truth before you can change the patterns you are often unconsciously repeating.

Adults also develop eating disorders from a deficiency of self-love and a desperate need for attention. Our current culture validates eating disorders by worshiping thinness. Obesity is rampant as well, which is the opposite extreme, and equally destructive. All extremes are dangerous if you move into them for lengthy time periods. Overeating has become a way to fill our emptiness: emotional, psychological, and spiritual. It can make the pain of emptiness subside within us and does not require us to count on others. We feel less vulnerable going to the refrigerator or the cookie jar than asking for a hug or a conversation. In her book *When Food is Love,* Geneen Roth writes that it is easy for children to turn to food to fill emptiness because it is often available when their parents are not. Once this process begins, it often continues as a way of filling our needs, *but food is not love.* Food and other addictions are often used as substitutes for love.[2]

Addictions can become "hole" stuffers that make us feel whole when we are actually digging holes that will swallow us, making real love impossible. Addictions destroy self-love. They eventually lead to self-destruction, unless you begin to love something inconsistent with the addiction. For example, if you are a smoker and can begin to practice love for breathing, this can become a healing path to self-love that helps overcome the nicotine addiction. Food addictions can be broken through the development of love for appropriate exercise and physical health.

Self-love involves a healthy balance of your eating and exercise regimes, your time spent alone and with others, your time for work and for play, and your style of giving and receiving.

BALANCING INTO WHOLENESS

EACH ONE OF us has an ultimate destiny that we will engineer to its end. I believe our ultimate destiny is to learn to love, and I know the most difficult part is learning to love ourselves. Until we learn to do this, regardless of how difficult, we will not be able to love others. Until we forgive ourselves, we are not able to forgive others. Until we are honest with ourselves, we cannot be honest with others. Until we behave so that we can respect ourselves, we cannot respect others. Until we are kind to ourselves, we cannot be kind to others. Until we can trust ourselves, we cannot trust others. Until we take care of ourselves, we cannot take care of others, yet each of these duo dynamics must be balanced between self and others. If we stay focused only on ourselves, we will end up lonely and unhealed, and if we remain focused entirely on others, we lose ourselves, having nothing to offer another.

Reflection Exercise

▶ Take an honest inventory of the above issues in your life.

▶ How do you balance meeting your needs and the needs of significant others?

▶ How do you balance your need for time alone versus time with others?

Dr. Ken Matheny, a wise professor of mine during graduate school at Georgia State University, held a seminar on this issue of balancing our lives when he realized how out of balance many of his students' lives had become. We were so intent on gaining insight into the lives of others in order to become superior counselors that most of us were forgetting we had a primary responsibility to keep ourselves healthy and balanced. He told us that our lives and relationships needed some healing work if we depended on any single activity or relationship to meet over 25 percent of our total affiliative needs, meaning our needs to connect to others. Most of us argued with him, insisting that his percentage was too low. I am now about the same age as he was at the time of this seminar, and I'm sure he was right.

Reflection Exercise

▶ List your affiliative needs: for friendship, for conversation, for feedback, for all aspects of love and intimacy, excluding sexual intimacy.

▶ Now make a list beside each need of the people, groups, and activities in your life that help fill this need.

▶ To what percentage are you counting on any one person, or group, or activity to meet your needs?

▶ Does any single adult depend on you to meet over 25 percent of his affiliative needs?

▶ How does it make you feel? And how does it affect your feelings about that person?

▶ How could you negotiate changing this without losing the love of this person?

▶ How could you be less extreme and more balanced into a healthier life?

A healthy life always involves intimate connections to other persons, but as beautifully expressed in *The Prophet,* by Kahlil Gibran, *"There must be spaces in togetherness."*

His point is that you have to have space in which you can maintain your unique individual wholeness to be able to participate in a whole and healthy relationship.

Self-love is appreciating yourself in the way Melody Beattie expresses it in *Codependent No More:* "You are the greatest thing that will ever happen to you. Believe it. It makes life much easier."

THE HEALER WITHIN

YOU ARE CREATED with the healing power to become as whole as your individual destiny allows. This is no easy task, considering all the myriad negative possibilities you encounter throughout your lifetimes. Paul Tillich, the late contemporary philosopher, stated, "The courage to be is the ethical act in which a man affirms his own being in spite of the elements of his existence which conflict with his essential self-affirmation."

The idea of being created equal is one of the bitterest pills we are supposed to swallow. It usually does not take long for us to realize that this idea is simply not true. Due to genetics, economics, cultures, and opportunities, some have advantages that make their lives healthier than others; yet we each have an assignment, so to speak, to live out an individual destiny. This destiny might involve overcoming great adversity, or it might involve accepting what we cannot change. When I look around I never feel that whatever comprises destiny plays fair. I am thankful that there is a greater plan for our universe than I am capable of grasping. My reach to understand always exceeds my ability to grasp the wisdom I seek.

I do know there seems to be a universal healing process to which every living cell has access. We can sense it, even though we may not understand it. It is innate within us or we could not survive. There is a life-force energy that perpetuates life in all living things, even though we may not be able to see it or measure it scientifically. We know it is there; otherwise a cut on a finger would not heal. We are all healers. Richard Gordon, a healer and author of *Quantum Touch,* writes, "No, I have absolutely no idea what water is," said the fish. "Why do you ask?" Like the fish who has no concept of water, in modern Western culture, we seem to have little conscious knowledge of the healing life-force that is the animating current of our lives, yet we feel it within us. We are most aware of it when we are feeling loved and connected to loving energy. Perhaps *it* is love.[3]

Many Eastern cultures base their entire healing systems on knowledge of the healing life-force. Tibetan medicine is founded in the Buddhist belief that the spiritual toxins of anger, pride, ignorance, frustration, and fear cause disease, and that living with the good intentions of integrity, kindness, and compassion for ourselves and all other living things is the path of staying well. Their system is not based only on the physical, but includes the emotional, mental, and spiritual. Healing the spirit is the highest form of healing, and love for all living things is the highest form of spiritual life. It is not an issue that someone may be physically deformed because that is simply form, but to be spiritually deformed—broken in spirit—demands healing attention.

This is not an issue of religion, but an issue of your personal belief system about life. Healing of every kind demands belief. Dr. Jerome Frank, professor emeritus of psychiatry at the Johns Hopkins University, cites a dramatic example of three bedridden patients who were not recovering after serious surgeries. Conventional medicine had done all that was possible and the concerned physician decided to try faith healing through a local healer, who claimed to be able to heal patients without touching them. On twelve different occasions, the healer projected his healing powers at the three patients, without any significant improvements in their conditions. The doctor was discouraged, but tried a different approach. He told the patients about the healer, which he had been too embarrassed to do in the beginning. He told them that he knew a healer who had amazing gifts of healing without any contact with a patient. He said that on a particular day this man would send healing energy to each of them. Within the following days, all three patients began to gain weight and to make remarkable improvement. In truth, the healer did nothing on that day. Dr. Frank established that our beliefs about outcomes may have a critical influence on healing.[4] Prayer and positive, loving thoughts may be the best medicines available.

Reflection Exercise

▶ Why do you believe you become ill? Include physical, mental, and emotional illness.

▶ Why do you believe you heal?

True healing goes beyond the physical and often involves a change in consciousness or in belief. It seems to be true that people who believe they will become victims of certain diseases are at more risk for contracting the disease than people who focus on positive health. It is also true that many people who believed they would be cured of a disease, regardless of its medical prognosis, have been.

The medically verified healings that have taken place at the shrine of Lourdes are among the most miraculous. Deepak Chopra tells of an Italian army officer who was dying of metastasized bone cancer that had almost dissolved one of his hip joints. After being blessed with holy water, his hip literally re-formed, and within a month, there was no trace of cancer. More than seventy scientifically authenticated healings have taken place at this particular shrine in the past few decades. There have also been hundreds of cases where there was no obvious physical healing, but persons claimed to have felt a spiritual healing that allowed them to be at peace with their illness. Some suggest that the differences in outcomes could be that many of us have not yet developed the ability to contact the power point of virtual reality, the Alpha and Omega where life is created; however, the only viable explanation is that we do not have all the answers.

To be able to relate to this virtual level of reality, great spiritual healers and teachers claim that we must free ourselves of negative emotions, and inhabit a state of pure love. Most of us find this next to impossible because we have been participating in negativity since shortly after our births. Healing requires we take a careful look at our negative emotions and do something to release them, regardless of whether or not they are justified. When we are hurt or abused, self-love elicits justified anger, but healing requires we forgive and let the negativity go. Holding on to negativity blocks the love that can heal our bodies and our spirits. Letting it go opens the channel so that love can flow from virtual reality through quantum reality to physical reality.[5]

Reflection Exercise

▶ What was going on in your life prior to the last time you were ill?

▶ Have you ever been sick from anger? What did you do about it?

▶ Do you tend to focus on your physical health more than your emotional and spiritual health?

It is possible for a physical condition to be cured without meaningful healing taking place. It is also possible for meaningful healing to take place without a physical cure. The difference is that when meaningful spiritual healing takes place, the physical condition does not carry as much negativity in our lives, as in the cases of Christopher Reeve and my friend Ann Marie.

This has also been the case with many people who have AIDS. Two personal friends of mine have died due to the complications related to HIV, but died filled with peace and love, whole in spirit, knowing they would remain that way. The homosexual community has formed support networks so that people with AIDS do not have to suffer or die alone. They have become an inspiration to the medical community as they extend loving support to any one and any family who has to endure the horrors of this tragic illness. When we look at the grander scheme of things, I cannot help but wonder if it took AIDS to wake us up to the fact that sex was never meant to be casual. AIDS and other STDs have provided a powerful stimulus for getting to know someone and developing a loving friendship prior to hopping into bed with them.

Recent research also indicates that safe sexual intimacy can keep us healthier, happier, more connected, and even more spiritually whole. One of the profound findings in the surveys being conducted in this field is that most participants in interviews on the subject of sexual pleasure and health are in agreement that honesty and sharing in meaningful friendship enhance the enjoyment of the sexual experience. Many report that a sexual experience with a loving partner is a spiritual experience.[6]

Reflection Exercise

▶ Evaluate your feelings about your sexual experiences.

▶ How do you feel about casual sex?

▶ Have you felt more spiritually whole after satisfying sex?

Sexual energy is the principal energy of our existence. It is innate to all of us. It can become a monster of destruction and disease or a healer into loving wholeness. I'll never forget one of my first conversations with Luigino, the loving husband of my friend Ann Marie, after they had been married a few weeks. He exclaimed, "I thought I had known ecstasy through some of my religious experiences, but now, oh-la-la, sex is the ultimate religious experience. Her body is the most wonderful thing I've ever touched." When she came out of the recovery unit following her mastectomy, he was waiting in her room with a diamond ring. He wanted her to know that she remained the jewel of his life. They have maintained a beautiful physical, emotional, and spiritual relationship because they are each whole and have healed into the wholeness of real love.

Ornish's systematic review of the scientific literature for his book *Love and Survival* has proven that when we feel connected socially and intimately, feel cared for and loved by others, we are much more likely to be happy and healthy. We are even less likely to become ill, and when we have an illness, we raise our chances of being cured and healed if our affiliative needs are well met.

He reports that the studies based on the number and structure of social relationships reveal significant findings, but he was most impressed by those that dealt with the *quality* of relationships. In a study at Yale, where 119 males and 40 females were undergoing coronary angiography, those who felt the most loved and supported had significantly less blockage in the arteries of their hearts. This result was independent of diet, smoking, exercise, genetics, and other more common risk factors.[7]

Our local paper carried the story about how Jeff and Emily Lyons discovered the healing power of love after she nearly died in an abortion clinic bombing in Birmingham, Alabama, where she worked. As she lay comatose in the intensive care unit hooked to wiring, tubing, and blinking devices, Jeff leaned close to her and continued to whisper, "I love you. I will be here every step of the way." At the sound of her husband's voice, Emily's pulse quickened and her flagging blood pressure climbed a bit. Her connection to the healing life force of love increased as long as she could hear his voice. Emily had to undergo thirteen surgeries to become whole physically, but she and the doctors credit Jeff's love as the most significant healing force. It pulled her through the painful skin grafts to heal her burns and the removal of nails and gravel that were embedded from her feet to her face. Some remain too deep to be removed. The doctors gave her little chance of ever walking again, or of reading again due to the burns in her eyes. She is able to do both. Jeff has been there every step of the way, encouraging her and loving her.

Reflection Exercise

▶ Do you have someone who cares for you enough to be with you through trauma?

▶ Whom do you care for enough to support through trauma?

▶ Have you been in such a situation that you needed someone to love you enough to be there through such an experience?

▶ How could you cultivate a relationship with this depth of love? Trust that you do deserve it.

THE HEALING WISDOM OF INTUITION

IN THE SAME way you possess a healing life-force, you possess a source of wisdom and healing that our culture has given short shrift—intuition. The late philosopher and psychologist, Joseph Campbell, in a televised interview with Bill Moyers, stated: "Medical technology, machines, computers, and all our other tools do not have a chance to save us as a human race. Only when we learn to trust our intuition will we find the resources of character to meet our destiny of learning to heal and to love, which are possibly the same thing."

The term *intuition* has been applied to the highest insights of the greatest philosophers as well as to the thought forms of primates. It describes a way of knowing things that are beyond our capacity of reason to discover. According to *Webster's International Dictionary*, intuition comes from the Latin, *"intueri,"* meaning to see within. "It may be a revelation by insight or direct knowledge, akin to instinct, or a divine empathy that gives us direct insight." It attests to the psychic ability we each possess. When you appreciate yourself, you can appreciate your intuitive, psychic ability to know when something is healthy versus unhealthy for you. You always know, but sometimes do not trust your knowing, or even sabotage what you know in deference to another's opinion. Learning to trust your personal inner wisdom is basic to our healing into wholeness.

Intuition alerts us to danger or evil. This is powerfully portrayed in the story of Patch Adams, which is an authentic record of a loving doctor who has devoted his life to helping persons who are denied care by the organized medical community. In the movie version, a young female medical student is enticed by a psychopath to come to his home alone. Her intuition had previously warned her about this person, but she denies it and tries to live up to the model of love Patch has exhibited in his free clinic. She pays with her life, which causes Patch to rethink the fine line between self-love and extended love for humanity. Self-love does not mean sacrificing our lives needlessly to prove a point. When you have a healthy love for yourself, you develop a keen intuitive sense of what is safe and what is not.

A horrifying personal experience taught me this lesson well. I was one of several chaperons for a Girl Scout camping weekend at an isolated woodsy spot several miles from town. It was close to midnight with each camper tucked into her sleeping bag when one little girl became ill with a fever and was throwing up. I knew her mother was at home alone with a new baby, so I volunteered to drive her home. On my return to the camp, I discovered to my dismay that I was very low on gas. I prayed that the last service station near the turn before hitting the dirt roads leading into our woodsy camping site was still open. I thought my prayers had been answered for there was a man just climbing into his truck by the gas station. I asked if I could still purchase gas, to which he responded, "Sure, if you'll come sit in my truck with me first."

My heart sank into the pit of my stomach. I slammed my car door and took off. He screeched off after me. My thoughts were racing. I did not have enough gas to drive back into the city, yet I did not want to lead him to our camp site, and I had no idea where else I might end up out in these boonies. I believed that if I ran out of gas I would be raped and possibly killed. For the first time in my life I considered how I might kill another human being. Interesting that this incident happened shortly after the opening story of this chapter when I had contemplated suicide for the first time in my life. But things had changed. I wanted to live, and I wanted to protect the women and girls at the camp—and I did not want to be raped or murdered. I was driving dangerously fast on unknown dirt roads, with this man, literally, on my tail, and the gas tank registering empty. I became acutely aware that I must devise a plan to kill a man if I wanted to save my own life. I planned to open my car door, pull the emergency brake, and dive out the door. A bad crash would be inevitable and I hoped he would be killed. The minute I had my plan, I felt calm and assured that I could do it. However, within an instant, I spotted a light in the distance and intuitively drove toward it, off the road, through a field, and into a yard. After crashing into the steps, I stopped at the porch of an old house. This awakened the entire household: a mother, father, grandfather, and at least seven children. My pursuer stopped his truck when he realized he was in someone's yard. The kind couple who lived in the house immediately sensed the problem and pulled me into their home. The grandfather was already calling the sheriff. My pursuer screeched off again—this time in reverse.

I believe we have guardian angels. I'm very sure that I had one with me that night, who taught me invaluable lessons about self-love and about the need to trust my intuition. Perhaps not important, but worthy of mention, is the fact that both my pursuer and my savior were of a different race and color than I. My angel could have been as well.

In retrospect, I've tried to analyze how I moved from being a "hole" person thinking of suicide three months prior to this incident, to a more whole person, loving myself and others enough to risk killing in self-defense. The process began with my connection to the message of the violet pushing up through the snow. I had to shift my mind from self-pitying to grasping that life always has cycles of hardships and joyous renewals. Healing required that I take responsibility for the circumstances I had created, and then apply my mental, emotional, and physical energy to changing them into a more positive situation. It did not help me, or my children, to continue to punish myself for a mistake. We all make mistakes, but it is possible to turn them into impressive teachers.

My greatest mistake was trying to limit my idea of love to a single relationship, hoping it would heal an emotional wound. I was looking to another for love that I should have been able to cultivate within myself. When this truth struck me with its full force, I had to take an honest inventory of the ways I had allowed my love life to become grossly distorted. I had to reconnect to the spiritual and find the power point within myself where my human needs and spiritual needs could fuse without conflict. We each possess an intuitive wisdom that will help us locate this point of power—the place where significant healing and love begin.

THE HEALING WISDOM OF DREAMS

INTUITION AND DREAMS are both connections to the quantum dimension of reality, or the transition zone between the physical and virtual dimensions, therefore both possess healing qualities. Every Native American tribe has a version of a "dream-catcher" story that explains the healing power of dreams. My favorite is a Muskogee legend of a young crippled boy and his grandmother, who made him a "dream-catcher." One night the child was feeling especially sad that he was not able to run and play like other boys. His grandmother said to him, " Sometimes, if you really believe in a dream, it comes true. I'm going to make you something special to help you catch your dream." She soaked four thin sticks and some sinew in water until they were flexible, then tied the sticks end to end to form a circle, across which she wove the sinew, leaving a small round hole in the center. The child exclaimed that it looked like a spider web. His grandmother explained that a Grandmother Spider had taught people how to make them long ago because spiders understood that while they slept, their webs would catch good dreams and make them come true. The hole in the middle of the web allows bad dreams and negative thoughts to escape.

She told her grandson that he had to believe that the dream-catcher would make his dream of becoming whole and being able to run come true. The child *tried* to believe, but each morning he awoke still crippled, with one leg withered and shorter than the other. He complained to his grandmother that the dream-catcher did not work. "It only works if you believe with all your heart," she replied.

That night, before he went to sleep, he prayed that the Creator would make his belief strong enough so that he would be healed. He dreamed that his legs grew strong and that he was playing stickball with the other boys. When he awoke, remembering his dream, he pulled back his blanket to look at his legs. His short leg had grown longer. He stood up and discovered that his dream had come true. He could walk. "Am I still dreaming?" the boy wondered, but he ran off to tell his grandmother how much he loved her.[8]

This legend is hundreds of years old, but contains the same elements for healing that are set forth today by healers of all traditions: a sincere desire, a pure heart, prayers, a strong belief, and love.

Helen Keller, born with monumental physical handicaps, but loved into spiritual wholeness by her teacher, Annie, said, "You cannot hold a torch to light another's path without brightening your own." We each are a part of a grander universe to which we contribute our energy, which can be used selfishly or compassionately. We are born equal in the sense that we each have access to the power of healing love—if we choose to believe in it and connect to it with pure intention.

EIGHT

Are You Ready *to* Accept *that* Lasting Love *is a* Choice?

> *NOT WHAT WE HAVE, BUT WHAT WE USE;*
> *NOT WHAT WE SEE, BUT WHAT WE CHOOSE—*
> *THESE ARE THE THINGS THAT MAR OR BLESS*
> *THE SUM OF HUMAN HAPPINESS.*
> —CLARENCE URMY, AUTHOR OF *THE THINGS THAT COUNT*

SINCE THE BEGINNING of recorded history, there has been debate over the extent to which we choose—or the fates choose for us. In the Myth of Er, at the conclusion of Plato's *Republic,* he suggests that prior to coming to Earth, souls gather and meet with the gods to choose the conditions of their future lives. These conditions include selecting parents to birth us, caregivers who will raise us, guardian angels to protect us, and a reason to take the risk of living in the perilous environment that is Earth. Our chosen reason establishes "our earth mission," so to speak. Plato believed that each of us has a special purpose to fulfill during any given lifetime that will further the advancement of our souls toward the goal of perfected love.

At the other end of the spectrum is the idea that everything is chaos, that life is purely happenstance, and that we are merely biological accidents, tossed about by the fickle hand of

Fate. The truth is probably a mysterious combination of both theories, which we may never fully grasp, although the explanation in Chapter Four of three interacting dimensions of reality offers a "theory of everything" that I am willing to accept as possible and probable. However, the ultimate reality that we must grasp imminently if human life is to continue on this planet is that love is always a choice for adults. Love is the responsible choice to be kind to others, our environment, and ourselves. With any awareness of current events, environmental issues, and the immensely confounding problems of overpopulation, we are forced to confront the dire consequences of the irresponsible choices we have already made. If we continue to squander and corrupt our most precious resources—safe water, clean air, and children—our time of choices will soon end. Reynolds Price, James B. Duke Professor of English at Duke University, writes in the profoundly insightful novel *Roxanna Slade*:

> The human heart is not built to live in crowded quarters with more than one or two other people unrelated by blood. Ganging strangers together in cities like termites hiving or stacked like logs is asking for just what we have in the world today—runaway madness, murder, rape, hatred, unthinkable cruelty to children, and hundreds of thousands of souls who wind up sleeping unshielded the whole year round in snow and rain. Thick swarms of people will one way or other be the cause of whatever end the human race undergoes.[1]

CONSEQUENCES

BEGINNING WITH THE choice to get out of bed each morning, or not, every choice you make has consequences. Often, these consequences are farther reaching than most of us consider. This was powerfully driven home to me by a friend, Martha McKinney, who presented a "children's sermon" in our church several years ago. Each Sunday, before the grown-up sermon, the young children are invited to the front of the church where they listen to a short story or participate in a learning experience. On this particular Sunday, Martha held up a small plastic Baggie and asked, "How many of these have you thrown away after using them only one time?"

The children responded with numbers ranging from ten to one hundred. She next asked, "How many plastic bags have you seen your parents throw away after using them one time?"

The children responded with numbers ranging from a hundred to millions! Many of us adults had red faces. Since then, I've washed and reused Baggies, plastic wrap, and tin-foil products many times before discarding them.

It is a small choice, but one with big consequences for the preservation of our planet. Martha's last comment to the children that morning was: "Anytime you think a small decision of yours is not important, just think what would happen if everyone on Earth made the same decision you made."

A precocious little boy giggled to his friend, "I wouldn't want to go swimming in our pool again."

Reflection Exercise

▶ Jot down the choices you have made within the past few hours.

▶ What were the consequences of each choice? How would another choice have altered what has happened within these hours?

▶ Who beyond yourself has been affected by these recent choices?

CRITICAL CHOICES

SOME DECISIONS HAVE more critical consequences than others, but even small choices, such as reusing plastic Baggies, can have lasting consequences for which we are individually responsible. Buddhists call it karma. Karma simply means that actions and consequences are connected. It is almost impossible to make a choice without someone or something being affected. Bo Lozoff writes in *We're All Doing Time:*

Every thought, word, and deed is a seed, which we plant in the world. All our lives, we harvest the fruits of those seeds. If we plant desire, greed, fear, anger, and doubt, then that's what will fill our lives. Plant love, courage, understanding, good humor, and that's what we get back. This isn't negotiable; it's a law of energy, just like gravity.[2]

We all use the expression "what goes around, comes around." Yet, most of us have found ways of denying that this concept applies to us personally. If I tell this one little lie. If I use Styrofoam for just one party. If I don't recycle this week. If I screw this good-looking stranger just once. If I pass this one truck over a double yellow line: *Five killed instantly and driver paralyzed from neck down.* Karma can happen in an instant, following one careless choice, or can happen over time with accumulated irresponsible choices, but consequences always occur. There will be accidents, and someone always pays. The price can be high. Granted, we live in a fast-paced, quickly changing world that pressures us to make rapid decisions. In the face of immediate danger, haste may be necessary, but it pays to think through the possible consequences of most decisions before we commit to them. Embedded in each of our brains is a tree full of "chattering monkeys" who remain eager to participate in our decision-making process.

The chattering monkeys who dance along the synapses of my brain often complicate decisions that should be easy to make. Every spring, knowing that bathing suit time is approaching, I begin to plan my annual diet. The instant my vanity monkey begins to whisper that it's diet-time, the greedy glutton monkeys begin to tempt me with thoughts of cheeseburgers, hot fudge sundaes, and cookies. They know I love cookies. The monkeys love choice time. It's high-energy time for them, but it's anxiety time for me. If I could make an over-all commitment to health, to loving myself enough to want positive health in every moment, I could make this decision process easier. Instead, I do constant battle with my monkeys, who endlessly argue among themselves. "Procrastinator" argues with "Just Do It," while "I Want" argues with "You Should." The monkeys are crucial to my understanding the many facets of myself. They keep me aware of my potential to cause harm through destructive decisions. I know I've made the right decision when they are silent—especially when "Doubt" loses interest in the discussion. Decisions are more responsible after we've listened to our monkeys, discussed the possible and probable consequences with them, and are honest with ourselves—often the most difficult part, due to our lack of introspection. Bo Lozoff credits a wise Medicine Chief with saying:

> *If you seek to understand the whole universe,*
> *You will understand nothing at all,*
> *If you seek only to understand your Self,*
> *You will understand the whole universe.*

You cannot understand yourself unless you are willing to examine and take responsibility for the consequences of your decisions.

Reflection Exercise

▶ List three major choices you have made within the past five years.

▶ What advice did your monkeys give you on each decision?

▶ What have been the consequences of these major choices?

▶ How have others been affected?

▶ Knowing what you now know about consequences, would you have altered any of your major decisions?

A CRITICAL CHOICE: LOVE VERSUS MONEY

THERE WAS A popular song in the Forties that went something like: "Dance, ballerina, dance, and do your pirouette in rhythm with your aching heart. Once you said his love must wait its turn, you wanted fame instead. We live and learn. So dance, ballerina, dance." This theme continued to a lilting, haunting melody that always made me feel deeply sad. It made quite an impression on me during my early days, as I dreamed of fame and fortune, while also dreaming of being a loving wife and mother. I remember wondering which was really the most important and why we could not have both. I've since learned: We *can* have both, but *not at the same time.* To succeed at either requires a priority commitment of time and energy. When that commitment is divided and scattered, the returns are substantially diminished.

During the many years I spent in my office as a marriage and family therapist, I listened to dozens of successful career women despair over the lack of love in their lives. They came to me to confess that they were lonely and depressed because they were not in healthy relationships, or were not in relationships, period. Many admitted going home at night and "vegging out" alone in front of the TV, then crying themselves to sleep. I would remind them of what Judy Garland so poignantly said: "In the silence of night I have often wished for just a few words of love from one man, rather than the applause of thousands of people."

Judy Garland, Marilyn Monroe, Elvis Presley, and hundreds of others chose money, fame, and the applause of thousands over learning to truly love themselves through standing in love with one significant other. We make choices to commit our time, energy, and talents to what we believe will make us happy. These famous, wealthy people destroyed themselves without the kind of love that brings peace and lasting happiness. Many people die longing for the kind of love they never chose to cultivate during their too busy lives. I've yet to hear a single story of anyone's dying longing for another dollar or another moment of fame. The most unfilled desire prior to death is for forgiveness and more time to give and respond to love.

NPR annually airs a program called "Women in the Shadows," which focuses on women composers who lived in the shadows of their greater composer husbands. Clara Schumann is an example frequently cited. It is stated that she was cheated of fame and fortune by her husband and children. A complex rage resonates in me when I hear comments like this. Not a rage that Clara Schumann was cheated, but a rage at the assumption that because she was talented, she could not have chosen to be a wife and mother. Clara Schumann could have been one who came close to balancing her life into wholeness. She had a loving husband who appreciated her support and children with whom she could spend time and to whom she was devoted. She spent her mornings, while the children were in school, composing and playing the piano.

She composed several lovely sonatas still frequently heard today. How can anyone say these sonatas could have been composed without the exact balance of love and work she had chosen? It is totally conceivable to me that she chose less fame in order to have more real love.

A contemporary and well-respected former First Lady, Rosalynn Carter, chose to commit the early years of her marriage to her family. Following a successful career as a homemaker, she now has a successful joint career with her husband as a homebuilder for thousands of needy people through the nonprofit organization Habitat for Humanity. She is the first to admit that she could not have been successful at both simultaneously. She cultivated skills in her homemaking career that opened the gate for her present career.

Reflection Exercise

- ▶ How do you balance your life between work and love?

- ▶ Which requires the larger quantity of your time and energy?

- ▶ Which gives you the most personal fulfillment?

- ▶ Which do you suppose will ultimately be the most important for lasting fulfillment?

- ▶ How could you redistribute your time and energy to create more love?

The things to which you choose to give the larger quantity of your time and energy usually work. The things you choose to neglect usually suffer or are not as successful. When homemakers and parents try to have a full-time career outside the home, it is usually your home life and relationships that suffer *because* you are more prone to take them for granted, while giving your priority time and energy to a career.

THE MOST CRITICAL CHOICE

HEADING THE LIST of love choices with lasting consequences is the decision to bring a child into the world. Regardless of whether you have chosen your parents or the circumstances of your birth, as Plato theorized, you do not have conscious choices as infants and young children about the ways you are treated by your caregivers. You cannot survive without them. Their choices shape the circumstances of your life. Their choices give you your original definition of yourself and of love. Love has basic requirements, as discussed in Chapter One. Love requires active care, responsible behavior, respect, gaining knowledge and understanding of your loved ones, and the commitment of your consistent time and energy to meet the needs of your children, if they are to feel loved. Love also requires an ability to forgive, a commitment to honesty, and a spiritual connection, which emerges from sharing who you are with those you love. In no situation are these requirements more critical than in raising a child.

Reflection Exercise

▶ How did your caregivers meet these requirements for loving you? (Check back to your answers to the exercises in the earlier chapters.)

▶ If you have children, how do you meet these requirements for loving them? How about other significant people or pets who live with you?

▶ How do you meet these requirements for loving yourself?

I was fortunate that I was able to stay at home while my children were preschoolers—and that stay-at-home mothers were valued by the culture during the early Sixties. Unfortunately, that value was shifting by the late Sixties. I did go to work full-time when my youngest daughter was five years old. It is difficult for any of us who have tried to raise young children while working full-time to assimilate the fact that violent crimes committed by young children have increased 500 percent in the past three decades.[3]

The contemporary women's movement has given women more choices and is to be commended for progress in that area. The saddest downfall of the movement is that women who choose to stay at home and raise their children are not honored and respected for their choice. I remember painfully a social event I attended in the late Sixties when a woman approached me with *that* question: "And what do you do?"

I replied, "I have four young children, so I stay busy."

With a look of total disgust, she muttered, "How utterly boring."

As she turned away, I wanted to throw wine in her face. I felt humiliated for doing what had felt right to me until that moment. I knew that more women were beginning to work outside of their homes, but it did not seem to make them more fulfilled. In fact, it seemed they were becoming more stressed and less happy in their relationships. However, I did decide to "test the waters" by taking an evening graduate course in child development. This led to my being asked to take a part-time job in a nursery school. This seemed like a good balance because I could enroll Karla, my youngest child, in my class and still be with her, while beginning a professional career. It could have worked, but I became overzealous about the latest theories and practices of child development—and forgot about marriage and home. Thus began some negative decisions that ultimately led to the end of my first marriage.

One of the most positive gains of the women's liberation movement is that many fathers have become more involved in childcare. David, a psychologist, and his wife, Ann, a television script writer, made the joint decision that he was more able to nurture their two sons on a daily basis than she. He is a natural nurturer and she is a dynamic career person who loves her work. She also loves her children, as do most working fathers who are not able to be with the children as much as they would like to be. Many couples have worked out sharing the responsibilities of raising their children and earning a salary. It doesn't matter which gender takes the lead, or if time with the children is equally shared, but it does matter that someone who loves the children be there.

A friend recently complained to me about her irresponsible adolescent son and wondered what she and her husband could do to get his respect and attention. I knew the boy had been in day care since he was three weeks old, as both parents held responsible jobs. They could have maintained a high standard of living on either one of their salaries. They had sent their son to the best summer camps and enrolled him in structured activities to keep him occupied. They had given him very little attention during the years when he most needed it. As a result, it would be nearly impossible to get his attention at this stage of his life. The parents had chosen money over love, a choice that always leaves children aching for more attention and love. This ache turns into anger and rebellion, which usually will receive parental attention—*negative* attention. Boundaries imposed by authority figures are not easily accepted by adolescents whose parents were not present to set limits and values for them during their younger years. It is during the preschool years that children set their internal boundaries that protect them for the rest of their lives. These important boundaries are initially developed through parental guidance, family values, and the limits established through earlier interactions within a family.

Much to the chagrin of a mother attending a professional dinner one evening, her young son called her to ask when she was going to be home. Several of us were in close proximity to the phone and heard the child's teary voice scream, "But you said you would be home now and help me with my science project! You lied to me! I hate you! You never keep your promises to me!"

Those of us who overheard felt heartsick for both of them, and hoped she would choose to go home. She could have left the dinner party at that instant and not missed anything significant. She chose to remain, explaining how her son always exaggerated. I seriously doubted that the child was the one stretching the truth.

One evening, as I was rushing around preparing to go teach an evening class, Karla began to call me from the bathtub, where she was taking her bath. I responded that I was running late, so could she please tell me whatever she wanted while I was in the next room. She yelled back that she couldn't do that. Alarmed, I ran into the bathroom. She grinned and said, "I just needed to look at you before you left me again."

I felt ashamed. I had been in too big a hurry running off to teach child psychology to give time to the psychological needs of my own child. I wanted to call off the class, but my professionalism at that time would not allow me to do that. I had convinced myself that I was a "good enough" mother, and I did not want to recognize the behaviors that contradicted this. I had made a choice that would give me a place to use my academic abilities, but I had a child who needed me to be more present because many things in her life had changed during that year to accommodate my needs. Karla paid me back during her adolescence, as she managed to do several things that forced me to rearrange my priorities. She once "borrowed" my VISA card and purchased an airline ticket to Paris, France. Upon discovering my missing credit card and my missing child, I had no reservations about canceling class that evening and heading for New York City to find her. I remain grateful that she got my attention in time for us to heal our relationship.

Our children usually even the score one way or another, but I wish I had known then what I have since learned about love's requirements. I wish the six-year-old who shot and killed his classmate in a Michigan elementary school in March of 2000 had had a chance to know love. This horrific tragedy is a wake-up call for all parents of young children.

This tragedy is not about guns or gun control. It is about no one being there for a young child who has needed love since his birth and has only known survival in a hellish situation of drug addiction and weapons. *Children do learn what they live.* Children raised in loveless hellish situations learn violence. They are filled with confusion and rage that will be taken out on themselves, on others, or both. This is an indisputable fact, but one our culture continues to deny. I find it appalling that we look for organizations to blame rather than insisting that our children have available parenting. Less than one year prior to this tragic case, two elementary school-aged boys killed a younger boy by throwing him from an upper floor in an urban high-rise apartment. Why did this horrific murder not receive as much publicity as the shooting murder? Especially when it is was reported that the child also had a knife, but the teacher had discovered the knife and taken it from the child. *Our culture does need better-managed gun control,* but a more critical need is for parents to love their children enough to be with them. If circumstances make this absolutely impossible, then we must love them enough to assure they will be cared for in a responsible and respectful situation. I realize that all of us parents make the best decisions we believe we can under the circumstances at any given time, but I also realize that often they are not wise decisions. Many alarms are going off to wake us up to facts we seem not to want to hear. Dr. Laura Schlessinger's latest book, *Parenthood by Proxy,* makes a strong and well-researched case for not having children if you won't be able to raise them responsibly.[4]

BALANCING YOUR LIFE VERSUS JUGGLING IT

MANY PRIMARY CAREGIVERS today do not spend enough time with a child to ensure that the child feels loved and valued. When a baby is rushed to day care, handled by others who are responsible for several other babies, then rushed home by tired parents who hope the baby will go to sleep early, there is little opportunity for a baby to feel adored. Babies need and deserve to feel securely adored. I do not mean to insinuate that working parents do not love their children. I mean that for children to *feel* loved, a primary caregiver must stay with them consistently enough to allow them to feel that their needs are of prime importance to someone.

Real love is not about sporadic quality time or about giving children expensive gifts to make up for a deficit of time and attention. Many parents try to buy their children's love by substituting new toys for their not being there. This is just another palliative that spoils children. Spoiled children do not know real love. They know how to manipulate parents, as Karla did me, because we feel guilty for not being present.

I was guilty, but our culture would not condemn me, for it *appeared* that I was *balancing* my professional and private life. In my heart, I knew I was *juggling* and praying that it would all hang together. It never does for long. I would gladly give twenty years off my life had I made other choices at that time. I could have spared my children some of their pain and allowed them to have more self-esteem had I tried harder to make my first marriage last longer. I was seduced by the big push to prove women could do anything we wanted, *which is definitely true;* but, I should have been more committed to my children and their father and less impulsive in my decision making. A different choice at that time would have spared me some bad karma and guilt, as well as given me more genuine fulfillment, because I would have been doing the right thing at the right time.

Penelope Leach, the British childcare guru, writes in her latest book, *Children First:* "Supermom is a myth, quality time is a conceit, infant day care is damaging, and the way most couples are scrambling to juggle work and families is bad for kids—and for parents."

In an interview for *The New York Times,* Dr. Leach stated: "Unless Western society allows children more time with their parents in early years, when I.Q., temperament, values, and a child's chances for success are largely determined, it will cost society more than it can afford later." Murder, suicide, others crimes of violence, drug addiction, and the astounding number of young children in the United States on prescription psychotropic drugs attest to the fact that the latter is upon us.[5]

Some have accused Dr. Leach of using "scare tactics" to threaten parents who choose to work into feeling guilty about working and placing their children in day care. My only answer to this is that no adult feels guilty without his or her own permission. Others do not make us feel guilty. If you are guilty, you know it. If you are not, you do not feel guilty. You may feel angry and want to defend your position, but the position of having children and then choosing not to have time to raise them is difficult to defend. This is a much deeper and more serious problem than our culture has been willing to address. The more children are left without appropriate family members to guide and protect them, the more rage and dysfunction we see in our children. The same trend is creeping into other cultures, as more parents are not at home and leaving children in day care and with sitters. A student of mine from Japan did her master's thesis on this topic and found the correlation in her country was similar to that in ours; the more children are primarily raised by other than family members, the higher the incidences of childhood crime and addiction.

We can and must change our choices about having and raising our children. Either do not have them or plan to raise them. Too many parents have chosen money over love, a choice we cannot afford to make if we want healthy, secure children. Our children need parental guidance more than expensive sneakers and designer clothes.

A conference was held the first week of May 2000, in Washington, D.C., to discuss the results of a recent survey assessing the needs of adolescents, as prioritized by a large population of adolescents. The adolescents themselves claimed their number one need was more time with their parents.

There is the argument that couples need two full-time incomes to survive, which is difficult to believe when it means paying childcare, additional transportation, more expensive and often less wholesome eating habits, and a wardrobe for work. When we consider what we lose in not raising our children and what our children lose in love, family values, and self-esteem, I cannot fathom that any monetary gains are worth it. Since the first edition of this book, I have received several letters from parents who were angered by reading this, until they discovered that it was true, and have written how grateful they were for "the wake-up" call. Single parenting definitely creates problems, but it took two to create the child, and at least two should be responsible for raising the child, even if it means an absent parent's salary is garnisheed for child support. It has been suggested that if the government took half the budget spent on finding new ways to blow up the world, and put that money into paying single parents to stay with a child for at least the first five years, most single parents could quit their jobs and see an increase in their incomes. Since we have enough warheads to annihilate the world fifty times over, this suggestion might truly be worth our political, policy-making consideration. If more parents were at home with pay from the government for effective parenting, it is guaranteed that less money would have to be spent caring for and rehabilitating children.

Reflection Exercise

▶ If you and your spouse have young children and are both employed full-time outside the home, take a very detailed and careful look at your budget.

▶ Look for some alternatives that might give you more time with your children.

▶ If you are a single parent and working full-time, what are some alternatives that might be available to you to provide more time with your children?

Our children are the most valuable assets in the universe. Raising them in a loving home is your obligation to them and to the world, *if you choose to have them*. It is also the most demanding and important career you will ever choose, and in the long term, the most fulfilling with the greatest rewards. As Roxanna Slade says to her daughter, who is leaving for a teachers college, "My chosen career of wife and mother was at least as hard as coal mining (and more confining—for miners can usually sleep through a night) and it required the mind of a general, a nurse, and a saint, not to mention other needs."

This is not to imply that *all* of any parent's energy or time should go into raising a child, or children. This can be overbearing, smothering, and unhealthy for parents and for the children. Your energy needs to be wisely distributed—like all valuable resources. Stay-at-home parents can use energy to do many stay-at-home jobs, including organizing and running a healthy home, which also requires an abundance of time and energy.

During my stay-at-home years, I ran a small catering business, which my children loved, as they got to sample all the goodies. They also learned to cook and bake, which the girls still enjoy, as do their families and friends. My oldest daughter Karen makes and sells American-style birthday cakes in Ecuador, which have become so popular that she's had to cut back on the business to have sufficient time with her children. Many mothers tutor, teach music, do freelance writing and consulting, form book clubs, music groups, and hundreds of other interesting activities to use their talents, stimulate their minds, and add income to the family. If you are bored raising children, you had best take a good long look at why you are using your children as an excuse to be bored. When you lack for something to do while raising young children, I would seriously question what else is lacking in your life. I know what was lacking in mine was an understanding of what my children required to feel well loved and secure. Choosing not to have children is certainly a commendable decision when you know you need a full-time career to feel validated. This is especially true in light of the fact that overpopulation will destroy the world. This is becoming painfully evident with the increasingly frequent water shortages we've been experiencing.

Whether you have children or not, any love relationship requires a daily, even hourly, commitment to love if the goal is to have love last.

Standing in a grocery checkout line recently, I read on a magazine cover *Minnie Driver Finds Lasting Love.* I laughed out loud. A man behind me said, "That does seem to be an oxymoron."

I agreed, but realized it was an oxymoron I had once believed—and one, sadly, that a large portion of our population tends to still believe. The only way love lasts is to choose to make it last. Regardless of whom you love, whether or not you have children, or how you spend your time, you will have moments of boredom, of longing for more, of depression, of stress, and of other negative feelings. Those feelings have nothing to do with love. They have to do with our choices and decisions about how we spend our time and energy. When I was complaining about a shortage of time to the gracious Eleanor Roosevelt, who was speaking at an event on the University of North Carolina campus in 1958, she informed me that one of her uncles had told her when she'd made the same complaint as a young woman, "Eleanor, you have the same twenty-four hours in each day that we all have. It is what you choose to do with it, how you set your priorities, that will make the difference."

Reflection Exercise

▶ What do you choose to do each day to love yourself?

▶ What do you choose to do each day to create loving relationships?

▶ If you have children, how could they feel more loved by you?

▶ How could your life be balanced to meet more of their needs? How could your life be balanced to meet more of your own needs?

▶ Include your significant others in a conversation about what they need most from you in order to feel more loved by you. Talk to them about what you need most from them to feel more loved.

▶ Are you living in accordance with your deepest values? If not, take a serious look at changing what could be changed.

LOVING HOMES

WHERE ARE THEY? What are they? I've had children in therapy ask me what I meant by a "loving home." One little girl actually thought I meant a house that could love her since no one was ever actually there until nighttime. I've stopped using the term—a sad pronouncement on modern day life. One of the blessings of our family's move to France was that as a foreigner, I was not allowed to work for a salary since we were able to live on my husband's salary. I'll never forget the first day the two girls, then ages eight and twelve, came home from school and I heard Karla scream with delight to her sister, "Mama's home!"

They came in and hugged me in a way they had not hugged me for a couple of years. In that moment, I knew what a mistake I'd made by working full-time the three previous years. But especially now, in the difficult transition to another culture, they needed the touchstone of my being at home. The time at home allowed me to begin writing more seriously while the children were at school and to develop more close friendships than would have happened had I not curtailed my professional activities. Of greater importance, I had time again to create a home. Homes should not be empty spaces. To be whole and to feel wholly loved, we all need to have a place called home, a group called family, a special tribe or clan to which we know we belong, that comes together in shared history, time, and space.

Mary Pipher, a family therapist, has written, in her marvelous book *The Shelter of Each Other, Rebuilding Our Families*:

> Today family members are often living in the same house, but often they are not interacting. Interruptions and pressures keep people from spending time together and from knowing each other. People define themselves by their possessions and lose all that really matters.[6]

THE THING THAT really matters, as my father reminded me in our final conversation, is love. Creating loving homes has requirements: committed time together, including sharing meals and conversations; sharing the maintenance of home; developing mutual interests, such as hiking, camping, sports, music; sharing celebrations and holidays, which build special memories that are often passed down through generations and perpetuate a sense of belonging; rituals, such as telling bedtime stories, sharing prayers, or even a special way of preparing something for a holiday meal or celebration; and family stories that reinforce memories and connections.

Karen, our daughter who lives in Ecuador, allows her three children to miss school on Thanksgiving and celebrates the traditional American Thanksgiving to keep the children connected to the ritual of her own childhood. This past Thanksgiving I was able to join them. When it was time for the televised Macy's parade, everyone piled onto big pillows placed around the coffee table, where she had put out homemade "monkey-bread" (cinnamon rolls) and hot-spiced tea, which I had made throughout her childhood. I felt happy tears rising from my heart of memories, but tried not to cry for fear the children would not understand that I was just deeply touched in a soft and loving way. Five-year-old Michael saved me when he said, "Mom, you have the tea in the wrong thing. You are supposed to use the one with the push-down top so we can get our own." He knew every detail of the ritual, and I'm sure that some day he will have a thermos with a pushdown top for his children to use while they watch television on Thanksgiving twenty-five years hence. I hope Macy's will still have a big holiday parade with Santa arriving at the end to welcome in the holiday season.

Following Michael's comment, his mother said, "You are right. I made a boo-boo," as she immediately went to put the tea in the right thing. He beamed, feeling important, respected, and loved. Karen's response was a small thing, like a good night kiss, but it created a big, loving connection.

Reflection Exercise

▶ How did your family of origin share special times?

▶ What rituals do you remember? Have you continued any of them in your present family?

▶ What new interests, rituals, and stories are being created in your present family?

Creating a loving home requires time and a willingness to make it happen. They are choices well worth making. This does not mean that children with a stay-at-home parent will never have problems. There are no guarantees that children will not have difficulties, but it does mean that the risks of serious behavior and self-esteem problems are less likely than when children are primarily raised by day care centers and baby-sitters, who cannot have the same loving connection to a child as the parents do. Not that baby-sitters cannot love a child, but when the child becomes more attached to a sitter than to a parent, the parent will feel a loss that is seldom restored.

IDEAL LOVE VERSUS REAL LOVE

CHOOSING SOMEONE WITH whom to have a child or build a family is another critical choice with monumental consequences. Chapter Five dealt with some of the reasons we may choose to fall in love with a certain person, but to marry and have a child with that person ups the ante considerably. These endeavors require "standing in love" in the ultimate sense. The decision to commit to a mate for life needs to be made from a joint committee of our heads, our hearts, and even our souls.

Standing in love is hard work, as John Osborne well expressed in a recent issue of *The Sun Magazine:*

> It's no good trying to fool yourself about love. You can't fall into it like a soft job without dirtying up your hands. It takes muscle and guts. And if you can't bear the thought of messing up your nice, clean soul, you'd better give up the whole idea of life and become a saint, because you'll never make it as a human being.[7]

HE'S SO RIGHT. A committed partnership, which marriage and parenthood should be, is not a choice you should make *if* you expect it to be easy. Falling in love and having sex are the easy parts. Growing together to stand in love is never easy. You rarely have a clue about how to swim through life with another until you are in deep water. You have some clues about what kind of love you want, but few about what kind you might receive. My friend Jan beautifully describes the kind of love most of us fantasize about receiving:

I want the kind of love where we each hear what the other has to say.

I want the kind of love where each of us can stand alone, and can also stand together.

I want the kind of love where wanting, not needing, permeates and giving, not taking prevails.

I want the kind of love that comes from strength, absent of fear and weakness.

I want the kind of love that reflects all that is good and whole—and therefore that which comes from God.

This is ideal love. It is what we all dream of experiencing and is a lofty goal for which to strive, but it is not reality-based, day in and day out human love. Real love between human beings is created from who we actually are, how we feel, and how we behave. Not one of us is without needs, fears, and weaknesses. Not one of us is good and whole all the time. Each of us is a combined mixture of positive and negative, and we are going to share both with each other. For a committed relationship to flourish requires an active decision to keep love and respect flowing between any two of us for the rest of our lives. A newlywed friend called one night distraught because she was hurt by and furious at her husband of less than a year. "If I love him," she asked, "how can I be so damn angry at him?"

Her question is a common one, but also an easy one to answer. The people you love most have the power to hurt you the most. They will make you the angriest, and will tap more deeply into your mess of emotions and behaviors than people to whom you are not so connected. When the consuming lust of new love wears off, you are faced with the reality of another less-than-perfect human being, be it your child, your spouse, your parents, or any other person you have chosen to love. Being angry is never a reason to end a relationship. It is an opportunity to work through a difficulty and to grow into a deeper understanding of love.

Two clinical psychologists, Connell Cowan and Melvyn Kinder, wrote a short book several years ago, called *Smart Women, Foolish Choices,* which could just as easily be applied to men. One of their main points is that we often make disastrous relationship choices because we hold onto unrealistic expectations around love.[8] We become addicted to the idea of "perfect love," when in truth there are no perfect human beings to love. We only fantasize that someone is perfect before we live with him or her, not realizing that he or she is carrying the same fantasy about us. Each of us knows that we are not perfect, but we work at fooling someone into thinking that we might be, without realizing they are playing the same game. We all play it. We all lose. It's reality time.

In reality, standing in love requires accepting yourself as you are and whomever you choose to love *as they are,* which is never who you want them to be *in every moment.* Standing in love certainly allows for the expression of hurt, disappointment, and anger, and even requests for changes, but it does not allow for bailing out just because you feel hurt, disappointments, and anger, without making every effort to resolve the causes of these negatives.

Reflection Exercise

▶ When was the last time you were disappointed in, or by, someone you love?

▶ When was the last time someone you love was disappointed in you?

▶ How did you resolve the disappointment?

▶ If it remains unresolved, make an appointment with each other to talk about the experience of your disappointment, including feelings and what you need to feel better.

One of the most devastating threats to relationship health is repressed negative emotion. We try to conceal our negative emotions thinking we will appear more lovable, but in truth, keeping them inside makes us bitches and jerks. Get them out, but be kind! Many clients will come back at me with "He won't love me if he knows the real me." Or "You have no idea how angry this could make her." Or "It's just too risky."

Risks

MY REPLY IS always that it is too risky to choose not to do so. Life is risky business. Love is risky business. Choosing to stand in love is less risky business. The following poem, author unknown, says what I believe to be true about taking risks:

> To laugh is to risk appearing the fool.
> To weep is to risk appearing sentimental.
> To reach out for another is to risk involvement.
> To expose feelings is to risk exposing your true self.
> To place your ideas, your dreams, before a crowd is to risk their loss.
> To live is to risk dying.
> To try is to risk failure.
> To hope is to risk despair.
> But risks must be taken, because the greatest hazard in life is to risk nothing.
> *The person who risks nothing, does nothing, has nothing, and is nothing.*
> They may avoid suffering and sorrow, but they cannot learn, feel, change, grow, love, or live.
> Chained by their attitudes, they are slaves, for they have forfeited their freedom.
> Only a person who risks is free.

Risks and choices cannot be separated. Every choice involves a risk. Some choices turn out to be mistakes, but mistakes can be transformed into valuable lessons. One of the most distressing love situations is that of a person making the same negative choice over and over again. This can involve choosing to marry one addict after another, thinking she can change *this* one. Someday we may learn that we can never change anyone except ourselves. It can involve choosing to have one child after another when there is no way to provide adequate care for the first one. These situations sometimes require that others participate in helping us make choices. This can be a loving friend, a therapist, or a group of people who care enough to want us to wake up to the consequences of our bad choices.

Reflection Exercise

► What risks have you taken today? This year?

► What has been your greatest emotional risk?

► What is a risk you would like to choose to take?

► What do your "chattering monkeys" have to say about it?

► If a risk you have taken turned out badly, what did you learn from it?

AFFAIRS ARE REAL RISKY BUSINESS

HAVING CASUAL SEX and having affairs while married are very risky choices, but choices frequently made in our culture. They are choices that can cause tremendous and far-reaching pain, but they do not have to end an established relationship—*if* the partners involved are willing to choose to love each other enough to use the lessons of their negative choices to strengthen their relationship. It is not easy, but it can be done. As I've mentioned in previous chapters, my husband and I are in a second marriage for each of us. Both of us have had affairs, which we deeply regret, but following these shattering experiences, we have learned valuable lessons about standing in love. An affair is an indication that a choice needs to be made—a choice to end one relationship, be it the marriage or the affair—in order to heal the marriage. A marriage cannot be healed if either partner's energy is spent on maintaining an affair.

There is quite a bit of hullabaloo going on today about whether to be honest about an affair. I come down on the side of honesty because I believe that, in most cases, the partner will find out, and then there will be greater pain with less possibility of healing the marriage. I also believe that dishonesty creates distance and is the enemy of intimacy, and therefore one of the greatest threats to standing in love. Most couples marry thinking their affair days are done. *Usually* women feel relieved and men feel a tad regretful; however, most couples discover their affair days are not necessarily over. Several recent polls indicate that over 60 percent of married people in the United States have affairs.[9]

My husband's desire to make the move to France for his job required that I resign from mine, which I agreed to do, but was still silently resentful. Rather than admit the resentment and appear selfish, I took it out by not being nice in little ways, such as not listening to him attentively and by being disagreeable. Love cannot stay vital with repressed resentment. What I did not realize at the time was that he had a French teacher who showered attention on him. *Voila!* The first devastating affair during our marriage began. He didn't tell, but got caught through his lies, and my resentment then exploded into unadulterated rage. I did realize that I was partially responsible for triggering the event, and that part of my rage turned inward, becoming almost immobilizing depression.

Recognizing I needed help, I located and made an appointment with a highly recommended French therapist. She thought I was terribly overreacting to the attraction that occurs frequently in Europe between language teachers and their American students. I then directed some of my rage toward her. She laughed it off, saying I should pay my husband back by finding a sexy male French teacher and be done with it. I stormed out of her office.

While riding the Metro back to our village outside of the city, I surprised myself by becoming amused by her attitude. I realized that she was probably wiser than I. She had certainly caught me off guard and diffused my anger at Tim. She had also accurately pointed out that I had choices. I began to see how one choice had led to another. I chose to move with him, then blamed him for my choice and resented him, which he could not understand, for I had participated in the decision. I stopped trying to explain and behaved like an iceberg. I made sure he felt as miserable as I was feeling. What I did not count on was someone else spending time with him who made him feel adored and desired. It hurt badly, but I woke up. We had another set of decisions to make. We chose to work at rebuilding the relationship and eventually pulled the marriage together enough to enjoy sharing activities and to survive the next few years in Paris as a family. To say the relationship was healed or that I had totally forgiven him would be stretching the truth.

After we returned to the United States, and the children had left for preparatory schools and college, I became professionally employed again in close proximity to the man, mentioned in Chapter Five, that I had been immediately attracted to, but tried to avoid, prior to our move to Paris. With my trust level in my marital partner still tentative and my wounds still raw, I was ripe for an affair. *Voila, encore!* My turn! I left the marriage and became involved with my idealized new love, who, of course, had his own share of unresolved problems and issues, which soon began to wreak havoc on our relationship. I learned that daily reality always diminishes the ringing of "the bells" and shatters the unrealistic fantasies.

Because Tim more or less expected me to "pay him back" and because we had remained friends throughout my involvement, we became closer friends and made an honest commitment to each other again. Since we were both guilty, we had some heavy forgiving to do, which was perhaps easier for us than when one partner remains "the sinner" and the other appears to be "the saint."

In the 1930s, psychologist Mary Borden wrote: "Not all of us are born lovers, or great lovers. We are normal people, feeble, fumbling, well meaning, bewildered, and lonely in the crowd of the world. What we really want is a friend or two, and a companion who will be glad when we are glad, sorry when we are sorry, stick with us through adversity, and last the course."[10]

We "last the course" when we choose to cultivate being that friend and companion. Lasting love is not about falling in love at all, but about standing there with another through adversities. We choose to open our heart to love at some point because someone has stood with us through a part of life. Tim and I have managed to do this through many challenging times. When any two people make this choice together, the magic and mystery of love unfolds.

An affair may be only one partner's choice, but it is usually the result of two persons' accumulated choices of repressing emotions, withholding information, and hurting each other through daily decisions. Those small choices mount up, just like the plastic Baggies we toss carelessly away after one use. We shut each other out by making choices and not considering their impact on our partner. The more frequently one makes an "I" choice rather than an "I–Thou" choice, the greater the risk of negative consequences on the relationship. This is not to say that some "I" choices are not in order, but again, we need to maintain a healthy balance between self and other.

Reflection Exercise

▶ Looking back at the choices and risks you listed in the earlier exercises of this chapter, how many were made from an "I" mode? How many were made considering the effects on others?

▶ For each major choice you made, how were others affected?

▶ How often do you consult people you love as you make choices?

▶ Do you consider yourself primarily a giver or a taker? Why?

A DELICATE BALANCE

CREATING A BALANCE between giving and receiving requires continuing the I–Thou choices necessary to maintain a healthy relationship. We tend to think of love as the choice to give, but at a deeper level, there is no real love unless we also open ourselves to receive. This means being vulnerable, which is risky, but necessary. Unless each partner is able to receive the love offered by the other, there is no genuine love relationship. In a complementary fashion, givers seek and find takers, while takers seek and find givers. Yet complementarity and balancing both come into play to create a healthy love relationship. If a giver over-gives without being vulnerable to receive, and a taker over-takes without ever giving, the relationship becomes one of control.

Takers tend to be more controlling than givers, but givers can control through over-giving, which causes their partner to feel obligated or overwhelmed. Givers tend to be more emotional while takers tend to be more analytical and rational. Takers tend to be more introverted, while givers tend to be more outgoing. The good news is that we can each be a bit of both. To keep a relationship balanced, we need to be.[11]

Reflection Exercise

▶ How could you better balance the roles of giving and taking?

▶ Have a discussion with your significant other on this topic.

▶ Is it easier for you to give or to receive?

In his brilliant novel *Ishmael,* Daniel Quinn identifies our cultural history of the past 10,000 years as one of Takers, who believe the universe was created for man to control. In our efforts to rule and control, we have devastated the world, which was thriving nicely prior to 8,000 B.C. From the beginning of life on Earth until 8,000 B.C. every living creature lived in a shared community. There were no wars for there was no reason to compete or to kill—except for food. No living species hoarded food. They ate what they needed to survive, and there was no scarcity. The universe and all that dwelled upon it lived in harmony. All creatures followed the peacekeeping law that they belonged to the world and must share its resources, allowing each species to evolve naturally through what I've called, in earlier chapters, cooperative competition.

As human beings evolved into creatures of choice, they chose not to trust the peacekeeping law of "live and let live" that had been operating for three million years of surviving as hunters and gatherers. The only purpose of hunting was to eat enough to survive. When man began the agricultural revolution, we began the destruction of the planet. This revolution has resulted in ceaseless competition for land in order to accumulate more food, which has in turn resulted in more for some and less for others. This led to wars over land. Land began to represent power. Choosing power over cooperative sharing has resulted in the mess we have made of the world.[12]

Unless we choose to stop defying our planet's natural peacekeeping plan and realize that we belong to the universe, not that it belongs to us, we will destroy ourselves with it. Choosing to live in cooperative community is our only chance for continuing to live at all. It requires that we give up our need to compete and conquer each other at any level. It requires that we choose to create more love for ourselves and all living things. Choosing is an individual decision and responsibility. *Our destiny will be created one choice at a time by each one of us alive on the planet today.*

The Power of Choice

WHILE A LOVING relationship is a committed choice made by two, love itself is a choice that can be made by all of us in practically every waking moment of our lives.

Viktor Frankl, a recently deceased psychiatrist and author, who survived the Nazi concentration camps—although his wife and children did not—has said that the only thing an oppressor cannot take away from us is our human choice of how to respond. In the face of evil and pain beyond what most of us could ever imagine, he chose to love the essence of life. He chose to see beyond the horror created by greed and jealousy. He chose to see God, within himself. It is our ultimate potential, the most difficult to achieve, yet Frankl proved to me that it is a choice. We tend to blame others and circumstances for our negative choices, which is comparable to giving up our positive and even greater power of responsibility.

Ram Dass, a psychologist, author, and contemporary spiritual teacher, tells a wonderful story about being stranded in a train station in India for two days. He had dysentery and was spending most of his time in the toilet, which was the embodiment of his mother's idea of hell. Squatting there in the filth, covered with flies, and suffering stomach cramps, he burst out laughing realizing that he was still "happy in his soul," that he could appreciate the humanness around him because he was at peace, content within himself, continuing to love himself and those around him. This does not mean that toilet paper would not have been appreciated, but it does mean we each have the power to maintain peace and contentment, to choose love in the face of any amount of "yuck."

Similarly, life and love relationships will have some "yuck." Being disappointed and hurt is yucky, but you still have a choice to forgive and work through the difficulties as long as the other person chooses to stand with you through adversity. If they do not, then the most loving decision you can make is to love yourself enough to walk away. If you choose to walk away in this manner, you will meet another who will welcome your love. This is the way of the peacekeeping plan. Our greatest power is our power of choice. Our only hope for survival on this planet is choosing love.

NINE

Are You Ready *to* Accept Help, *if* You Need it?

ALTHOUGH THE WORLD IS FULL OF SUFFERING, IT IS FULL ALSO IN THE OVERCOMING OF IT.
—HELEN KELLER

RETICENT CARMEN FINALLY showed up for her therapy appointment with me, after making and canceling two previous appointments. I felt both relieved and concerned. When she first called, she gave no specific reason for wanting to see me, but she asked for an evening appointment so she would not have to miss work. I complied, but she called at her scheduled appointment time with a legitimate-sounding excuse and asked to reschedule. Again, I complied, and again, she called at her scheduled time to reschedule. This time I heard anxiety and tension in her voice, so I risked asking why she was in such conflict over showing up. There was a long pause, then Carmen blurted out: "Because I'm going to die if I don't come, and maybe I'd rather die than deal with all this torment. I'm afraid you'll try to save me, and I'm also afraid I'm not worth saving."

She'd gotten my attention. "I promise you that I cannot save you if you are really determined to die," I replied. "But I have a strong feeling you don't want to die and that underneath your fear, you are a courageous woman, or you would never have called."

Now I'd gotten *her* attention. "Then maybe I'll show up next time," she said softly. She did.

As she sat in my office, Carmen's guarded demeanor and anxious voice told me that she was terrified of making any kind of real connection. I deduced that she was dying of loneliness. I knew that I would have to proceed with great caution or she would bolt for the door. Before she could talk about herself, she asked about me—my philosophy of therapy and of life. I shared what I believed to be appropriate. Then she caught me off guard. "Do you ever hurt? I mean *really* just hurt," she wanted to know.

"Yes," I replied simply. "You have to know real hurt to understand real hurt."

Taking her first deep breath, Carmen said she was willing "to try to trust me." I assured her that was good enough for starters. Tentatively, she began to share her story. Over the next several weeks, I learned that Carmen's father had been a physician and an alcoholic. During his office and hospital hours, when he was publicly visible, he was a concerned and sensitive physician. He was also active and visible in a local church and a respected pillar of the community. By evening, the stress of keeping up this image would send him straight to his gin and his "girls," referring to Carmen and her mother. After a few strong drinks, he would begin to accuse his wife of failing to appreciate him after he'd slaved to give her a beautiful home and everything else she wanted. She would feel guilty and try to please him, or calm him. When her efforts to mollify him failed, she would often resort to going to her room and having a few drinks to calm herself. Sometimes he would come after her, drunk and demanding. Carmen would hear shouting, beatings, and screaming, and would go to her room to hide. If her father had not been satisfied by whatever he had done to her mother, or had not passed out, he would come looking for her. He would profess to love her, call her his little darling, and beg her to comfort him by sitting on his lap and fondling him. Usually, fondling was not enough. The abuse began when Carmen was nine years old.

Carmen was an only child, bright, musically talented, shy, and deeply tormented. She wondered if this were the way all fathers acted, but she didn't know, for she'd never dared ask another soul. She did know that Daddy wanted his "love" for her to be their special secret. The reality that he beat his wife and sexually abused his young daughter remained a secret for almost forty years. Both parents took their guilt and shame to their graves. People had commented at each of her parents' funerals that Carmen's grief was so deep she couldn't even cry. The truth was that her rage and grief were so deep *over their lives* that she could not even *feel*. Carmen had had three marriages to alcoholic, abusive men. She never left them. Each left her, telling her she was "no good." She believed it.

Prior to her first call to me, Carmen had watched an Oprah episode in which four women had discussed openly their own stories of being sexually abused—in front of a live studio audience and ten million TV viewers. Each of these women told a story similar to Carmen's, but each had gotten into therapy, come to trust the therapist, gained insights and confidence, and now seemed to be enjoying her life. Carmen claimed that her real incentive to call me was not to tell her shameful secrets, but to discover how these women could "spill their guts" to the entire world and not die of shame.

Reflection Exercise

▶ Can you relate to any of Carmen's feelings? Write down the ones you can relate to, and why.

▶ Have you ever had counseling or psychotherapy? If so, what motivated you to make the first call?

▶ How did therapy help? If it did not help, why not?

Little by little, as I gained Carmen's trust, she began to pry open the lid from her holding tank of fears and secrets. Gradually, she learned that since she'd actually survived all the horrors of her childhood, she would also survive discussing them. Cleaning out the "secret tank" that had kept her a prisoner for all these years freed up a tremendous amount of energy that she'd been using to keep the lid tightly shut. Carmen now knows she does not have to remain a victim to the secrets or the memories that have tortured her for so long.

It has taken courage and fortitude, of which I knew she had plenty, to have survived the accumulated "yuck" of her past. She has begun to make some healthy choices, including playing in a symphony orchestra and developing new friendships with people who respect her, for she's beginning to respect herself. She claims that the most valuable lesson of therapy was to become aware that *her history did not have to be her destiny.*

Carmen had lived in an intrinsically destructive, tightly woven web. She had no definition of love, for she had only known abuse cloaked in the guise of love. Although her mother did not physically abuse her, neither did she protect her daughter, for she had become a victim of "learned helplessness," a phenomenon which frequently occurs when personal ability to change events is extinguished by what one believes to be overpowering circumstances.[1] Not protecting a child from abuse is passive abuse. Carmen had to accept that she could not change the past, but she could stop trying to deny her wounds. Repressing and denying wounds, shame, and guilt have a way of deepening their pain. When you store memories and pain deep in your psyche, they gain an insidious power in your unconscious.

This part of the unconscious is what Freud referred to as "the boiling cauldron, which will boil over later in life," meaning that these stored memories often seem to produce in us a need to repeat the experiences later in life, even when we know the outcome could be destructive. It is as if we are unconsciously programmed to do the same thing, hoping for a different outcome. This is often evident when a child who was hurt by his parents' divorce buries the hurt, and then years later will divorce when he has children close to the same age he was at the time his parents divorced. It is a bewildering tendency, and much more apt to happen when you repress earlier wounds, or are afraid to take your parents off the pedestal upon which you placed them in your childhood.

BEHAVIORAL PATTERNS

In his groundbreaking book, *Emotional Intelligence,* Daniel Goleman explains in scientific detail how our emotional memory works. Essentially, there is a preverbal part of our brain, the amygdala, which scrutinizes incoming information (including experiences) for its emotional weight. If an experience or piece of information has emotional significance, it is more apt to be remembered. Because our emotion-charged amygdalas respond faster than our rational neocortexes can process information, we tend to automatically react to stimuli that have caused us extreme pleasure, pain, or fear in the past. Forever after, when we are in a similar situation, we will instinctively react the same way we did as young children. Although we can learn to be more in charge of our behavior as adults, we continue to have the same initial childhood reaction.[2] You probably know adults who still scream and cry to get what they want when they want it. We usually refer to them as "childish," or unreasonable.

When I was young, my brother and his friends loved to sneak up on me and scare me when I was involved in something and not paying attention to my surroundings. I would automatically scream and jump. When my husband quietly enters a room where I am busy, I have the same response, much to his delight. The response is deeply patterned. I'm often terribly embarrassed by it, because I know it is an overreaction, but I can't seem to control it.

Reflection Exercise

▶ Give yourself permission to remember a painful event or situation from your childhood that remains unresolved. Have you set up any situations in your adult life that may repeat the same dynamics?

▶ Do you still have patterns from childhood that you instantaneously and automatically repeat?

▶ Have you consciously tried to change any of them?

▶ Did the behaviors serve a useful purpose for you in childhood?

▶ Do they have any useful outcomes in your adult life?

Therapy can help you "reprogram," that is, change a reaction or behavior that is no longer appropriate or useful, *if* you are committed to changing it. However, if you believe it serves, or could serve, any useful purpose, you probably will not change it. It only took someone's saying to me after he had triggered my "scare response," "Good God, you'll never have to worry about intruders, your scream would send anyone running back into the night." I've stopped trying to change the response. However, repeating negative relationships to abusive partners serves no useful purpose. It is a pattern that needs to change. Even when there could be a difference in past reality and the way you remember it, due to the emotional impact of the experience, *what feels true in your minds is true for you,* and is what must be dealt with in therapy, or in a relationship.

Consciously, Carmen had told herself that she never wanted to marry and certainly never wanted to have children. She claimed that she did not believe in childhood. One of her primary issues in therapy was trying to understand what drove her to marry three men like her father, and to have a child with one of them. When your conscious thoughts and your behaviors collide, you are usually stuck in an unconscious pattern. When the pain of the actions and behaviors accumulates to the point that you no longer trust yourself to act or to choose wisely, you need help.

How Does Therapy Help?

Everyone who calls for a therapy appointment is searching for a structure through which she can make sense of her life and continue it with less pain and more love. Just picking up the telephone to make a therapy appointment can help. It is an admission to yourself of pain that you have probably tried to deny or repress. It also is an admission to yourself that there may be hope of healing the pain. If you hear a receptive voice on the other end of the line, that hope is increased. I've had many clients admit that they felt so much better after the initial call, just knowing they had possessed the courage to make the call, that they considered calling back to say they did not need to keep the appointment. This happened for Carmen, but she didn't trust her first act of courage, so she had to cancel and go through calling again to reinforce that she could reach out for help. She admitted that when she called to cancel, she halfway hoped I would tell her I would not see her since she waited until the last minute to cancel her appointment. It is important for the therapist to acknowledge that this is totally normal for someone who has never called a therapist. I've learned that the people most in need of attention and emotional, psychological healing are the most reluctant to ask for it. They need validation for making the initial call.

After the initial call, which allows the client and the therapist to acknowledge the existence of the other, the process of good therapy is similar to the process of building any healthy loving relationship. As stated in earlier chapters, the deepest need of every human being is to have his existence acknowledged, and this is closely followed by needing another to empathetically share in our existence. This is true from the moment of our first breath until the moment of our last one, when our physical form is transformed back into love itself. Life on Earth is too difficult for any of us to go it alone without love. If you have not been able to participate in a healthy, loving relationship due to loneliness, depression, past abuse, or unconscious patterns that eventuate in your making destructive choices, you need to consider looking outside yourself for help.

BUILDING A LOVING THERAPEUTIC RELATIONSHIP

THE WORD "THERAPY" means healing attention. Love is created between any two people or a group of people through the sharing of healing attention. Healthy love relationships are always therapeutic. Similarly, healthy therapy, as Freud stated when he said that healing never begins until a patient feels loved by the therapist, must involve a genuine love, *without exploitation,* of a client. My acknowledgment of Carmen's courage was her first adult experience of even considering that she might be truly worthy of love. When you meet any person, it is a good policy to acknowledge something positive you notice about them, for in so doing you will give them the gift of positive energy. It is sad to me that our culture has become so suspicious of compliments that when they are bestowed, many of us question the motives of the giver. This transforms what should be positive into negative energy.

My mother-in-law has a good remedy for this: When she gives any of us a compliment or a gift and we play the "Oh, you shouldn't have" game, she replies with, "Unless you can accept it and say thank you, I'll take it back."

Reflection Exercise

▶ What is your first reaction to a compliment?

▶ How often do you compliment others?

▶ How often do you compliment yourself? Are you able to recognize your own best qualities?

▶ What has someone said about you lately that shocked you into looking more deeply at your qualities, or negative traits, or behaviors?

After I had complimented her for her courage, Carmen needed to check out my level of honesty by questioning me about my life, which is not a bad policy before we invest in a relationship with anyone. She had been so damaged by the guises and self-aggrandizement of others that she did not want to set herself up for similar situations in therapy. Therapists who want to play the role of "god" are one of the major reasons therapy can fail. Therapists are just as imperfect as anyone else, and usually it is our personal pain that serves as our impetus to become therapists. I freely admit I've made many mistakes and do not hold all the answers to anyone's problems—especially not my own. But I am committed to joining in the search for answers with other searchers, be they my clients, friends, children, or any others, who are committed to the search. I am positive that the aforementioned have helped me discover as many things about myself as I have helped them discover about themselves.

Once contact is established, the next step in building a healthy relationship is listening—an art that is developed through mutual sharing and responding. Many children do not have the validating experience of being listened to. Carmen certainly had not been listened to. Her father never shut up and her mother, who rarely talked or listened, had died inside, like the domineering next-door neighbor's wife in the psychologically profound movie *American Beauty*. Their story is quite similar to that of Carmen's family, and to thousands of other families. In the movie, the next-door family, the Fitts, is headed by an aggressive bully of a father who hides his insecurities behind a false image of being in control. His wife, Barbara, a victim of learned helplessness, has given up on love, and life. She cannot defend her son from his abusive father or even offer support to him because she has ceased trying to support herself. The son, Ricky, finds the courage to defy his father through developing the support of his next-door neighbors, the Burnham's, headed by the mother, who dominates her depressed husband, Lester, and their daughter, Jane. This movie brings almost all of our repressed feelings to the screen, making them bigger than life, which is why the movie has been a hit in every country where it has been shown. It clearly shows how false images, repressed feelings, and negative love choices can kill us. In the movie, no one listens to anyone, except the two teenagers, who listen to each other and exhibit how falling in love can lead to standing in love through horrendous difficulty.

When Carmen was a child, she had essentially stopped talking, which is why people assumed she was shy. Her truth was that no one had cared enough to listen, so she made the assumption, often made by children, that anything she might say would not be considered important. Parents and teachers tend to talk at children more than listen to them. If our goal is to create a loving relationship, we must listen to a person's story, and share our own, when appropriate.

One afternoon, when I was a teenager, my father sat listening to a church member's complaints for over an hour while I killed time with my homework in the next room, waiting for him to keep our date to play golf. I was irritated with both of them. When the woman finally left his office, I confronted him with "Why did you have to listen to her carrying on like that when you had something else you'd rather do?"

He thoughtfully replied, "I guess I didn't have to listen, but what I've learned is that if you listen to anyone long enough, they will say something important because they run out of *nothing* to say. It sneaked through her complaining that she is terrified that she will die alone, and lonely."

"So what can you do about that?" I quipped.

"Listen to her more."

He had given me one of the most valuable lessons of my life in how to be a good therapist—and a loving person.

Reflection Exercise

▶ Evaluate your listening skills in your next conversation. Think about what you have heard—and may not have heard.

▶ What do you believe the person talking was feeling and did not say? Consider checking it out with him or her.

▶ Why do you think most of us are prone to not say what we really feel?

▶ How could it change your life, if you did express your deepest feelings?

▶ How could it change your life if your significant others expressed their deepest feelings to you?

Each of us has something important to share when we know someone cares enough to listen, but most of us do not express our deepest feelings because we doubt that anyone cares deeply enough to handle them with love. Carmen had years of profound experiences to share. The more I listened, the more she shared, and the more we both learned about the capacity of human beings to endure suffering and to heal into love. Creating love always involves listening. The best therapist learns to "hear" what the client is not expressing and probes the silence, but this has to be done in a safe and loving way. It is a skill worth developing for each of us. A prison inmate, who participated in a human relations group I led at a local penal institution, impressed me deeply when he requested of the group: "Hey guys, I don't express myself too good, but I'm really hoping you can hear all the things I'm *trying* to say. So you need to listen hard to what I'm not saying. You know, listen with your inside ears."

We knew he meant the ears of our hearts, which are the ears we need to keep tuned in to truly hear the people we love.

Several years ago, a student gave me the following poem, by Keith Pearson of Melbourne, Australia:

> When you listen, you affirm me,
> But your listening must be real;
> Sensitive and serious,
> Not looking busily around,
> Not with a worried or distracted frown,
> Not preparing what you will say next,
> But giving me full attention.
> For this tells me that I am a person of value,
> Important and worth listening to,
> One with whom you will share yourself.

When you are listened to attentively, trust and a safe place are established for you to become more fully yourself. Your truest and deepest self is usually a joyous, loving person, who has often gotten lost—sometimes buried alive—in negativity heaped upon you by others who, in turn, are just passing on the negativity that has been heaped upon them. Therapy can be a way to start shoveling yourself free of that negativity and to learn how to stop spreading it around.

People tend to think that therapy is about advice, but the best therapy rarely has to do with giving advice. It has to do with careful listening to help another discover more of herself. Through an evolving process of self-discovery, you will discover what you really want. Carmen, like almost all of us, wanted to better understand herself, her history, and her desires. She needed to discover that she could heal and be loved while she simultaneously developed love and respect for herself. Once you have a structure or belief system in place that allows you to engage responsibly in creating real love, you begin to heal toward wholeness—the goal of therapy, and of love.

Reflection Exercise

▶ How therapeutic, or healing, is your love for the people you love?

Reflection Exercise (continued)

▶ In what way are you healed by their love?

▶ How could each of you participate in more healing into wholeness?

▶ How could you cocreate a safe place where real love can happen?

Healthy therapy should always model a healthy relationship. They both require: the courage to connect; sharing enough to establish honesty, trust, and respect; attentive listening one to the other; and setting mutual goals for the relationship. There would be no need for therapists if we each followed these steps in our relationships.

HEALING INTO HEALTHY RELATIONSHIPS

ON A RECENT episode of National Public Radio's *Prairie Home Companion,* Garrison Keillor told a story of a female relative whom he had known when she was a young, powerful girl. He claimed she had been a rebel and a creative whiz at mischief making. Keillor had been awed by her strength and her ability to stand up to anyone—especially her parents. Years later, Garrison and this relative became reacquainted as adults. He was struck by how overwhelmingly angry she remained at her parents. She was still rebelling against these now elderly and feeble people, clinging to her childhood image of them. To Keillor, it felt as though she were carrying two giant stone statues around on her back. These statues controlled her life more than her parents had ever controlled her when she was a young rebel.

Keillor asked the profound question that all therapists wonder when we encounter this phenomenon: "Why can't she grow up and see them as they really are today?"

The sad answer is that she made her anger at them—for their inability to set limits for her as a child—the driving force of her adult life. Because she felt stronger when she was angry and rebellious, she became afraid to let go of those stances for fear that she would become weak. We are reluctant to give up anything we perceive as having worked for us, especially when we believe it protects us from being vulnerable to people who have hurt us in the past. And often, we simply do not want to let them off the hook. It is always easier to blame our lack of love on our parents or other caregivers than to forgive them and get on with creating the love we need in our adult lives. In reality, blaming them denies us our personal power of choice.

FORGIVENESS

CAROLINE MYSS, A renowned medical intuitive, claims that we are a culture addicted to the power of our wounds. We tend to love the privileges that our wounds and sicknesses grant us, and therefore avoid the work of healing and the choice of forgiving.[3] She has a valid point. Many people come into therapy or a new relationship primarily seeking sympathy for past abuses and for ongoing problems. It is a terrible thing to have been abused—emotionally or physically—but it is just as terrible to limit and define the rest of our lives by having been an abused child. It is equally painful not to learn to forgive. In her book, *Why Me, Why This, Why Now,* Robin Norwood writes of a woman with whom she worked who freely admitted that she hated her mother and realized that this hate was hurting her more than her mother. Nevertheless, she did not want to gain insight into her mother's life because if she began to understand her, then she might have to forgive her, and if she forgave her, she feared that she would be vulnerable to being hurt by her again.[4]

Reflection Exercise

▶ What is your deepest wound? How would you rate its impact on your life?

▶ How do you define yourself by your wound(s)?

▶ What gifts have you received through being wounded? These could be insights, opportunities, relationships, or abilities you would not have cultivated without the wound.

Although Carmen's parents were no longer alive, she still felt that if she forgave them, she would renew her vulnerability to future abusers. It is amazing how complex a web we weave to protect ourselves from being vulnerable. I had to reassure Carmen that the same innate power that allowed her to survive being wounded was still hers and could be used to create a more rewarding life for herself. Holding onto anger at her parents, her husbands, and herself was draining her of her real strength. Anger is a deceptive demon that fools us into feeling superior while it robs us of our ability to create the love we crave. You have to be willing to be vulnerable and to expose your delicate emotions to have sustaining love and intimacy in your life. It is not easy, and the more you have been abused, the more courage it requires, but equally true, the more abuse you have survived, the more transforming power you possess. Choosing to forgive only adds to that power. The key to building love while simultaneously protecting yourself from further abuse is to move slowly while establishing trust and intimacy.

Reflection Exercise

▶ What happens to your body when you hold onto anger?

▶ Practice breathing it out and see what happens to your body.

Choose to breathe in your personal power as an adult. Your parents no longer rule your life, regardless of what they once did to you. You deserve your power of choice and your chance to love.

MARCEL PROUST WROTE that the real voyage of discovery is not in seeking new landscapes, but in developing new eyes—a new perspective on our past. Being abused by caregivers says nothing about you, but says everything about how wounded and sick they were. Your adult eyes are not the same as your child eyes, *unless you refuse to grow up*. A wise and loving therapist, friend, or partner can help you heal and grow up. It is never too late, until this lifetime is over, and

I have a deep suspicion we will just be sent back for another try at forgiveness unless we are willing to do it this time around.

Of all the unfinished business we bring into therapy and have dragged into each of our relationships, holding onto resentment about what someone has done to us is at the top of the list. Like Garrison Keillor's relative, we carry resentment around until the resentment itself begins to control us and keep us miserable. We tend to think that forgiving someone makes us wimps, or that forgiving means condoning something evil. I once attended a workshop with family therapist Steve Andreas, whose primary work is helping people learn to forgive. He was working with a man who was reluctant to forgive a colleague who constantly put him down in professional situations. Steve asked, "If you forgave him, are you afraid that you could not maintain your resolve to protect yourself against his put-downs?"

"Yeah. I feel like he would just keep insulting me and trying to make me feel inferior to him," the man admitted. "Forgiving him is like giving him the upper hand, which is exactly what he wants."

Steve explained that this is our most common fear about forgiveness. We have to understand that being compassionate and forgiving requires great courage, and that it does not preclude our protecting ourselves from more abuse. He suggested that the man in the workshop develop a plan to talk with his abusive colleague and request no more put-downs. Requesting a behavioral change is always permissible, and having another person present as a witness is often a good idea. To be effective, forgiveness must transpire from a place of true compassion. Steve explained that the colleague of my friend in the workshop probably had an underlying sense of inferiority, since most abusive people have been abused and are suffering from feelings of inadequacy.

Reflection Exercise

▶ Does this hold true for people you choose not to forgive?

▶ What do you think would happen if you forgave them? How could it help you? How could it hurt you?

Reflection Exercise (continued)

▶ How could you forgive and still protect yourself from further abuse? It is certainly permissible to request a behavioral change and establish boundaries, as Jan did with her father in Chapter Five.

The deepest truth about not forgiving is that it rarely harms the person you refuse to forgive, *but it always hurts you*. You are more likely to repeat destructive patterns that lead to your being abused when you hold onto the destructive patterns of past abuse. Carmen's three marriages to abusive alcoholic men were the only proof she needed to see the truth of this statement. Life seems determined to teach us how to untangle this intricate web of abuse by giving us more and more challenges until we figure out that developing compassion for ourselves and others is the only way out. We become stronger and the abuse stops. I believe it is a matter of redirecting energy. When you take charge of your own energy, strengthen it through developing a greater understanding of yourself and others, make choices to forgive, and join in creating compassion, the power of real love puts an end to being abused—and to abusing yourself.

In her insightful *The Book of Qualities,* J. Ruth Gendler writes:

"Forgiveness" is a strong woman, tender and earthy and direct. Since her children have left home, she has embarked on an extended walking tour visiting ruins and old monuments, bathing in rivers and hot springs, traveling through small villages and large pulsing cities, tracing the currents of sorrow under the stories she hears. Sometimes the city authorities and officials don't want her within their gates. If the people want her there enough, she always manages to find a way inside. Forgiveness brings gifts wherever she goes. Simple ones, a three-stranded twig with leaves growing yellow, a belt she wove on the inkle loom, a little song that grows inside you and changes everything. She brought me a silver ring from the South with a pale stone, pink with a hint of brown. When I had asthma, she taught me how to breathe.[5]

Forgiveness is a breath of fresh air. It is a gift to ourselves when we seek improved mental and physical health. A story that has been passed down through generations of Lakota Indians tells of a family who sat in judgment of an orphan boy's life. He had killed their son. Their grief and anger were immense at this boy and one by one, they stated, "Kill him." Then the elderly grandfather spoke: "Killing him would not bring our beloved son back to us. It would reduce the number of our young hunters. I think there is a better way. Why not adopt him and teach him the ways of our son?"

The family and other members of the tribe saw the wisdom of this idea. The young man grew into a devoted son and became a tribal leader in his old age.

GUILT AND SHAME

THE EMOTIONAL STATES of guilt and shame can be as crippling to our souls as unforgiving and repressed anger. There may be a real reason to feel them, but there is also a good reason to forgive ourselves and let them go: Chronic guilt and shame create negative energy that alienates us from love. It has been said that guilt is something others impose upon us, while shame is something we impose upon ourselves. Guilt may tell you that you have behaved badly, but shame tells you that you *are* bad. When either of these emotions are present in your life, you need to ask forgiveness from anyone you may have hurt and forgive yourself. To do this deeply difficult work, most of us need the help of a loving friend or a therapist, who can help us understand that *we are far more than the worst thing we have ever done.*

Many painfully lonely adults, filled with guilt and shame, were yesterday's abused children. Even though they have forgiven their parents, they have not yet forgiven themselves. As young children, we usually deny abuse because our dependence upon our caregivers requires that we convince ourselves they love us. Children keep the abuse a secret in order to maintain what little love they might receive. However, by adolescence, most abused children believe they must somehow have caused the abuse by not living up to their parents' expectations. This intensifies repressed anger, while adding guilt and shame to compound the problem. In adulthood, they tend to either abuse themselves or stay connected to others who abuse them—which is a form of self-abuse. Self-abuse is a desperate cry for loving attention.

Reflection Exercise

▶ Are you abusing yourself in any way? If so, how?

▶ Are you abusing others in any way? If so, how?

▶ How do you feel getting in touch with either set of answers?

▶ What causes you to feel guilt or shame in your present life?

▶ Have you shared your negative feelings and thoughts with anyone? If you have not, I encourage you to make an effort to do this.

▶ What could you do to change any abusive situation in your present life? Do it. Then give yourself the gift of forgiveness, letting go of guilt and shame.

REASONS TO SEEK THERAPY

IF YOU DISCOVER that you are unable to deal with reality without employing defense mechanisms, as discussed in Chapter Three, or are not able to forgive or to reduce the guilt, shame, and suffering in your life, you need the help of a therapist, or a therapeutic loving friend, with whom you feel safe enough to be totally honest. Sometimes you need this help in order to get out of your own way. It is easy to become stuck in your own negative thinking. The late Bob Hoffman often said, "Negative thinking leads to stinking, which really blocks loving."

When I was suffering through the terrible process of deciding to separate from my first husband, I knew that I would deeply hurt the people I loved most, my children and my parents. Overwhelmed by guilt and shame, I sought the help of a therapist. Instead of delving into my childhood, helping me untangle webs, give up my illusions, and face reality, he asked me what kind of "masterpiece" I wanted to leave the world when I made my final exit. The question caught me totally off guard. He then explained that each of us comes into the world with a canvas, an easel of colors, and many brushes. In our early years, our caregivers train us to paint a certain way and guide us in our choice of colors, but as we mature, we make our own choices and the painting will become our own. He pointed out that for most of my adult life, I had continued to paint what I thought my parents wanted me to paint.

Reflection Exercise

▶ Consider how this analogy might hold true for your life. What have you painted thus far?

▶ What kind of masterpiece do you want to paint during this lifetime?

I admitted that he was right and that my rule-bound artwork no longer appealed to me. I was purposefully smearing the lines and messing up the symmetry. Until the recent past, I had not considered that my happiness could be contingent upon anything other than following the rules and values taught by my parents. I was also painfully aware that when I went back to graduate school, I had begun behaving more like an irresponsible adolescent than a mature adult. The big problem was that I had discovered that there was more excitement out in the world than I seemed to have in my life. I had grown up without really growing up. I was making my husband miserable and was becoming more and more dissatisfied with myself. I had a feeling of wanting to break free, even though I had a nice husband and four children.

Essentially, I was a thirty-four-year-old adolescent, without a clue how to untangle myself from the web that had defined me since my birth. I did not know who I was or what I really wanted. All I knew was that I wanted out. I wanted to be free from something that kept me tied down, but I certainly did not understand webs, illusions, families, suffering, love, or myself. Therapist Anne Wilson Schaef says that trying to live up to everyone's expectations is like always wearing a girdle that is too tight.[6]

Dr. Schaef claims that when we have worn the girdle so religiously that we have lost contact with the person inside, we have to step free. My therapist agreed with her. I stepped out of my girdle and created the scenario that opened Chapter Seven. I left my husband, moved out to a farm with my children, and put myself in real psychological danger. The problem was that I had changed everything without really dealing with anything, which was a mistake—a mistake that I still feel some guilt over. In retrospect, I believe my therapist and Dr. Schaef were right, but I needed to take more time to work through underlying problems, such as being less impulsive and more patient. I continue to work on forgiving myself for hurting all those who were adversely affected by my behaviors, as I continue to work on developing into a more loving person. I have a deep suspicion that this guilt probably drove me into graduate school to become a marriage and family therapist.

RESOLVING THE PAST, EMBRACING THE PRESENT

MANY YEARS LATER, after remarrying, doing some painful growing up, obtaining my professional degrees, and opening my office where I saw families and groups, Rob and Ellie showed up.

She was a frail woman and an alcoholic. He was an imposing-looking man and the CEO of a relatively large company. He needed to be needed, and she needed someone to look after her. Rob's father had been an alcoholic and had died of alcohol-related complications. The youngest son in the family, Rob had suffered the most abuse from his father. He was filled with guilt and shame, but still claimed to love his father, explaining that his dad had been good to him when he wasn't drunk. Rob had taken care of his father the last few years before his death, and in watching him suffer, Rob claimed that he had forgiven him and made peace with their past. He also promised himself that he would never touch an alcoholic beverage. Instead, he married one—someone who could not stop drinking.

When Ellie got drunk in public, Rob always made excuses for her and blamed himself for her antics. When she berated him in public, he would laugh it off. He would take her home and tuck her into bed, praying she would stay there. She controlled his emotions and a large portion of his life. He eventually lost his job because he was afraid to leave her at home alone. It was clear to me that Rob's unresolved grief and shame over his father had been transferred to his wife. During a therapy session, I suggested to him that perhaps he had never let go of his father and still felt shame for not being able to "save" him. He stared at me in abject amazement, and exclaimed, "You might be right." He had not been receptive to attending ACOA (Adult Children of Alcoholic) meetings until that minute. Now, he said he would go, but did not want to go alone. I called Carmen, who had become active in an ACOA group and was happy to take Rob to her meeting.

Through this group, Rob began to see how his strength to nurture had become a weakness, and how his wife's addiction had become a controlling "strength." Several in the group urged him to divorce her, which he did not want to do. Other group members solicited my advice and offered to help him organize a family meeting so that family members and a few of their closest friends could supportively confront her about the problems caused by her drinking and urge her to seek help. Those of us involved planned to address the problem as belonging to both Rob and Ellie, which it did. Rarely is it true that one person is totally innocent and the other totally guilty, one good and the other bad, or one strong and the other weak. Human interactions are more complex and interdependent than they may appear on the surface—one of the reasons an insightful therapist may be needed to get to the underlying dynamics of a problem.

During the meeting, we began to point out how their relationship had become a power war, which Ellie was clearly winning. She expressed that she felt strong when she manipulated him into looking after her, but that she had not realized how she had made him her slave.

When she verbalized this powerful truth, Rob burst into tears, which seemed to instantly dissolve his armor. He became totally vulnerable in her eyes for the first time, and she became aware of how the power of honesty was greater than the manipulative power she had previously relied on. Shortly after this experience, Ellie checked herself into a twenty-eight-day treatment center, where she began to heal. Rob continued to be active in the Adult Children of Alcoholics group, and began to see how his unresolved deep issues with his father had patterned his marriage.

In a private therapy session I regressed him back in memory to a special time with his father and had him express all the feelings he had repressed over the years. After cleansing his psyche, he offered heartfelt forgiveness of understanding rather than a false forgiveness out of pity to his deceased father. In subsequent sessions, he was able to release years of accumulated guilt and shame and to forgive himself. He had to learn that love is not abuse, but that love does involve pain, and also heals pain. Over time, he and Ellie have continued to deal with their distorted perceptions of love. Gradually, they have restored themselves into real love, accepting its painful moments as challenges.

Rob recently introduced Carmen to his older brother, Steve, whose wife had died of cancer two years before. Step-by-tentative-step, Carmen and Steve are building a relationship. Just a few weeks ago, I saw the four of them, Rob, Ellie, Carmen, and Steve together at a symphony concert. Remembering the roads they had each traveled to get to this place in their lives, I felt happy tears forming, and gave Carmen a hug. We laughed, reminding each other of her first call and those cancelled appointments. She barely resembled the reticent, fearful woman I had met four years earlier. Each of the four had known deep suffering, guilt, and shame. Each had changed profoundly through reaching out for support, giving up defense mechanisms, choosing to forgive, and connecting to love. They had done the work required to make the transition from repeating destructive patterns into the healing wholeness of healthy, honest relationships.

Reflection Exercise

► List the most important transition points of your life.

► What precipitated each major transition?

► How did you gain support through your transitions?

> ## *Reflection Exercise (continued)*
>
> ▶ How had you changed when you reached the other side of a transition?
>
> ▶ What did you give up and what did you gain as your life changed?
>
> ▶ What did you learn about love with each marked transition?

THE COURAGE TO CHANGE

IT IS ALWAYS easier to "rot in your ruts" than to change. Change requires awareness, which often requires that you see things you would rather not see, that you give up the defense mechanisms that may have served you well, and that you take risks. While a good therapist can guide and support you through these processes, he cannot do the work for you.

My eldest son, David, was almost twelve years old when his father and I separated. He behaved as though he totally accepted our coming apart. To my knowledge, he never cried and even comforted his younger siblings when they expressed grief over the separation. David claimed to love living on the farm, and in many ways, became "the man of the house." He seemed to thrive after we made the move to Atlanta, made new friends quickly, became a baseball star, and rarely complained about not having the standard of living that we had enjoyed as an intact suburban family. He always seemed to "roll with the punches."

What I did not know was that David was developing a drinking problem to help him "roll" along. By his junior year in college, he had become addicted to nicotine, alcohol, and rescuing damsels in distress. He had literally become "the knight in rusty armor." His addictions were his armor to protect him from feeling and dealing with all the repressed pain that had accumulated since his father and I divorced. When I tried to get him to admit the problems the breakup had caused him, he would say, "Forget it, Mom. I'm a big boy. I'm a little depressed sometimes, but who isn't these days?"

I wanted to believe him, so I also denied his problems. I put on my own armor, rationalizing that he had always managed well and that my actions had not really harmed him. Several years later, while he was staying with us for his youngest sister's wedding, I could no longer rationalize that he was without problems. At the reception, he was the life of the party, flirting with every female present, even my twice-his-age friends, and drinking twice as much as anyone else. When the bartender alerted me that David was overdoing it, I watched him in action, and was horrified. I brought him into the garage, where we had a real heart-to-heart. He was drunk enough to let his feelings fly. Much of what he had kept buried inside for years surfaced. We both ended up in tears, and he ended up going into a treatment program the next week.

In treatment, he discovered that one of his major underlying problems had been keeping me, his therapist mother, on a pedestal. Believing that our relationship depended on his keeping me there, he had never admitted to himself that I had fallen off many times. In a later conversation about this, it struck me like a bolt of lightning that I had done the same thing with my father. I totally idealized my father, who was a big-time rescuer; I'm a rescuer, and I had passed on the legacies of parental perfection and rescuing to my son. In a perverse way, rescuing can become a buffer that allows us to focus on others' problems while denying our own.

We need to wake up to see how our "boiling cauldron" of unresolved fears and pains patterns our lives until we make a conscious choice to get beyond the past. We do not have to remain a victim of the past, but we must be willing to experience ourselves as we truly are: a powerful energy system, that can make choices to heal, to forgive, and to change behaviors that have destructive consequences, once we become aware of them.

People often spend years in therapy trying to work through familial interactions and relationship patterns, erroneously thinking that all of the unfinished business in all relationships must be resolved before real love can happen. Thankfully, this is not the case, or we would never get out of therapy or have time for real love in our lives. It is the case, however, that if you are an addict, you must learn to make different choices, and change patterns that keep you "stuck" with addictions and other negative behaviors. The process of positive change requires that you connect to your true self—your spiritual self that knows right from wrong.

David needed to be assured that my love was not contingent upon either of us being without faults. Together, we've had to learn that standing in love means stepping off the pedestal, giving up defense mechanisms—addictions included—and being together as real people who deserve to love and be loved. As his mother and a therapist, I have no power to change him, but out of my love for him, I can support him through the changes he is presently making in his life. None of us can change another. We can only be present with another, listening and connecting, connecting and listening, which the best therapy and love have in common. Change is a process of transformation over which we have little control. We have to give up the known, the familiar, and reach out for the unknown, as the knight in rusty armor was finally able to do.

The best metaphor for this process I've read is one written by Danaan Parry, author of *The Essene Book of Days,* comparing life to a series of trapeze swings. He writes that most of us spend our lives hanging on for dear life to our trapeze-bar-of-the-moment, which allows us to feel safely in control. We are feeling secure enough with what we have become used to, when off in the distance, we see another bar swinging toward us. We know it has our name on it, and that to grow, we must reach for it, which requires releasing our grip on the present bar and hurtling across space to grab the new one. It is terrifying. But the drive to reach our potential, to fulfill our innate need for growth, forces us to release the old and fly out across the void toward the new. Regardless of the number of times we repeat the process, it is always frightening because there are no guarantees or safety nets. Change requires a leap of faith into the future. Before the bar of the future is in our grasp, we experience soaring through the dark void of "the past is gone and the future is not yet here." It is in this void that change, growth, and transformation really happen.[7]

BEYOND THERAPY

THIS METAPHOR FEELS true to me. It is not therapy that changes us, but the journey we each must make from what we know to what we are seeking between therapy appointments. Change happens as we expand beyond our past and reach for what we may become when we discover the courage within ourselves to risk reaching out. The real change agent in the process of transforming negative into positive energy is self-love.

In reaching out to another we begin to trust in our ability to cocreate love. Walt Whitman illustrates the process in his exquisite poem about a spider:

A noiseless patient spider,
I marked where on a little promontory it stood isolated,
Marked how to explore the vast vacant surrounding,
It launched forth filament, filament, filament, out of itself,
Ever unreeling them, ever tirelessly speeding them.
And you, O my soul where you stand,
Surrounded detached in measureless oceans of space,
Ceaselessly musing, venturing, throwing, seeking the spheres to
connect them,
Till the bridge you will need be formed, till the ductile anchor hold,
Till the gossamer thread you fling catch somewhere, O my soul.

The most valuable aspect of therapy is the forming of a connection between your truest self and someone who will really listen as you spin out your story, chapter after chapter. When you are truly listened to, you learn that you have something to say worth listening to, and you learn, in turn, to listen to yourself. Within yourself, you have all the makings of love—the power to forgive, to understand, to take the leap of faith, to learn to fly, and to connect. Ultimately, the still small voice within you is your best therapist, but in order to hear it, you have to stop running, stop defending, stop rescuing, be still, and listen to its wisdom. When you do this, you will discover that everything you have experienced thus far anchors you in the lessons of love, so that you can build the bridge to connect to another in love. This is the primary purpose of human existence.

TEN

Are You Ready *to* Discover Your Raison d'être?

THE TRUTH IS THAT THERE IS ONLY ONE TERMINAL DIGNITY—LOVE.
THE STORY OF LOVE IS NOT IMPORTANT—WHAT IS IMPORTANT IS THAT
ONE IS CAPABLE OF LOVE. IT IS PERHAPS THE ONLY GLIMPSE
WE ARE PERMITTED OF ETERNITY.
—HELEN HAYES

EVERY RELIGION AND school of thought has its version of a creation story, and each creation story ends with the creation of human beings. Most of these ancient stories share the theme that we were put on earth to learn to love—to love the earth and take care of it, and to love each other. We have been searching for an understanding of what love means and how to find it ever since.

According to one ancient Eastern creation story, after the gods created the Universe with the stars, sun, moon, seas, mountains, trees, flowers, animals, and humans, they realized that all of these beautiful and wonderful creations needed a Truth to live by. They agreed that the Truth should be Love, but they had a problem deciding where this Love should be placed so that human beings could have a great adventure searching for and discovering it. Knowing that humans especially liked adventure and that the nature of their life was passion, the gods were sure that human beings would value love more if they could discover it through a passionate adventure.

Some of the gods thought it should be placed at the top of the highest mountain where brave and strong humans would find it and bring it down to distribute to all other living beings. Other gods suggested that the treasured Truth of Love be distributed among the stars, so that when these adventuresome beings began to explore space, they would be rewarded by discovering True Love. But the wisest god, the ancient Absolute, said, "I think we should hide the treasured Truth of Love inside the heart of every human being. They will look all over the Universe, but will be overjoyed when they discover it inside themselves, where it will have been since the beginning of time."

The gods agreed that this would be the perfect place to hide the Truth of Love. They also agreed that each time a new baby was born, the baby would bring a tiny new piece of love into the Universe. Gurdjieff, an Asiatic Russian mystic who explored the interaction of our psychological and spiritual natures, characterized a newborn baby as the purest manifestation of our deepest self, because the infant has not yet been contaminated by a culture's inhumanity.[1]

Perhaps this story explains why we look into the face of new baby and are filled with instant love. It is easy and natural to love an infant. When an infant's needs are met, the infant smiles and settles into contentment. The adult caregiver feels rewarded and a genuine love attachment is born. But as babies grow up, love becomes more elusive and illusionary. During the process of growing up, many of us learn to block our responses to what people call love, because we've lived with people who have tried to control us, betrayed us, lied to us, and abused us in the name of love. We've searched for it in many wrong places and we've been hurt and disappointed when we've found what we thought was lasting love. We've gotten the Truth of Love confused with power, control, obsession, addiction, lust, and self-involvement.

In *A Little Book on Love,* contemporary philosopher Jacob Needleman writes that there are two kinds of love that must be combined if we are to know real and sustaining love in our lifetimes. One is the sexual love that draws us to the great earthy sensual forces. This is the intense state of "falling in love," when our bodies long to join totally with another. People might say, "I'm so in love I can't see straight."

They are correct. The other has a spiritual nature and is more complicated, as well as being more difficult to achieve. It requires that we join in a search for our selves in the universal world, that we truly connect our spiritual essence to the same in another. This kind of love helps us search for Truth, perhaps the Truth that is hidden deeply enough in our hearts to afford us the great adventure planned by the gods. The challenge of sustaining love is bringing these two oppositional forces—one that seems to arise from our animal nature and the other from our divine nature—together so that one serves the other. Needleman refers to this combined love as intermediate love.[2] It is this intermediate love that we humans need to create if we want to experience passionate and sustaining love relationships.

Reflection Exercise

▶ Where have you searched for love, only to be disappointed in what you found?

▶ What have you discovered that can feel like love in the beginning, but not be sustaining love? This includes relationships that are initially filled with lust, but in a few weeks, or months, tend to peter out.

If you do have sustaining love in your life, what has been required to cocreate it and to have it last?

BROKEN HEARTS AND SCAR TISSUE

MOST ADULTS HAVE survived several broken hearts in our search for sustaining love. Each time our hearts are broken, or even cracked a bit, scar tissue forms in the healing process. This scar tissue forms a layer of protection around our hearts, but it also makes it more difficult to reach our most delicate part—the parts that create and nurture sustaining love. Herein lays one of love's most complicated and puzzling paradoxes.

To be able to love, Carmen, and millions of other neglected and abused children, have to devise ways to protect themselves physically, emotionally, mentally, and spiritually, while still hoping that love can happen for them. At what point does the scar tissue become so thick and hardened that there is no way to discover the deeply buried treasure of the Truth of Love? In working with groups of convicted prisoners, I've yet to find a single one who did not hold out some tiny hope that love might still happen in his life.

Alan was in prison for life for killing his mother and her boyfriend. He claimed that he felt safer in prison than he had at home with his mother, who had abused him and his sister and allowed her boyfriends to abuse them for as long as he could remember. When he was four years old, his mother had stabbed him with a carving knife on Thanksgiving because he had reached for a piece of turkey before she gave him permission. His grandmother happened to drop by and took him to the hospital, but lied about how he had been wounded. By the time he was ten, he promised himself and his sister that he would kill their mother and anyone else who abused them. At age seventeen, he did. He expressed no regret for his crime at his trial and was declared incorrigible by the courts. Having been incarcerated for three years and having caused no trouble during this time, he was allowed to join our human relations group.

As a way of giving each meeting a focus, I would ask a member of the group to draw one Rune, from a collection of twenty-five kept in a velvet pouch. Runes are small stone oracles once consulted by ancient Norse warriors for special divination before a quest. Each Rune bears a different message. Ralph Blum, an anthropologist and author of *The Book of Runes,* has explored the origins of the Viking Runes and reinterpreted their meanings in terms appropriate for contemporary spiritual seekers.[3] Alan drew the Rune called "Signals," which alerts the seeker to the possibility of new life through new connections. I asked him to read aloud from Blum's interpretation:

> Even scoundrels and arch-thieves can be bearers of wisdom. When you draw this Rune, expect the unexpected. The message is always a call to new life. You need to address your need to integrate unconscious motive with conscious intent. Drawing it tells you that a connection with the Divine is at hand.

All sixteen of us in the room were awed by the message and by the shift in Alan's voice as he read. No one dared speak as he carefully closed the little book. After waiting for the message to sink into our minds and hearts, Alan looked into the eyes of each of us around the room and gently said, "You guys have helped me understand this and helped me discover some good in myself. I love you guys—and you, too, Paddy. I've never said those words before in my life." There was not a dry eye in the group. Even the two officials who were posted to guard the men during the session had to use the Kleenex. I've never again questioned the power of love to pierce through the thickest scar tissue.

Reflection Exercise

► When has love surprised you by breaking through your scar tissue?

► When have you observed others caught by love in an unsuspecting moment?

► Have you ever been deeply aware of love when experiencing grief or pain?

VISIBLE SCARS

WHEN TIM AND I married, twenty-six years ago, he gave me a choice between a wedding ring and a custom-built, ten-speed bicycle. This was no real choice, since we loved riding bikes together and I was tired of panting up hills on my six-speed while he surged ahead on his ten-speed. He would often circle back to be sure I was going to make it, but I found this kindness a bit humiliating. After I chose the bike, he made a ring from one of the spokes for our wedding ceremony. We have ridden through several sets of bicycles and over many bumpy roads throughout the years.

On a lovely summer afternoon a few years ago, we had planned a fairly vigorous ride. Tim was delayed at work, but thought he would still be home in time for our ride. I waited and waited and by the time he showed up, I was really annoyed. It was getting close to dusk and my better judgment said, "Forget it," but in my irritation, I said, "Let's go," knowing we would be caught by darkness and have to walk up the final hills to home, which he would hate. In a perverse way, I thought this would remind him to come home on time for the next ride. I was definitely processing through my dark side. Being energized by negative emotion, I rode ahead of him, which does not happen often. Darkness fell, but we rode on. Going fast downhill, I lost control when my bike slipped on gravel that I couldn't see. I hit the road face first. There was a moment of searing pain, and then my only awareness was blood—blood in my eyes, blood and goo where my nose and mouth had been. My only thought was that I had to end my life before Tim reached me because I could not abide the thought of his having to live with a faceless, blind woman. I prayed to die. I thought I had.

My next awareness was his turning me over and screaming, "Oh God, oh God, this is really bad." I felt no physical pain, only shock at the thought that I wasn't dead—yet.

I was sure that no loving God would keep me alive in the shape I was going to be in. I was wrong.

Vaguely, I could hear Tim talking to himself almost hysterically about how to get help on a dark, seldom-used country road. Then car lights appeared. Tim ran out into the middle of the road and flagged down the car. Moments earlier, he had given me his shirt to hold on my face to try to stop some of the bleeding. The shirt had absorbed enough blood that I realized I could see out of one eye, so I was trying to decide if I still wanted to die, if I were only half-blind. Simultaneously, I was amazed that I felt no physical pain.

By the time we made it to the emergency room of the nearest hospital, I realized that I was probably going to live with half a face and *maybe* I could handle that. But I did not want Tim to have to live with me. I did not think the "for better or worse" of our wedding vows could stretch to this level of "worse." Throughout the whole ordeal, Tim had been saying, "I love you, I love you. It will be all right." I couldn't take it in because I didn't think he had any idea how really ugly I would be after this. I had had an ugly attitude several hours before, but I knew we were going to be dealing with big-time physical ugliness after this mess healed, if it ever would.

Shortly thereafter, a doctor began picking the bits of gravel and tar out of the bloody spot where my face had been and poking needles into the wounds to numb the tissue. Intense physical pain began, and again I was sure that I would die. Then one of the most unusual and amazing phenomenon I've ever experienced occurred. The words of the Lord's Prayer began to roll through my mind, followed by the 23rd Psalm: "The Lord is my shepherd, I shall not want . . . ," which I had not consciously quoted in years. Within a few seconds, I became totally calm and free of pain, although the doctor was still poking needles into my face. As I repeated these beautiful words from the Bible that I had memorized in childhood over and over in my mind, a feeling of being connected to an encompassing divine love flooded my entire being. I forgot about living or dying. Neither seemed to matter. I felt as deep a love in my body as I had ever experienced.

I tried to look up at Tim, who had been standing beside me, holding my hand, to let him know I really was going to be fine, but he had disappeared. A nurse was helping him onto the gurney beside mine while asking another nurse for the ammonia, explaining that he was about to pass out. I wanted to tell him to say the Lord's Prayer and he would feel better, but I couldn't talk as the doctor was stitching my top lip back in place. Knowing that my husband wasn't too keen on praying, I decided I'd best send the next round his way. I was filled with a profound feeling of love and appreciation for him and for the healing life-energy that surrounds us.

A superb plastic surgeon was called the next morning, and after four hours in the operating room where he carefully placed several hundred stitches, he had my face back together. Visible scars remain, but I now refer to them as "scars of love," for they are a constant reminder of the healing love I felt the night of the accident from my husband and from the ultimate healing power. The entire emergency room experience has been the only portion of time in my conscious memory when I felt I was encased in a womb of protection, feeling that my only task was to stay connected to the source of energy available to me.

As a result of this experience, I learned that sustaining love reaches far beyond physical appearance and that our personal definitions of "better" or "worse" are trite compared to what real love can accept.

Reflection Exercise

▶ Remember any experience you have had when you had no ability to control any aspect of what was happening to you.

▶ What happened to sustain you through the experience? Giving birth to an infant would definitely be in this category and, for a male, I imagine watching your child being born would be an equally powerful one.

▶ How would you define sustaining love at this point in your life?

Many of the personal stories related in earlier chapters also illustrate this concept of discovering how your passionate connections can be brought into the service of your more divine nature to help create sustaining love. Carmen, Ann Marie and Luigino, Jan and her father, Alice and her husband, and the entire Albertson family were all deeply wounded, but when their passions combined with their spiritual nature of searching for a greater Truth, they gained the kind of love that sustains us through adversity. Misplaced passion has broken many hearts and lives, but when combined with spiritual love, sustaining love is created. This does not mean the end of frustrations, fears, anger, quarrels, and struggles, but it does offer us a path through them—a path of forgiveness and openness—and ways to rebuild trust through honest communication and searching together for the Truth of Love.

Jacob Needleman agrees that honest communication, which is the life blood of a healthy love relationship, is based upon an ability to truly listen to one another. Genuine listening is an ability developed over time and requires that we are mature enough to put our personal agenda aside to hear what another is trying to say—to take in a point of view that may differ from our own and work to understand it. Maintaining a healthy relationship is a struggle, but a struggle well worth the effort, for without the struggle, we could not appreciate the joy. Human nature is funny that way. We seem to require a relative frame of reference to remain passionate. Without passion, we exist, but do not fully live.

DIFFICULT DILEMMAS

THERE IS A difficult dilemma when we are faced with the question of why passion, healthy relationships, and the Truth of Love become available to some—including the scoundrels and arch-thieves—and yet seem to be totally beyond discovery to others who *appear* to be searching for them diligently. Persons who come into the universe with severe genetic pathologies, personality and character disorders, or have had no opportunity to experience love are left floundering without a clue. We wonder if the gods forgot to hide the valuable treasure in their hearts. It doesn't seem fair. It is not fair from our limited ability to comprehend the whole.

In the extraordinary movie *The Green Mile,* we have a clear presentation of *unfair.* John Coffey, a black man, who is good in the ultimate sense of morally good, pays with his life for a bad white man's deeds, representing the ultimate pathological evil. There seems to be no Truth of Love portrayed here. We can say, "It is only in the movies," but in fact it is a story that has been reenacted ad infinitum, ad nauseum in every society where there is prejudice and control of one group by another.

Deep Reflection Exercise

▶ Do you believe it is within the realm of possibility that we must create evil and psychopathology to balance the wholeness of human nature?

▶ Do we need mental illness and evil to understand mental health and goodness?

▶ Do we need fear and hate to understand love?

▶ Reflect on any negative thoughts you have had in the past few days. If you do not think you have had any, try to drop your denial and search your thoughts again.

We must accept that there is unfairness and evil in the world, but most of us tend to deny our own ability to generate unfairness and evil. *This kind of denial puts us a step closer to causing harm to ourselves and others.* When you deny your dark side, you begin to separate parts of your psyche that must be integrated for you to be psychologically healthy. When you separate any aspect of yourself from other aspects, such as the way Carmen's father did in the preceding chapter, you create a dangerous zone within your mind where destructive thoughts breed and can be manifested into destructive behaviors.

A plausible explanation for the presence of evil and negativity is that the vibrating impulse of energy from which original life began combined positive and negative currents, just as we combine the positive and negative poles of a battery to create power. Each of us can recognize positive and negative energy within our own bodies. It may be manifested through our "chattering monkeys," or simply through our moods and attitudes, which can change instantly in the wake of new events or thoughts. I can be feeling positive and excited, as I was on the afternoon of the disastrous bike ride. But the later it became without hearing from Tim, the more negative my mood became. By the time he came home, I was in a place of real negative energy, although I denied it. There is no doubt in my mind that my repressed irritation at him led to my riding carelessly, which, in turn, contributed to causing the accident. As events then began to happen beyond my control, I had to surrender to whatever happened. I was very lucky that I was with someone who loved me enough to intercede with positive energy and save my life. John Coffey, in *The Green Mile,* was not so lucky. The circumstances that led to his arrest and death sentence were controlled by prejudiced people who feared and therefore rejected him. Prejudice is an evil that runs rampant in the world today and often causes us to miss love.

Reflection Exercise

▶ Get in touch with your prejudices. How do you act on them?

▶ Get in touch with any prejudices you may have had and have given up. How has that changed you?

I am aware that I am prejudiced against "right-to-lifers" for I fervently believe any female should have a right to make her own decision about having a child, especially when there could be a health risk or when the child could not be cared for properly. I base my prejudice against the antiabortion movement on personal experience and having worked with scores of children who have been abused by parents and caregivers who did not want them and could not care for them. I have watched some of these children grow up and abuse their children. I've remet several of them in prisons. I feel sick about their lives and the lives that have been harmed by them. Perhaps if they had been aborted, the world would have been spared some negativity and pain. Yet, at a much deeper level, I am also aware that each person's life has a purpose. Once I begin any kind of personal connection with a troubled person, such as the prison inmate, Alan, my prejudice unravels. I do not have anything upon which to stand because I know my understanding is limited to my experience. I have to come face-to-face with that part of me that would like to think I know better than the Absolute, that I have some right to control others' decisions. I do not, and bottom line, I cannot. I have to back off—and accept what is beyond my understanding.

I have to accept that others have a right to disagree with me, that there is pathology I cannot cure, that evil happens, and that we live in a less than perfect world. It causes me great angst, but it should not cause prejudice. It is a difficult dilemma, brought poignantly to my attention in an E-mail I received from a niece last year. I have not been able to locate the original author, but am indebted to her or him for the following story.

There once was a King who offered a prize to the artist who could paint the best picture of peace. Many artists submitted pictures, but two really impressed the King. One was a picture of a calm lake, which mirrored towering mountains and a beautiful blue sky with white fluffy clouds. It was a perfect picture of peace.

The second picture had mountains that were rugged and bare and an angry sky from which rain fell and lightning flashed across. A waterfall tumbled down the mountain, crashing on the rocks below. At first glance, the King did not think this painting would qualify as peaceful at all. But looking more deeply, behind the waterfall, there was a tiny bush growing from a crack in the rocky surface. In the bush, a mother bird had built her nest and was sitting peacefully on her eggs.

The King chose this picture and explained, "Peace does not mean being in a place where there is no turbulence or hard work. Peace means to be in the midst of those things, and still be calm in your heart."

The Absolute, as well as those gods who hid the Truth of Love inside our hearts, quite possibly would agree with this King. There is no challenge to peace or love, no way to grow us into it, without our having to make daily choices about utilizing our positive and negative energies. Working out a way to tame the negative aspects of ourselves into the service of love may be our greatest adventure. It may also be the only way to create sustaining love.

Evolving Consciousness

BOTH POSITIVE AND negative impulses have been, and remain, necessary for the survival of human beings. The evolving homo sapiens species had to be aggressive to eat, but also had to be nurturing to raise their offspring. We continue to have the same positive and negative impulses, but we now have many more choices about how to develop and utilize them. The ways we choose to use our energies become most obvious in our "seeking" behaviors. As a species, humans have always been searchers—searchers for food, attention, sex, power, status, wealth, excitement, romance, peace, love, truth, and, above all else, for meaning.

Meaning is assigned to each of these desired objects by the culture in which we live, and that culture, in turn, is designed by our level of conscious awareness. Our conscious awareness is designed by a configuration of psychological structures, which form an internal representation of our outside world. And all of these things tend to shift in accordance with the ways in which our consciousness evolves.

Just as there are two oppositional kinds of love that must combine to form sustaining love, and two oppositional basic energies, there are also two types of consciousness that seem to evolve simultaneously.

One is programmed by earth forces, manifested through our search for financial gain as our source of power and control. The other is programmed by spiritual forces, manifested through our ongoing search for compassion, openheartedness, and the Truth of Love.

James Hillman, Jungian analyst and author of *The Soul's Code*, and Plotinus, the greatest of the later Platonists, have written that we essentially are "soul beings," who choose to become human so that we can continue the development of our souls. With our soul's choice to take on human existence we must choose the circumstances of our lives, which work together to fulfill the mission required by our souls for advancement toward the goal of total compassion.[4]

Yet, even a cursory look around us, indicates that as a culture, we have chosen to apply most of our energies to searching for financial gains and accumulating things in a competitive, technological market rather than applying them to cultivating compassion. All the while, we continue to cry out, "Is this all there is?" We will create *what is* through our commitment to that which we choose to seek.

Deep Reflection Exercise

▶ For what am I searching?

▶ What is missing in my life?

▶ Where do I direct my energies?

▶ What are the results of my directed energy?

▶ How do I obtain personal power?

The Osage, a Sioux tribe of Native Americans, have a legend that deals with the tribe's search for what they felt was missing in their lives. They looked at the ways the insects and animals lived and realized that these beings seemed more content to occupy their place on Earth than humans. They decided that each clan should choose an animal or insect to guide them in their search for contentment. Most clans sent their best runners out immediately to search and explore for a symbolic creature, but one clan was late. Their best runner took so much time preparing for his search that other runners were already returning with animals to be the life symbol for their clan. They had chosen the deer, the eagle, and the buffalo. There were not many suitable animals left from which this late runner could choose, but he set out anyway, and was so busy searching that he didn't see a spider web stretched across his path.

He ran into it and screamed as he tried to pull the spider's sticky web off his face and body. When he spotted the spider up in the corner of the web, he was furious and yelled at it. "You silly little thing," he shouted," why did you build your house over this trail and cause me to run into it?"

"For what are you searching that you cannot see where you are going?" the spider asked

"I'm looking for a life symbol to guide my clan," the irritated runner replied.

"Why don't you choose me?" asked the spider.

Laughing derisively, the runner asked the spider why she thought she would be a good life symbol. "Where I am, I build my house," the spider calmly replied. "And where I build my house, all things come to it. I never have to search the earth without direction and without knowing for what I am searching."

The runner understood the spider's wisdom and returned to his clan with the spider.[5]

Like the spider, our essence already encompasses everything we need to create meaning, passion, and sustaining love, but we tend to use much of our energy to create destructive competition, to try to control, to feel superior, and to gain corruptive power.

According to Charles Tart, a professor of psychology at the University of California, in his book *Waking Up, Overcoming the Obstacles to Human Potential,* we enter the world as the pure essence of our *basic* nature with characteristics, potentials, and limits, but this does not mean it is our *ultimate* nature. This basic nature is then shaped, bent, conditioned, developed, and repressed in the process of enculturation—to make us "fit in" to the expectations of those who are in charge of us. We become the fly trapped in our culture's web instead of the spider creating from our essence what we deserve. As we encounter new events and new knowledge, we make adjustments to our characters and our personalities, and over time we evolve into whatever survival demands of us. This is the basic way we seek to protect ourselves, but it is killing us while we sleep tangled up, feeling that something is missing but without a clue about what it could be. If we stay asleep, life may be easier, but not fulfilling.[6]

If you are born and raised in a negative situation, you do possess the ability to influence the situation, or to leave it, after attaining an age of independence. One of the most difficult of all human dilemmas is to know when it is more beneficial to fit in, to try to alter, or to leave the culture to which you have become accustomed. When you are in enough pain, you will try to change something; therefore, pain might be necessary for the continuing evolution of consciousness. Since the beginning of recorded time, the evolution of consciousness has alternated between individual and group experience. This alternation exists in an overall movement as well as in smaller movements, which may begin within one individual. Examples would certainly be Buddha, Jesus Christ, Socrates, Karl Marx, Madame Curie, Golda Meir, Eleanor Roosevelt, and hundreds of others. When a movement begins within one individual, it is carried over into his or her relationships, then into a community, and then into a culture. Violinist Roberta Guaspari, who began the East Harlem Concert Violin Orchestra, is a powerful contemporary example of a tenacious woman with a dream that has transformed hundreds of lives, and inspired millions of others. The movie *Music of the Heart* tells her story and offers hope for anyone who has a passionate dream that could transform what seems to be a negative life event into a beautiful and positive cultural shift.

My dear and poetic friend, Suzanne Moffat, captures this idea in *Circles:*

> In the morning's early half-light
> The garden compost steams,
> From earthy hidden depths,
> From darkly heated central core—
> Circle of potential,
> Rich and fertile.
>
> Suddenly—
> First sun rays
> Filtering through fog,

Searching for life,
Thirsting for beauty—
First sun rays strike gold!

Set radiant fire to fairy-spun lace
Filigree-woven by web-spinning spiders,
Encircling the darkly fecund mound—
Light embracing shadow.

Myriad dew-sparkled intricate webs
Glisten and glow
Gossamer snowflakes
Gleam fog from above
Shine steam from below
Fiery light swirling
Beyond centered dark.

Prismatic lace charkas
Whirling with colors
Interlacing of circles
So delicately strong . . .
So magnetically wondrous . . .

We each have the potential to transform what could be considered
negative into positive when we utilize our ability to see beauty in a
mud puddle. The mud puddle, compost pile, bicycle accident,
divorce, disease, or even death can serve as a springboard for us to
choose to wallow in the negative aspect or rise up to create new opportunities. Our choice will have interactive effects that are ongoing.
Interlocking spiraled webs within the context of larger webs can conceptualize this process. The spirals have alternations that interact
within each single web as well as within the context of the whole,
which represents a cosmic consciousness, of which we each are a part.

During any given period, an individual may need to gather his
energies into his personal being for personal growth, as I certainly had
to do when I closed my therapy practice to apply my energies to healing myself and my personal relationships. I would never have made
this choice without the triggering negative of "the affair" mentioned

in the Introduction, but the benefits have been healthier relation-ships in which I, and those I love, feel more loved. The benefits of this love interact throughout my relationships and surroundings, which interact with others to stimulate change throughout a larger network of interwoven webs. Each of these interactions has con-tributed to my being able to write this book, which I pray will con-tinue to interact throughout larger webs, and influence others to look more closely at how each choice we make will affect the creation of compassion—or bring us closer to extinction.

Reflection Exercise

► Evaluate your past twenty-four hours by giving yourself a point for each thirty-minute segment of time you have spent engaged in positive behaviors which could perpetuate sustaining love, including for yourself.

► Subtract a point for each thirty-minute segment of time you have spent harming yourself or another, including negative thinking.

► During the past twenty-four hours, how have you expressed appreciation for any living thing?

► During the past twenty-four hours, how have you harmed any living thing?

► Has this been a typical twenty-four-hour period for you?

UNTANGLING WEBS

CONTEMPORARY SCIENTISTS, PHYSICISTS, the Dalai Lama, the late Gurdjieff, Deepak Chopra, and other spiritual teachers are convinced that unless we are willing to wake up to the ways we are creating destruction in the world today and begin to put our prime energies into creating compassionate love for all living things, we will devolve into extinction within the next few centuries. The only way we are able to create compassion is to see deeply into our own natures, including the negative, or potentially evil, aspect of our selves. As long as we stay tangled and asleep in the powerful competitive web that we have woven from false beliefs about what love is and what it requires of us, we will fulfill this sad prophecy. There is a way to wake up. The power is within each of us, but we will have to choose to access it and use it to weave a stronger web—one that values love over money, that respects and appreciates differences, and is designed through cooperative competition rather than the deadly competition of war.

Our present cultural web has lost the deeper meaning of power, as well as of love. Power is most visible as physical power, but in our obsession with the physical level of reality, we tend to discount the quantum and virtual levels of reality, as explained in Chapter Four. The virtual level, the level of the spiritual, of good, of God, is the level of the Truth of Love. The quantum level, which connects the other two, is the level of the mind, the place where we exercise choice, or free will. This is also the level at which everything is connected, bound together through the interaction of subatomic particles. If you focus only on the physical, you see separation, and deny the reality of connection.

If we deny our connectedness, and persist in seeing ourselves as separate, we become confused about meanings—the meaning of love, of life, of Truth. Our confusion breeds fear. When we are afraid of our own potential, we become afraid of the potential of others. Fear of others leads to trying to gain power over others, or even to extinguish them, as evidenced by the behaviors of this past century's ultimate evil person, Adolf Hitler. When separation and fear combine, evil and pathology eventuate.

At the deepest level, psychopathology is an *unawareness* of connection. Focusing on separateness directs our energy away from love, and in so doing creates the space in which evil dwells. If I see myself as separate from others, I can hurt others without feeling the hurt within myself. If I see myself as connected to others, I cannot hurt others without awareness that the hurt will return to me. Although at the quantum and virtual levels this separateness is an illusion, at the physical level it is very real and very painful. The ultimate goal of compassionate, sustaining love is unity. The ultimate goal of evil is separateness.

Reflection Exercise

► How connected do you feel to others?

► How does your life affect others?

► What is your deepest desire? Would others be helped or hurt by its fulfillment?

We cannot afford to be confused about what we desire and about how we are trying to fulfill our desires. I cannot believe that any sane human being desires to create evil, but I do believe that many have become so confused about love and how we are connected that they use their power negatively to feel superior to others as a replacement for love.

Each of us belongs on the planet, deserves to be valued, and to have the "wonder-full" experience of love in our lives. We are human beings searching for spiritual experiences and are simultaneously spiritual beings living out the difficult human experience in an effort to restore love in our lives. Every life is a love story unfolding, and at some point in every life, we will share the same story, for it is a universal story. It is the story of creation, of birth, of suffering, of death, of wounds that we must get beyond, of connections we must be willing to understand, of choices, of hopes, and dreams—and of searching for fulfillment.

Ultimate Reflection Exercise

► Reflect carefully upon the most fulfilling moments of your life.

► What have you contributed to the universe?

► What have you taken from it?

> ## Ultimate Reflection Exercise (cont'd.)
>
> ▶ What do you consider the purpose of your life, your raison d'être? Do your heart and mind agree on your answer?
>
> ▶ What are you doing to fulfill your purpose? What are you doing to oppose your purpose?
>
> ▶ How can you best utilize your energies and personal powers toward fulfilling your purpose?
>
> ▶ How do you think you will be remembered after your death?
>
> ▶ What would you like to have written on your tombstone?

Erich Fromm has written: *"Love is the only satisfactory answer to the problem of human existence."* We will find the Truth of Love when we are willing to look *where it is—in the heart of every man, every woman, and every child.* When we look deeply enough we will discover that we are more alike than different, that we each need love, that we are all afraid, and that we each possess an ultimate potential to forgive and to stand with others in love. Only when we truly learn to live love, can there be peace in the world.

Are You Ready *to* Stand *in* Lasting Love?

*LIFE IS ETERNAL, AND LOVE IS IMMORTAL, AND DEATH IS
ONLY A HORIZON, AND A HORIZON IS NOTHING
SAVE THE LIMIT OF OUR SIGHT.*
—ROSSITER WORTHINGTON RAYMOND

SITTING IN A large circle of people with whom I'd
shared a weeklong workshop on developing our intuitive abilities, I listened as two men told intensely moving stories of
tragic childhood abuse. They agreed that the suffering
imposed on them by alcoholic parents had forced them to
develop their intuition to survive. They had learned to pick up
subtle signals in the moods and behaviors of their parents,
which would give them clues to be quiet or get out of sight. I
was deeply saddened by their stories, but I could hardly imagine the kind of pain they were sharing. What concerned me
the most was that neither of them had ever told anyone. I
could not imagine *not* "squealing" when someone hurt me as
a child. In fact, I was not silent about much of anything. My
mother was a teacher and my father was a preacher. My family was full of words. Words were our fix.

I became a teacher and a therapist so that I could help "fix"
people with words of wisdom, words of comfort, words of

encouragement, or by listening to their words. I did not believe there was any pain so deep that talking or writing about it would not help.

At the conclusion of the workshop session that morning, I realized that I was feeling somehow guilty for having had so few real tragedies in my life. I was concerned that I might be less competent as a therapist because I had never experienced pain so deep that I chose to suffer in silence rather than talk about it. I was aware that such suffering existed and that enduring it did seem to make some people not only more intuitive, but gave them a stronger spiritual core. I was aware that when I suffered I searched for words to help heal me. I searched my mind for healing thoughts. I read. I talked to myself, or to anyone else who might listen. When there was no one to listen, I wrote letters—to whomever, including to myself, and often to God. I prayed. I tried to meditate, which was difficult because words would quickly move into the space that was supposed to remain empty. I was acutely aware that I had never known the depth of pain that forms a spiritual rite of passage.

As I walked along the pathway back to my cabin, lost in these thoughts of suffering and of non suffering, someone stopped me to say there was a note for me pinned on the cabin door. Suddenly I remembered that my daughter, Karen, and her husband, Saadin, living in Ecuador, were due to have their second child on this very day and my heart quickened its pace. The first was a beautiful little girl, Nina, now two years old. Nina was the connecting center of love and joy in our transcultural family. Through ultrasound, we knew that this second baby was a boy, already named Nicholas. His birth, as the first son of his generation, would ensure the survival of the family name, especially important to the Ecuadoran grandparents. My excitement mounted. I began to run toward the cabin.

Five words were scrawled on a pink slip, tacked to the cabin door: *Your grandchild died this morning.* My world shattered as if a nuclear bomb had exploded inside my being. My mind knew only one word: No, No, No! There was agony so deep that it felt as if every fiber of my being were being ripped into shreds. I ran like a wounded feral animal into the nearby woods. I screamed and cried. I hit trees and beat upon the ground. I wanted to tear the world apart. Instead, I tore the pink slip into tiny pieces and hurled them at God. My soul screamed at Him to take the words back and change them. I now knew real suffering. I knew what it was to have to bear the unbearable.

After venting enough pain to be able to get back in touch with a portion of reality, I realized that I didn't even know whether the note referred to Nina or Nicholas. I was assuming it was Nina, as there had been no message about the birth of Nicholas. I stumbled out of the woods and ran for a telephone. All the international lines to South America were busy; I yelled at the operators until a merciful one finally placed an emergency call through to get me hooked up with a relative who could tell me what happened. Nicholas had been born that morning with the umbilical cord around his neck. He was dead. Everyone was grief-stricken.

I never returned to the workshop. Instead, I got on the first flight I could take to Ecuador. I cried until I was exhausted, but now my tears were for Karen, one of the kindest and most loving souls on this earth. I could not believe that I had not been there for her. I'd sent her sister, Karla, to be present for the birth, and I'd planned to follow ten days later, after completing my doctoral examinations. They no longer mattered. The only thing that mattered was that I had a daughter suffering beyond measure in a Third World country where there was no professional to help her deal with the death of her son. My heart was breaking over and over again.

When I finally arrived at her door, there were no words that could begin to touch the grief, the compassion, the sadness, and the love. Karen's gentle blue eyes seemed to be looking up from the torments of hell. My heart broke from an even deeper place. We sank beneath the sadness and held onto each other like two drowning victims. We shared our raw pain in silence. For the second time in two days I knew total powerlessness.

I could not give Nicholas life. I could not heal Karen's pain. I could not explain to Nina why she didn't have the little brother she had been joyfully expecting. I could not lessen anyone's suffering. I could only be there and suffer with them in silence.

Ecuadoran laws required that the baby be buried before sundown on the same day he was born—and died. At the hospital, Nicholas had been wrapped in a sheet and handed to his father, Saadin, the only person to hold him before he was buried. Saadin said that he was a beautiful, perfectly formed baby, who already had the face of an angel. Karen was never able to see or hold him, a regret she will carry to her grave.

We planned a graveside service for the next day. With heavy hearts, Karen, Saadin, Nina, Karla, Saadin's parents, his sister, and I met outside the cemetery, where flower vendors sat along the high stone wall separating the busy highway from the cemetery grounds. We bought flowers from them as we entered the cemetery. Each of us grandparents wondered if we had the spiritual strength to support our grown children through saying farewell to this beautiful baby, who had known life only in Karen's womb. I had prayed that God would help me find words that might offer some solace to my family, especially my daughter and Saadin, but no words seemed to touch the pain.

Saadin and his father had buried Nicholas in a special section of the cemetery reserved for the graves of infants and young children. It was high on a terraced hillside with flowers everywhere. The view included a vast expanse of sky with the majestic Andes Mountains decorating the horizon. In the center of this sector of the cemetery was a white stone statue of an angel. Her wings reached out to gather in the souls of the small bodies buried there. We stood locked in a compassionate silence. Karen looked at me, expecting me to speak. No words came. The emotions that bonded us were stronger than words could have ever been. We embraced, forming a tight circle over the tiny grave. Differences in culture, language, age, and religion dissolved as the eight of us became one.

After a few moments of deep, silent connection, a gentle breeze began to blow and a soft rain began to fall. We knew the angel had folded Nicholas under her wings and they had flown past us on the breeze. We also knew that God was sharing our tears. Two-year-old Nina leaned over and lay her flower on Nicholas's grave. Each of us followed her lead. There was no need for words. Our hearts were joined beyond words.

Nicholas taught us that the voice of love is beautiful and powerful without words. He showed us that words don't heal suffering. *Only standing together in love begins the healing of broken hearts.* Souls can communicate clearly in silence. Prayers can be offered and answered without words.

This past year, seven years since our family first stood at Nicholas's grave, we stood there again, his two little brothers now widening our circle. We wanted Matthew and Michael to know their brother who came and went without words, but with love. The angel statue smiled.

I smiled back through tears—tears that seemed to spring from the depths of a place beyond myself, even beyond my soul. They felt as though they were rising from an endless ancestral pool formed by the billions of tears shed throughout the ages by all who have had to experience grief and powerlessness to know true gratitude and love.

As the others in our group began to busy themselves pulling weeds and planting flowers on Nicholas's grave, I felt drawn to the angel statue as if her power had enveloped me and somehow held the very essence of my soul. My awareness of the physical plane dimmed as I was absorbed into a connection with the angel, who seemed no longer a statue, but was transformed into pure light in the form of an angel as real to me as myself in that moment. I knew beyond all doubt that Nicholas was still with us, embracing us in an eternal love that has no separation or boundaries. His physical body died to show us that eternal life is a gift of love, not based on religious belief, race, class, or color. It's given as a part of the universal law: Energy forms are never lost, only converted and transformed. Love is the glue that holds the universe together. Fear is the force that separates, forming a space in our minds where evil breeds. There will be no evil when we choose to fill all the spaces with kindness and love. Love comes in varied containers—from the touch of a kind hand to the magnificence of a martyr for a noble cause. Fear comes in varied containers as well—from rejecting an aspect of ourselves that might prevent us from self-love, which is necessary to love others, to acts of crime and violence. Fear, not hatred, is love's opposite.

Each moment in which we choose love, we create a bit of heaven on earth. Heaven *is* love. It is in our hearts and our consciousness. We need not fear physical death. It is a way for us to graduate to the heaven that is eternal love, once our lessons here on the physical plane have been learned.

I felt myself trembling as the angel gently released me from this powerful communion. I now knew Nicholas had simply graduated early, for he already knew what I was still struggling to learn and live—the truth of Pierre Teilhard de Chardin's quote:

> Love alone is capable of uniting human beings in such a way as to complete and fulfill them, for it alone takes them and joins them by what is deepest in themselves.

I shifted my gaze from the angel to my family. There were no words to convey what I'd just experienced. I could only join them in love, the love from which we each have come, and to which we each will return, when we learn that it is all that really matters.

When we really, truly understand that love is all that matters, we will pass it on to others, who will pass it on to others—ad infinitum. We are the creators of what will be. This work cannot be left to the churches, certainly not the politicians, the therapists, or even to our children. We are the ones who must stand in lasting love. The only time is now.

Johari Window

THE JOHARI WINDOW is an exercise designed by two men, Joe and Harry, who wanted to expand their self-knowledge and their knowledge of each other. They each took a piece of paper and marked it into four equal portions. (Put a dot in the center of the page, and then draw a vertical line from the top to the bottom and a horizontal line across the center.) Designate the first section: Things Generally Known by Both of Us about Me; the second is Things You Know about Me (that I may not admit, or that I've repressed, or denied); the third section is Things I Know about Me (that I may not so readily share, but will trust you enough to share a few; and the last section, New Knowledge about Me (that is always discovered in the process of working through your window). Work through each of the four sections together. The more honest and openhearted you remain through the experience, the more powerful and helpful the experience will become. Sharing this experience during a relationship will help ensure "standing in love." It is based on the theory that we carry an image of ourselves that is usually not the same image that others have of us, which often causes conflict in relationships.

Example: My husband and children usually describe me as self-confident and sometimes controlling. I know I'm more prone to try to control when I'm feeling a bit insecure and out of control. What we all learned was that I often feel too responsible for everything, and try too hard to make everything "right." As a result of doing this exercise with my husband and two of our adult children, I'm learning to ask for help when I feel I need it rather than trying to take charge to make something happen.

Paul Harvey on
Columbine High School

For the life of me, I can't understand what could have gone wrong in Littleton, Colorado. If only the parents had kept their children away from guns, we wouldn't have had such a tragedy. Yeah, it must have been the guns.

It couldn't have been because half of our children live in broken homes and get to spend an average of thirty seconds a day in meaningful conversation with a parent.

It couldn't have been because we tend to treat our children as pets and our pets as children.

It couldn't have been because we place our children in day care centers where they learn their socialization skills among their peers under the law of the jungle, while employees who have no vested interest in the children look on and make sure that no blood is spilled.

It couldn't have been because we allow our children to watch, on the average, seven hours of television a day filled with the glorification of sex and violence that isn't even fit for adult consumption.

It couldn't have been because we allow (and even encourage) our children to enter into virtual worlds in which, to win the game, one must kill as many opponents as possible in the most sadistic way possible.

It couldn't have been because we have spoiled our children with material things to the point that they equate material things with love.

It couldn't have been because many parents today try to raise children only in spare time.

It couldn't have been because we teach our children that there are no laws of morality that transcend us, that everything is relative, and that actions don't have consequences. What the heck, the president gets away with it.

Nah, it must have been the guns.

Excerpts from the letter to the court from Dennis Shepard, father of Matthew Shepard

(BEATEN TO DEATH IN OCTOBER 1998)

YOUR HONOR, MEMBERS of the Jury,

A TERRIBLE CRIME was committed in Laramie 13 months ago. Because of that crime, the reputation of the city of Laramie and the state of Wyoming become synonymous with gay bashing, hate crimes, and brutality, but yesterday you showed the world that the city of Laramie will not tolerate hate crimes. My son, Matthew, paid a terrible price to open the eyes of all of us to the unjust and unnecessary fears, discrimination, and intolerance that the gay community face every day.

My son did not look like a winner. He was small for his age—weighing only 110 pounds and standing only 5'2" tall. He was uncoordinated and wore braces from the age of 13 until the day he died, 50 days before his 22nd birthday. But in this brief life, he showed the world that he was a winner. He was a gentle, caring soul, who proved that he was as tough as anyone. He was tied to a fence, robbed, ridiculed, beaten to a pulp, and left alone to die. But I know that he wasn't really alone. He had the beautiful night sky that he used to look at through his telescope, the smell of sage and scent of pine trees from the Snowy Range he loved, and he had God, to whom he was devoted. Matt is now a symbol—some say martyr, putting a boy-next-door face on hate crimes. Matt would be thrilled if his death would help others. He tried to use his best judgment when he took a stand, and when he quietly let it be known that he was gay, he didn't advertise it, but he didn't back away from the issue either. He knew there were dangers, but he accepted that and wanted to just get on with his life's ambition of helping others. He showed me that he was a lot more courageous than most people, including myself, and I'll always be proud of him.

My son died because of ignorance and intolerance. I can't bring him back, but I can do my best to see that this never happens to another individual again. I hope my son will be remembered as a symbol for encouraging respect for individuality, for appreciation of differences, and for tolerance.

MAY WE EACH remember Matthew and support the cause of justice and human rights for which he died. Perhaps this wise and loving father's letter sums up the entire manuscript.

Chapter Notes

PREFACE

[1]Menninger Clinic Report, May 2000.
[2]Rosenblatt, Roger. "The Killing of Kayla," in *Time,* March 13, 2000.
[3]de Mello, Anthony. *Awareness: The Perils and Opportunities of Reality.* New York: Doubleday, 1990.

INTRODUCTION

[1]de Saint-Exupéry, Antoine. *The Little Prince.* New York: Harcourt Brace & Co., 1943

CHAPTER ONE

[1]Fromm, Erich. *The Art of Loving.* New York: Harper & Row, 1956.
[2]Nash, Madeline. "Fertile Minds," in *Time,* Feb. 3, 1997.
[3]Harlow, Harry F. "Basic social capacities of primates," in *Human Biology,* 1959, 31.
[4]Ibid, plus Stone, L. Joseph and Church, Joseph. *Childhood and Adolescence, A Psychology of the Growing Person.* New York: Random House, 1957.
[5]Harlow, Harry F. "The heterosexual affectional systems," in American Psychologist, 1962, 17.
[6]Bowlby, John. *Attachment and Loss.* New York: Basic Books, 1969.
[7]Evans, Paul and Bartolome, Fernando. *Must Success Cost So Much?* London: Grant/McIntyre, 1980.
[8]Gould, Roger. *Transformations.* New York: Simon & Schuster, 1978.
[9]Durant quote cited in: Wall, Ronald E. *Sermons for the Holidays.* Grand Rapids, MI: Baker Book House, 1989.

Chapter Two

[1]Hamer, Dean, and Peter Copeland. *Living With Our Genes: Why They Matter More Than You Think.* New York: Doubleday, 1998.

[2]Ibid.

[3]Hillman, James. *The Soul's Code: In Search of Character and Calling.* New York: Random House, 1996

[4]Sandmaier, Marian. *Original Kin.* New York: Dutton, 1994.

[5]Pittman, Frank. *Private Lies.* New York: W. W. Norton, 1989.

[6]Fulghrum, Robert. *From Beginning to End.* New York: HarperCollins, 1996. Starhawk. *Walking To Mercury.* New York: Bantam, 1997.

Other suggested readings applicable to this chapter:

Covey, Stephen. *The 7 Habits of Highly Effective Families.* New York: Golden Books, 1997.

Pearsall, Paul. *The Power of the Family.* New York: Doubleday, 1990.

Also used: Poem by friend, Charles James

Chapter Three

[1]Underhill, Evelyn. *The Life of the Spirit and the Life of Today.* New York: Harper and Row, 1922.

[2]Assagioli, Roberto. *Psychosynthesis.* New York: Penguin Books, 1965.

[3]Gray, John. *What You Feel, You Can Heal.* Mill Valley: Heart Publishing Co., 1984.

[4]Poem by friend, Kathleen Payette

Chapter Four

[1]Hallowell, Edward. *Connect.* New York: Pantheon Books, 1999.

[2]von Bertanlaffy, Ludwig. *Perspectives on General Systems Theory.* New York: Braziller, 1975.

[3]Pearce, Joseph Chilton. *The Magical Child.* New York: Dutton, 1977.

[4]Ferrucci, Piero. *What We May Be: Techniques for Psychological and Spiritual Growth.* Los Angeles: Jeremy Tarcher, Inc., 1982.

[5]Dossey, Larry. *Healing Words.* New York: HarperCollins, 1993.

[6]Chopra, Deepak. *How To Know God.* New York: Crown Publishers, 2000.

[7]Wilber, Ken. *A Brief History of Everything.* Boston and London: Shambhala, 1996.

[8]Williams, Margery. *The Velveteen Rabbit.* New York: Avon Books, 1975.

[9]Eiseley, Loren. *The Star Thrower.* San Diego: A Harvest/HBJ Book, 1978.

[10]de Mello, Anthony. *Song of the Bird.* San Francisco, CA: Harper, 1985.

[11]Lozoff, Bo. *We're All Doing Time.* Durham, North Carolina: Human Kindness Foundation, 1985.

[12]Weiss, Brian. *Many Lives, Many Masters.* New York: Fireside Books, 1988.

Poem by Stan Dale and my childhood story remembered through Jon Kabot-Zinn's *Wherever You Go, There You Are*. New York: Hyperion, 1994.

CHAPTER FIVE

[1]Hoffman, Robert. *No One Is To Blame*. Oakland, CA: Recycling Books, 1988. The Hoffman Quadrinity Process is a therapeutic experience designed by the late Bob Hoffman to enable participants to let go of the past and begin a loving present.

[2]Hendrix, Harville. *Getting the Love You Want*. New York: HarperCollins, 1989. IMAGO Relationship Therapy is a therapeutic experience designed by Harville Hendrix to teach couples how to help heal old wounds and "to stand in love."

[3]Weiss, Brian. *Only Love is Real*. New York: Warner Books, 1996.

[4]Gottman, John. *Why Marriages Succeed or Fail*. New York: Simon & Schuster, 1994.

[5]*Ibid*.

[6]Fisher, Helen. *The Anatomy of Love*. New York: W. W. Norton, 1992.

[7]Keen, Sam. The Passionate Life. New York: HarperCollins, 1984.

[8]Godwin, Gail. *The Good Husband*. Westminster, MD: Ballantine, 1994. Poems by friend, Suzanne Moffat.

Other suggested readings applicable to this chapter:

Buscaglia, Leo. *Loving Each Other* and *Bus 9 to Paradise*. New York: William Morrow & Co., 1986.

Donovan, Mary Ellen and William Ryan. *Love Blocks: Breaking the Patterns that Undermine Relationships*. New York: Viking, 1989.

Keen, Sam. *To Love and Be Loved*. New York: Bantam Books, 1997.

Love, Patricia, and Robinson, Jo. *Hot Monogamy*. New York: Dutton, 1994.

Proust, Marcel. *Time Regained* and *Swann's Way*. (Translated from French) New York: Vintage Books.

CHAPTER SIX

[1]Gray, John. *Men are From Mars, Women are From Venus*. New York: HarperCollins, 1992.

[2]Tavris, Carol, and Carole Offir. *The Longest War*. New York: Harcourt Brace Jovanovich, Inc., 1977.

[3]Fisher, Robert. *The Knight in Rusty Armor*. Hollywood, CA: Wilshire Book Co., 1990.

[4]Tavris and Offir. (c. 2)

[5]Brown, Rita Mae. *Venus Envy*. New York: Bantam Books, 1993.

[6]Hendrix, Harville. *Keeping the Love You Find*. New York: Simon and Schuster, 1992.

[7]Coville, Bruce. *My Teacher is an Alien*. New York: Simon & Schuster, 1989.

Other suggested readings applicable to this chapter:

Assagioli, Roberto. *The Act of Will*. New York: Penguin Books, 1973.
Dyer, Wayne. *Manifest Your Destiny*. New York: HarperPerennial, 1997.

CHAPTER SEVEN

[1]Ornish, Dean. *Love and Survival: The Scientific Basis for the Healing Power of Intimacy*. New York: HarperCollins, 1998.
[2]Roth, Geneen. *When Food is Love: Exploring the Relationship Between Eating and Intimacy*. New York: Dutton, 1991.
[3]Gordon, Richard. *Quantum Touch*. Berkeley, CA: North Atlantic Books, 1999.
[4]Benson, Herbert. *Timeless Healing: The Power and Biology of Belief*. New York: Fireside, 1997.
[5]Chopra (c. 6, Chap. 3)
[6]Ogden, Gina. "Sex and the Spirit: The Healing Connection," in *New Age Journal*, Jan–Feb, 1999.
[7]Ornish (c. 1)
[8]Max, Jill, ed. *Spider Spins a Story*. Flagstaff, Arizona: Northland Publishing Co., 1997.

Intuition source: Welles, Paddy. *Intuitive Processes as Constructed by Psychics, Mediums, and Therapists, with Possible Application to Family Therapy*. Ann Arbor, Michigan: UMI Dissertation Services, 1988.

Other suggested readings applicable to this chapter:

Dossey, Larry. *ReInventing Medicine: Beyond Mind-Body to a New Area of Healing*. San Francisco: Harper San Francisco, 1998.
Dossey, Larry. *Recovering the Soul*. New York: Bantam, 1989.
Hendrix, Harville, and Helen Hunt. *Giving the Love that Heals*. New York: Simon and Schuster, 1997.
Locke, Steven and Colligan, Douglas. *The Healer Within*. New York: Dutton. 1986.
Rosanoff, Nancy. *Intuition Workout* and *Use Your Intuition*, published by Element.

On Self-Love:

Beattie, Melody. *The Language of Letting Go*. New York: A Hazelden Book, HarperCollins, 1990.
Beattie, Melody. *Co-Dependent No More*. New York: HarperCollins, 1989
Schaef, Anne Wilson. *Meditations for Women Who Do Too Much*. San Francisco: Harper San Francisco, 1990.

CHAPTER EIGHT

[1]Price, Reynolds. *Roxanna Slade.* New York: Simon and Schuster, 1998.
[2]Lozoff (c. 11, Chap.3)
[3]Statistic from State of America's Children Address, NPR, Jan. 2000.
[4]Schlessinger, Laura. *Parenthood by Proxy.* New York: Harper, 2000.
[5]Leach, Penelope. *Your Growing Child.* New York: Knoff, 1986
[6]Pipher, Mary. *The Shelter of Each Other: Rebuilding Our Families.* New York: Ballentine, 1997.
[7]Osbourne, John. "On love" in *The Sun Magazine,* Chapel Hill, NC.
[8]Cowan, Connell and Kinder, Melvyn. *Smart Women, Foolish Choices.* New York: Penguin, 1985.
[9]Loftus, Mary. "Frisky Business," in *Psychology Today,* Mar.–April, 1995.
[10]Spring, Janis A. *After the Affair.* New York: HarperPerennial, 1996.
[11]Boszormenyi-Nagy, Ivan and Barbara Krasner. *Between Give and Take.* New York: Brunner-Mazel, 1986.
[12]Quinn, Daniel. *Ishmael.* New York: Bantam, 1992.
Poem by friend, Jan Rainier.

CHAPTER NINE

[1]Seilegman, Martin. *Helplessness.* San Francisco: Freeman, 1975.
[2]Goleman, Daniel. *Emotional Intelligence.* New York: Bantam Books, 1995.
[3]Myss, Carolyn. *The Anatomy of the Spirit.* New York: Crown, 1996.
[4]Norwood, Robin. *Why Me, Why This, Why Now.* New York: Crown, 1994.
[5]Gender, J. Ruth. *The Book of Qualities.* Berkeley, CA: Turquoise Mountain Publishers, 1984.
[6]Schaef, Anne Wilson. "Life Beyond Therapy, Living Your Process," in *Lotus Magazine,* Fall, 1992, vol. 2, no. 1.
[7]Parry, Danaan. *The Essene Book of Days.* Cooperstown, New York: Sunstone Publications, 1989.
Source for descriptions of Defense Mechanisms: Duke, Marshall, and Nowicki, Stephen. *Abnormal Psychology, A New Look.* New York: Holt, Rinehart, and Winston, 1986.

Other suggested reading applicable to this chapter:

Weiss, Brian. *Through Time Into Healing.* New York: Simon and Schuster, 1992.

CHAPTER TEN

[1]Tart, Charles. *Waking Up: Overcoming the Obstacles to Human Potential.* Boston: Shambhala, 1987.
[2]Needleman, Jacob. *A Little Book on Love.* New York: Dell, 1998.
[3]Blum, Ralph. *The Book of Runes.* New York: Oracle Books, St. Martin's Press, 1982.

[4]Hillman, James. *The Soul's Code: In Search of Character and Calling.* New York: Random House, 1996
[5]Max (c. 8, Chap. 6)
Poem by friend, Suzanne Moffat.

EPILOGUE

This chapter is a true and personal story dedicated to my grandson, Nicholas, and to three of my dearest friends who have graduated into absolute lasting love during the completion of this book: Leah, Judy, and Ann Marie.

Suggested reading applicable to this chapter:

Callanan, Maggie, and Kelley, Patricia. *Final Gifts.* Bantam Books, 1982.
Gibran, Kahlil. *The Prophet.* New York: Alfred Knopf, 1923.
Levine, Stephen. *Who Dies? An Investigation of Conscious Living and Conscious Dying.* New York: Doubleday, 1982.

Acknowledgments

THERE ARE SEVERAL significant people to whom I am especially connected and for whom I am deeply grateful. I love each of them in special ways and for special reasons: my brother, Edwin; my sister, Beth; her husband, Bud (who was the first real boyfriend with whom I fell in love); my first husband, Wayne (who was the first man with whom I made love and we consequently made four wonderful children, but began to walk down different paths after thirteen years together); my most special friends: Carol, Martha, Jan, and Jean, who have remained in my life through thick and thin; and the members of the Welles family, especially Annie and Wellesie, who have accepted me and my children into their extraordinary clan.

To Charlie Williams, CEO of Geist and Russell Publishers, I owe half my soul for believing in me and my work enough to accept the book for publication in the hardcover edition in 2001. Without the editorial competence and continuing encouragement of editor Marian Sandmaier and of my friends, Peg Gallagher, Suzanne Moffat, and Pat Lawton, all editors extraordinaire, this book would not exist. For this revised paperback edition, my deepest gratitude goes to Matthew Lore, publisher of Marlowe & Company, and to Sue McCloskey, assistant editor for Marlowe, who have given new and profound meaning to the term "All Best." They are the best and have challenged me to do my best. To Kae Tienstra, publicist for both editions, I express loving appreciation for your tireless work, your trusted friendship, and for convincing Ellen Greene to take me and the book under her professional agent-wings.

There are a few contemporary, talented thinkers, sages, who have had a profound influence on my ideas and life. At the top of this list is Sam Keen, whose writing, thinking, courage, and curiosity have challenged and validated me for over twenty years. Harville Hendrix's ideas on love and marriage have helped me sort through masses of confusion about our choices of love partners, and his IMAGO therapy improved my marriage. Harville and his wife, Helen Hunt, exemplify the concept of "standing in love." Brian Weiss and Larry Dossey, two of our generation's most brilliant, courageous doctors and creative authors, have revolutionized the healing process. Both have expanded my mind and touched my soul. With fame and overwhelming professional demands, they have maintained humility and kindness. I am blessed by having had each of these powerful, gentle men as teachers.

There are numerous other friends, teachers, clients, colleagues, and students (especially Georgia, who has participated in each of these roles) with whom I have shared loving, learning experiences. My life has been enriched by each of you and I am thankful for your participation in my journey. There are those who have taken serious issue with my ideas, some who have disliked me and might consider themselves foe rather than friend; however, you also have your place as important teachers in my life, and I appreciate you. There are some persons I may have hurt, and to you, I want to say, I am truly sorry. There are a few who have hurt me, and it seems important that you know you have mellowed me, and, in some broad karmic sense, have helped me grow in love. *Merci a tous!*

Permissions